A -∅

Computer-Assisted Language Learning

Computer-assisted language learning (CALL) is an approach to teaching and learning languages that uses computers and other technologies to present, reinforce, and assess material to be learned, or to create environments where teachers and learners can interact with one another and the outside world. This book provides a much-needed overview of the diverse approaches to research and practice in CALL. It differs from previous works in that it not only surveys the field, but also makes connections to actual practice and demonstrates the potential advantages and limitations of the diverse options available. These options are based squarely on existing research in the field, enabling readers to make informed decisions regarding their own research in CALL. This essential text helps readers to understand and embrace the diversity in the field, and helps to guide them in both research and practice.

GLENN STOCKWELL is Professor in Applied Linguistics at Waseda University, Japan.

Computer-Assisted Language Learning

Diversity in Research and Practice

Edited by

Glenn Stockwell

CAMBRIDGE
UNIVERSITY PRESS

CAMBRIDGE UNIVERSITY PRESS
Cambridge, New York, Melbourne, Madrid, Cape Town
Singapore, São Paulo, Delhi, Tokyo, Mexico City

Cambridge University Press
The Edinburgh Building, Cambridge CB2 8RU, UK

Published in the United States of America by Cambridge University Press, New York

www.cambridge.org
Information on this title: www.cambridge.org/9781107016347

© Cambridge University Press 2012

First published 2012

Printed in the United Kingdom at the University Press, Cambridge

A catalogue record for this publication is available from the British Library

ISBN 978-1-107-01634-7 Hardback

Contents

Figures

Tables

Contributors

GORDON BATESON is an associate professor at Kanagawa Gakuin University, Japan. He majored in computer science at Imperial College, London University and, after graduating, worked as a programmer for several years at a major software house in the UK, creating and maintaining database systems. His special interests are cross-cultural communication and uses for music and technology in education. Since 2005 he has been one of the core programmers of the Moodle learning management system. He is in charge of the HotPot module and its successors, the QuizPort module and the TaskChain module. Apart from programming, he has published articles on innovative uses and adaptions for Moodle, such as a Moodle on mobile phones, anonymous fora on Moodle, Moodle as a team-teaching tool, and promoting student motivation to study online using aspects of game theory.

JOHN BRINE, Ph.D., is an associate professor at the University of Aizu, Japan. He received his Ph.D. in educational computing from the University of Toronto and has taught in universities in Canada, Japan, and New Zealand. His research interests are concerned with the cultural and collaborative aspects of learning, and applications of network-based communications to second language learning. His current work involves the design and development of methods and modules to be used in learning management systems to provide students with tools to process and manipulate texts, both socially and individually. He is the principal investigator of a research project funded by the Japan Society for the Promotion of Science to implement a distance computer science course for a Vietnamese university using a learning management system and flexible language acquisition tools being developed at the University of Waikato, New Zealand.

PAUL DANIELS has spent twenty years teaching English in Hawaii, Indonesia, and currently in Japan. He is an associate professor at Kochi University of Technology in Shikoku where he teaches English language to engineering students. He has recently published a textbook entitled *Science English* and has extensive experience in developing technology-enhanced courses in both online and blended learning environments. He is active in developing language learning modules for the course management system called Moodle (moodle.org) and his current research examines how technology can be used to reinforce content-based and project-based instructional models. He has published numerous journal articles in the area of CALL, specifically on course management systems and mobile learning. He has extensive experience designing language learning curricula that integrate technology with traditional textbook-based courses.

PORNAPIT DARASAWANG, Ph.D., is Dean of the School of Liberal Arts, King Mongkut's University of Technology, Thonburi, Bangkok, Thailand. She teaches in the M.A. and Ph.D. programs in applied linguistics and has been involved in training teachers at all educational levels for many years. She has been involved in projects through the Ministry of Education to establish language support programs around Thailand. Her research interests are in learner autonomy, learner training, and self-access learning.

ROBERT FISCHER, Ph.D., is Professor of French/Applied Linguistics and Chair of the Department of Modern Languages at Texas State University. He served as Executive Director of the Computer Assisted Language Instruction Consortium (CALICO) and Editor of *CALICO Journal* since 1997. He has also directed several grant-supported projects to develop and disseminate CALL authoring tools. His primary research interests lie in instructional design and student use of CALL materials.

PHILIP HUBBARD, Ph.D., is a senior lecturer in Linguistics and Director of English for Foreign Students in the Stanford University Language Center. He has been active in computer-assisted language learning (CALL) for over twenty-five years. During that time he has authored a number of software programs for learning English and has published articles on CALL theory, research, methodology, courseware evaluation, teacher education, learner training, and listening. He co-edited *Teacher Education in CALL* (2006) with Mike Levy and most recently released a four-volume edited series covering the whole field, *Computer Assisted Language Learning: Critical Concepts in Linguistics* (2009). He is an associate editor of *Computer Assisted Language Learning* and serves on the editorial boards of *Language Learning and Technology*, *CALICO Journal*, *ReCALL*, and *Writing and Pedagogy*. His current research focuses on language learner training for technology environments with a particular emphasis on online listening.

E. MARCIA JOHNSON, Ph.D., is Director of Student Learning, University of Waikato, Hamilton, New Zealand. She completed a Ph.D. in educational computing at the University of Toronto and has taught in several countries. This has included educational technology in teacher education programs in Canada, English language learning for university students in Japan, and applied linguistics with a focus on computer-assisted language learning, in a language teacher education program in New Zealand. She is project director of a multidisciplinary research team funded by the Teaching and Learning Research Initiative, Ministry of Education in New Zealand, which is exploring information and communications technology (ICT)/eLearning practices across several disciplines and with students from diverse backgrounds at tertiary level in New Zealand. The research has been designed to address issues of tertiary-level pedagogy, e-pedagogy, and research with the goal of building eLearning capacity, leveraging pedagogical change, and closing participatory gaps for students and lecturers. Her research interests also include technology implementation in developing economies (Vietnam), particularly using open source software tools and open educational resources.

MARIE-NOËLLE LAMY, Ph.D., came to the Open University from a background in linguistics to lead a team in charge of creating the university's first ever program of distance-taught languages, spanning proficiency levels from beginners to advanced. This program used technology to assist the development of skills, prioritizing interactive speaking (in real time, via audiographic tutorials online, in groups of ten to fifteen students connecting from different places and sometimes distant countries or even continents). Between 1999 and 2005, she oversaw the roll-out of one such system to about seven thousand students of French, German, and Spanish, studying at a distance with the Open University. Her research, within the Centre for Research in Education and Educational Technology, is directed at the pedagogical and epistemological implications of changes in the way that we learn, teach, and communicate in second languages with technology. She is a member of the editorial boards of the journals *Language Learning and Technology*, *ReCALL*, *Distances et Savoirs*, and *Apprentissage des Langues et Systèmes d'Information et de Communication (ALSIC)*.

HAYO REINDERS, Ph.D., is Adjunct Professor at the University of Groningen in the Netherlands, editor of *Innovation in Language Learning and Teaching*, and Convenor of the International Association of Applied Linguistics (AILA) Research Network for CALL and the Learner. He was founding Director of the English Language Self-Access Centre at the University of Auckland and Visiting Professor at Meiji University in Japan. Hayo is regularly invited as a plenary speaker on autonomy, CALL, and out-of-class learning, and is a speaker for the Royal Society of New Zealand. His most recent books are on teacher autonomy, teaching methodologies, and second language acquisition.

KENNETH ROMEO, Ph.D., is an academic technology specialist for the Language Center and an instructor in the English for Foreign Students program at Stanford University. He has initiated research on language processing and a wide variety of assessment issues, including individual speaking assessment and large-scale assessment using online learning management systems. He is currently responsible for the technical aspects of all online formative and summative assessments in the Language Center, as well as spoken placement and exit exams for undergraduates studying foreign languages and listening tests for graduate students in English as a second language (ESL) courses. His research interests are in a paradigm for curriculum development that can be both applied to and extended beyond current web-based technology.

GLENN STOCKWELL, Ph.D., is Professor in Applied Linguistics at Waseda University, Tokyo, Japan. He teaches a range of English language subjects and several applied linguistics subjects, including second language acquisition, second language teaching methodology, and computer-assisted language learning. His research interests include computer-mediated communication, mobile learning, and the role of technology in the language learning process. He is co-author of *CALL Dimensions* (2006) with Mike Levy, and published widely in international journals in the field of CALL. He is Editor-in-Chief of *The JALT CALL Journal*, and member of the academic advisory boards and review boards of the journals *ReCALL*, *Computer Assisted Language Learning*, *Computers and Education*, and *CALICO Journal*.

NOBUE TANAKA-ELLIS, Ph.D., completed her doctoral studies in the field of CALL at the University of Melbourne. She is currently teaching English as a foreign language (EFL) at Waseda University in Japan. She has lived in Australia, Japan, the Netherlands, Singapore, and the UK, and taught both English and Japanese at universities in Australia and Japan. Her research interests include computer-mediated communication, second language acquisition, task-based learning, collaborative learning, intercultural communication, and first language interference in second language learning. She has published in international journals and presented at conferences internationally.

Abbreviations

ADSL	asymmetric digital subscriber line
BBS	bulletin board system
BECTA	British Educational Communications and Technology Agency
CALICO	Computer Assisted Language Instruction Consortium
CALL	computer-assisted language learning
CASLA	computer-assisted second language acquisition
CELL	computer-enhanced language learning
CMC	computer-mediated communication
CMS	content management system
CSS	cascading style sheets
CVS	concurrent versions system
DL	digital library
EFL	English as a foreign language
ESL	English as a second language
ESP	English for specific purposes
EUROCALL	European Association for Computer Assisted Language Learning
GIT	global information tracker
GNU GPL	GNU General Public License
HTML	hypertext markup language
IIEP	International Institute for Educational Planning
IM	instant messenger
L1	first language
L2	second language
LMS	learning management system
LOM	learning object metadata
MALL	mobile-assisted language learning
MEXT	Ministry of Education, Culture, Science, and Technology (Japan)
MIT	Massachusetts Institute of Technology

MMORPG	massively multiplayer online role-playing game
MOET	Ministry of Education and Training (Vietnam)
MOO	multi-user domain object oriented
MP3	moving picture experts group-1 (or -2) audio layer 3
MSN	Microsoft network
MUVE	multi-user virtual environment
NBLT	network-based language teaching
NPC	non-playing character
OCW	OpenCourseWare
OECD	Organisation for Economic Co-operation and Development
OER	open educational resources
OSS	open source software
PC	personal computer
PC	playing character
RETRAC	regional training center
RSS	really simple syndication
SALC	self-access learning center
SCORM	sharable content object reference model
SDK	software development kit
SEAMEO	Southeast Asian Ministers of Education Organization
SLA	second language acquisition
SMS	short message service
SNS	social networking system
TALL	technology-assisted language learning
TELL	technology-enhanced language learning
TESOL	teachers of English to speakers of other languages
TOEIC	test of English for international communication
UNESCO	United Nations Educational, Scientific and Cultural Organization
VLE	virtual learning environment
VoIP	voice over Internet protocol
WiFi	wireless fidelity (also Wi-Fi)
WYSIWYG	what you see is what you get

1 Introduction

Glenn Stockwell

Introduction

Computer-assisted language learning (CALL) is a field that has featured as the theme of books, journals, and academic conferences over the past few decades. There are several internationally refereed English-language journals in the field, emanating from the US (*CALICO Journal, Language Learning and Technology*), Europe (*ReCALL, Computer Assisted Language Learning*), and Asia (*CALL-EJ, The JALT CALL Journal, PacCALL Journal*), as well as numerous publications in many other languages. Since its beginnings over half a century ago (see Levy, 1997), there has been an increasing range of technologies available to CALL practitioners (see Stockwell, 2007a) founded on different theories (Hubbard, 2008) and pedagogies (Beatty, 2003). While this increase in range has the potential to provide welcome variation and diversity, it can also be overwhelming, and the range of variables can seem immense both to teachers new to the field and to those who have established themselves in one particular aspect of the field. One of the best ways of managing diversity is to be aware of the issues involved in it, so for that reason, this book sets out to investigate the various aspects of diversity and to present this in a digestible manner. The diversity we see in CALL may include diversity in the technologies, diversities in the environments in which CALL is used, diversity in the pedagogies employed, diversity in the users of CALL, and diversity in the methods used to research and further our understanding of CALL. Each of these diversities has the potential to change the way in which we view, use, and even evaluate CALL.

This chapter forms the foundation of the book by looking at a number of key issues that are pertinent to the field of CALL as it is presented in the following chapters, starting with a description of the theme of diversity, discussions of theory in CALL research and practice, the affordances of technology and the issue of learner autonomy in CALL, and finally, an examination of the use of the term "CALL." This is followed by an overview of the structure and content of the book.

Some key issues

The theme of diversity

Diversity refers to things that are different and varied. There are times when we value diversity, such as when we are deciding on what to eat, what to wear, or even what type of television we may choose to buy. There are also times, however, when diversity can have a restricting effect, such as when we have too many choices – often with limited information – and we find it difficult to select from the range of options available (see Lehrer, 2009). Viewing diversity as a merit or demerit is conceivable also in CALL. Having a range of options from which to choose can be a positive point in that it is possible to select what is most appropriate to our given situation, but on the downside, the increasing number of choices that are available can make it difficult to decide what is best. Those who are new to CALL may find themselves daunted by the sheer range of technologies that exist, with little idea of how to break into the field, and even those with experience of technologies – including technologies in the language classroom – may struggle to keep up with the ongoing developments, not only in the technologies themselves but also in how they are used.

This book deals with various aspects of diversity, but it is only possible to cover a small portion of the possibilities that diversity in CALL research and practice might encompass. Technology is perhaps the most obvious aspect, given that it is what immediately comes to mind for many when CALL is discussed. Typical questions from those who are new to the field – even experienced language teachers – often include "what program is the best for teaching a foreign language?" or "how good is such-and-such a product for learning a language?" These questions, while seeming valid at face value, fail to take into consideration a number of critical factors about the environment in which a program may be used. That is to say, people would be far less likely to ask "what textbook is the best for teaching a foreign language?" without including some kind of qualifier regarding language skills or areas, level of the student, the means of teaching, and so forth. Everything in CALL occurs within a context, and this context will have an enormous impact on the choice of the technology and how it is used. We have seen numerous examples in the literature where generic technologies have been used in language teaching, ranging from word processing (Dall, 2001), email (Stockwell and Harrington, 2003), and chat (Darhower, 2002), through to podcasting (Rosell-Aguilar, 2007b) and mobile phones (Kiernan and Aizawa, 2004). We can also see examples of technologies that have been developed by CALL practitioners themselves, with detailed descriptions of how they work and how they may be used, including software for teaching endangered or minority languages (Ward and Genabith, 2003; Cushion, 2004) and sophisticated intelligent feedback systems (Tokuda and Chen, 2004). Why is there such a diverse range of technologies being used? Put simply, they vary because of the individual context within which they are used. The context is an extremely complex combination of factors, including the learners, the mode of instruction, the learning goals, the institutional environment, the experience and policies adopted by the teacher, and so forth, and each of these have an effect on decisions about technology.

The learners are perhaps one of the most diverse and constantly changing aspects, in terms of their backgrounds, goals, expectations, and even their lifestyles. They are typically the end users of the CALL materials and activities that they engage in and, as a result, it is up to CALL practitioners to constantly bear in mind who the learners are and what they want to achieve. Learners who have never used technology before for learning purposes may first need to overcome their expectations – and perhaps even their fears – of what using technology in language learning entails. Equally difficult to contend with might be a situation where learners have used CALL before but had a bad experience, meaning that the negative preconceived images that they have of CALL will need to be replaced with more positive ones in order to encourage them to engage with CALL in a more active manner. Learners' experiences of using technology for non-educational purposes will also likely have an effect on their expectations of technology in the classroom. If, for instance, learners are used to using a particular text-chat program to communicate with friends and family, but the text-chat program that they are required to use for educational purposes lacks features or functionality that are found in the program they use in their everyday lives, this is likely to have an effect on their opinions and attitudes towards not only the educational chat program but possibly also chat for language learning. In this way, learners' particular experiences with using technology in their everyday lives will naturally impact their acceptance and perceptions of technology for language learning. While it might be expected that experience or regular use of technology outside of learning situations can be linked to increased use for language learning, caution should be exercised before making assumptions that this will necessarily be the case (see Barrette, 2001). Added to this is the fact that learners constantly change in their own experience and preferences as a result of what they do both inside and outside of the language classroom, so there is some danger in viewing them as a static and unchanging entity. Furthermore, teachers need to keep in mind that learners will often do things that are not expected (see Chapter 2; Fischer, 2007), and at the same time not do things that are expected (Tanaka-Ellis, 2010), meaning that teachers find themselves in a position of needing to monitor the learners to ensure that learning goals are being achieved, even if there is some variation in how learners go about doing this.

The mode of instruction may shape and at the same time be shaped by the learning goals and the institutional environment. For example, while newer technologies used in distance education have opened up a wide range of pos-sibilities for language teaching that were not previously possible (see Chapter 5 for a discussion), there are still some limitations in what can be taught through distance education when compared with face-to-face environments. The instructional mode may also influence the technologies that are available. For institutions that offer exclusively distance education, such as the Open University in the UK or Universitat Oberta de Catalunya in Spain, technology takes on an immediate and central role for many aspects of instruction, and such institutions need to ensure that they have stable and good quality technol-ogy so that instruction can be carried out smoothly. In contrast, in institutions where the instruction is almost exclusively face-to-face, there may be some-what less of a need to use technology for instruction, making administrators less likely to dedicate money and resources on state-of-the-art technology. In these examples, the mode of instruction that has been adopted by the institution (i.e. distance vs. face-to-face) has a direct influence on what technologies are available to teachers and students, which in turn has the effect of expanding or limiting the technological options in the language learning environment. Where technology already exists in an institution, many teachers are faced with a situation where they need to adapt their teaching to that technology. One of the most common examples is when an institution adopts a learning manage-ment system like WebCT, and teachers find that their teaching revolves around this environment (e.g. Campbell, 2004). Other teachers may take a more pro-active position, and while it might be possible to ask their institution to pur-chase new technologies to achieve certain learning goals, financial constraints may necessitate self-development of technologies either individually (e.g. Lee *et al.*, 2009) or collaboratively (e.g. Corda and Jager, 2004), use of free or open source materials like Moodle (e.g. Hunter, 2008), or capitalizing on technolo-gies that learners already possess, such as mobile phones (e.g. Kiernan and Aizawa, 2004) or MP3 players (e.g. O'Bryan and Hegelheimer, 2007).

Finally, the experience and beliefs of teachers will also have a large impact on technology use. There has been an increasing body of work on teacher education in CALL (e.g. Hubbard and Levy, 2006; Hong, 2010), arguing that training in CALL, be it formal or informal, is necessary for more systematic and balanced integration of CALL. Being more experienced with CALL, how-ever, is not an accurate predictor of "innovative or integrated" use (Kessler and Plakans, 2008, p. 277), so this suggests that there are other factors at play which affect whether or how technology is used in the language classroom. These may include, for instance, teachers' policies towards the use of technology for teaching, or even just an interest in technologies. Teachers who are interested in but inexperienced with technologies can compensate for a lack of skills with enthusiasm, resulting in either a broad use of relatively limited technologies, or constant experimentation with the latest technologies on an ongoing basis.

Alternatively, teachers may choose to not use technology, not because of a lack of knowledge, but rather because they have strong views about what should or should not be taught using technology, and even if technological options are available, they may reject them in favor of non-CALL means.

Thus, the context will greatly impact not only what technologies are available, but what technologies are used and for what purposes. The diversity that is present in the context makes for an immense range of factors for CALL practitioners to consider regarding technology usage, and thus to make informed decisions, they need to be keenly aware of their individual context, bearing in mind its highly changeable nature. To conclude this discussion, it should be noted that diversity is also present in the way that this book has been approached. The authors of the chapters have approached the different aspects of the chapter in varied ways, in terms of the length and angle of their discussion of the general issues, the types of examples chosen and how they are presented, as well as the implications they raise. The very concept of diversity itself is perceived and approached differently, but perhaps this illustrates the difficulty in trying to put the field of CALL into neat boxes. It is a field that by nature is divergent and dynamic, and for this reason, we might argue that diversity in CALL is something that is not only inevitable, but also something that is necessary to provide the best options for the myriad contexts in which it is used.

Theory in CALL research and practice

Theory can provide "a context and a view of language and language learning" (Levy and Stockwell, 2006, p. 135) when undertaking both research and practice. The relationship between theory and practice is a bidirectional one, where, as Egbert (2005, p. 5) claims, practice "informs theory but theory should also inform practice so that not so much of our teaching is based on trials and errors." Given its obvious importance, why does it not appear as a chapter in this book? One of the main reasons is that CALL practitioners are predominantly consumers of theory, choosing to "review, select and apply theories produced by others" (Levy and Stockwell, 2006, p. 139), and considering the scope that any theory of CALL would be expected to encompass, it is not surprising that there are no overarching theories in CALL. A single theory could not possibly account for the complexities that now make up the CALL field, and it is natural that there will be multiple theories to attempt to account for these complexities.

What theories, then, feature in CALL? In a review of CALL theories cited in the *CALICO Journal* from June 1983 through to September 2007, Hubbard (2008) noted that there was a very wide range of theories that were used in the articles that were published over this time, but the overwhelming majority of these occurred only on a single occasion. Theories that appeared at least three times over this period included activity theory, cognitive theory of learning, education theory, government and binding theory, Jung's theory, lexical functional grammar theory, sociocultural theory, sociolinguistic theory, generative theory of multimedia, pedagogical theory, phonological theory, item response theory, schema theory, learning theory, and (second) language acquisition theory (p. 392). Of these, theories pertaining to second language acquisition or linguistics were by far the most common, making up thirty-eight of the ninety articles that included reference to a theory. If theories relating to learning are grouped (i.e. educational theory, pedagogical theory, and learning theory), these make up a further twenty-seven articles, which, combined with language acquisition and linguistics, comprise sixty-five of the ninety theories that appeared at least three times in the corpus. This is a clear indication of the fact that although the theories used are quite varied, there is still a strong tendency to focus around theories from education or second language acquisition.

At the very minimum, any theory of CALL needs to take into consideration two aspects – the learning of the language, and the interaction between the learner and the technology through which they are learning. The first of these two aspects relies heavily on existing theories in second language acquisition (SLA), and a look at the CALL literature shows that there is quite a body of research that refers to theories used in SLA research, such as the interaction hypothesis (Stockwell and Harrington, 2003; Yanguas, 2010), constructivism (Felix, 2002; Weasenforth *et al.*, 2002), sociocultural theory (Tanaka, 2005; Warschauer, 2005), and activity theory (Blin, 2004; Gromik, 2005). Each of these theories has a very solid position within research on CALL, providing a different perspective on the language learning process that is facilitated by the technology (see Levy and Stockwell, 2006, for a discussion).

The second aspect of the interaction between the technology and the learner has received far less attention, but there have been a few attempts to consider the impact of the technology on how learners learn a second language using technology. Perhaps one of the most notable distinctions that has been raised in this regard is that of the tutor and tool. A tutor evaluates learner output and responds according to this output, whereas a tool does not evaluate learner output, but rather serves to "augment learner capacities" (Levy, 1997, p. 184). Inherent in CALL as a tutor is "teaching presence" (see Hubbard and Bradin-Siskin, 2004), where the computer simulates the presence of the teacher in the learning process. Considering this pseudo-teacher position where the computer takes on characteristics of a teacher, then the effect of the instructional design built into the tutor will affect how language learning occurs. In contrast, given that a tool is used by learners to achieve other objectives – such as using a word-processor to write an essay or email to communicate with native speakers – the design of the instruction is not inherent in the technology, but rather based on how the teacher chooses to use the technology to achieve pre-determined goals. It is natural for this distinction to have an impact on any theory that might be used in CALL, but in both cases it is important to bear in mind that the primary objective is learning a second language, and to that end, it would be expected that a view of how to learn a language must be included in the instructional design.

Theory does have an important place in CALL, and useful discussions may be found in Levy and Stockwell (2006), Hubbard (2008), and a special issue of the *CALICO Journal* (2011). An excellent general resource on theories in second language learning has been provided by Mitchell and Myles (2004). It should be pointed out that while a detailed overview of theories has not been included in this book, theory has not been ignored, with reference made to sociocultural theory (Chapter 4), semiotic theory (Chapter 6), and activity theory (Chapter 7) in relation to the individual examples of research and practice.

Affordances of technology

Originally coined by Gibson in 1977, the term "affordances" has appeared with increasing regularity in a wide range of genres over the past few years, and in simple terms may be defined as what something makes possible (see Hutchby, 2001). Discussions of affordances in CALL contexts most commonly center around the enabling or restricting capabilities of technology in language learning, and the term is used to refer to how technology may help or hinder the learning process. Affordances of different technologies make them useful in facilitating learning in different ways. In listening, for example, technologies such as audio-conferencing software make it possible to speak to someone in real time even if separated geographically. Other technologies, such as portable MP3 players, allow learners to carry audio recordings with them and listen to them at a time and place that is convenient, such as at home or even on a busy train. While both of these technologies may be used to give learners access to speech from a teacher or native speaker, they both do this in very different ways. In audio-conferencing technologies, the communication can be two-way, where learners can speak as well as listen, but until recently this could only be done from a desktop computer without incurring prohibitive costs. In contrast, an MP3 player is very convenient in that audio recordings can be listened to almost anywhere without particularly causing irritation to people around, but the recordings must be made in advance, and there is no interactivity in terms of speaking to an interlocutor.

While technologies possess inherent affordances, the manifestation of these affordances will differ depending on the user. The same technology used by two people will not necessarily be used in the same way, and depending on experience, skills, and knowledge of what the technology can do may lead to very different results. To provide an example that keeps on the theme of listening, Windows Media Player is a commonly used technology for playing audio or video media on computers. Most teachers would be quite familiar with the functions of playing, pausing, or moving to a particular point in the media, but it is likely that a considerably smaller proportion of teachers would know about the function which allows the media to be slowed down or sped up (see Romeo and Hubbard, 2010). Thus, for teachers with knowledge of this extra function of Windows Media Player, the technology has an additional affordance than it does for teachers who are not aware of it. Accordingly, the *actual* affordances of a technology are the culmination of both the inherent affordances of the technology and the user's depth of knowledge of the functions.

With advances in technological developments, it naturally follows that the capabilities of computers and other devices will improve, and this will have an effect on their affordances. Affordances of the latest laptop computers, for example, are exponentially better than those of laptop computers just a decade ago, in terms of speed, size, weight, and functionality. Where modems were still often used for connecting to the Internet at that time, these days we have wireless broadband, meaning that Internet access is not only faster and more stable, but it can be accessed from a far wider range of locations. Many laptops come complete with built-in microphones and video cameras, making video-conferencing something that can be done wherever there is a quick Internet connection, provided that the necessary software is installed (much of which is now available for free). Even the traditional concept of a laptop itself has been challenged by emerging technologies such as tablet computers that operate through the use of a touch screen, smart mobile phones, and other Internet-capable handheld devices that fit somewhere between these two. These allow not only even more portability but also some additional features not available on many laptops such as on-screen handwriting recognition, where writing can bypass the need for any kind of keyboard at all. The implications of these affordances are significant for their application in teaching and learning of languages as well.

While the affordances of technology have improved tremendously – and will likely continue to do so in the future – we need to bear in mind common misconceptions of technology suggested by Bax (2003), that a technology would be inherently better if it had more features and that the mere existence of technology means that it will be successfully implemented into the curriculum. The huge range of affordances of technologies means that it becomes increasingly important to keep up with what these technologies are actually capable of to avoid failing to capitalize upon potentially useful functions. In saying this, however, care should be taken to not fall into the trap of assuming that the existence of these affordances will make them better for learning in lieu of a carefully designed curriculum that integrates the specific functions of technology to achieve particular learning goals.

CALL and learner autonomy

 The concept of learner autonomy has received relatively constant attention in both CALL and non-CALL language learning literature over the past several decades. It is an important concept which has been defined as "the capacity to take charge of one's learning" (Benson, 2001, p. 8) or "experiencing oneself as the origin of one's behavior" (Dörnyei and Ushioda, 2011, p. 25). It is important to note here that self-study does not equate with autonomy. Self-study does not take into consideration the factors that lead learners to study by themselves, whereas for learning to be autonomous, learners must be able to seek out, recognize, and capitalize upon learning opportunities for themselves. Learner autonomy is often cited as an advantage of CALL, generally based on the fact that learners can work alone in their own time, but to assume that learner autonomy is a natural feature of CALL is somewhat naïve. Learner autonomy is a product of a range of factors including motivation, training, experience, culture, the educational environment, and social interactions with peers and teachers (Little and Dam, 1998; Benson, 2001; Blin, 2004). The link with motivation is no doubt a strong one (Dörnyei, 2001), but motivation itself is only related to learners' *willingness* to take responsibility for their learning, not the practical skills of *how* to actually go about undertaking the learning itself (Ushioda, 1996), and most learners will need training of some kind in order to be able to do this (see Chapter 3). Learner autonomy is a constantly changing condition that is manifest in different behaviors and, even if learners are autonomous in some aspects, it does not mean that they will be able to apply this autonomy to all areas of their learning (Schwienhorst, 2003).

 While it is possible to provide activities through CALL that learners can undertake individually, engaging in CALL does not necessarily make them more autonomous (Benson, 2001), despite some of the claims that have been made in CALL research (Blin, 2004). Technology can provide opportunities for learners to work autonomously, but having access to this technology is no guarantee that they will actually do so. Certainly, learners are able to work autonomously using CALL, but only provided they have reached a sufficient level of autonomy that prompts them to take the initiative to learn of their own accord. In most cases, becoming autonomous is a gradual process that requires transitions from teacher-dependence to self-dependence and from fixed content to variable content (Healey, 1999). CALL materials that allow practice of a certain skill or area, then, could not be considered as enhancing learner autonomy unless they played a role in facilitating these transitions, rather than just being a source of activities that learners can undertake without teacher supervision. Simply undertaking activities without teacher presence is not an indicator of autonomy. If, for example, students complete listening activities outside of class because they are required to have them done by the following class, this would unlikely be considered as autonomous, even though they were done without direct teacher supervision. If, however, students felt – of their own volition – that they wanted to improve their listening so decided to spend several hours completing the listening activities before the next class, this would be closer to what might be considered as autonomous learning.

Learner autonomy in CALL is complex, and certainly dependent on factors that reach far beyond the technology itself. Development of CALL materials that can support – or even contribute to – learner autonomy is not an impossibility, but it requires an understanding of these complexities at the design level. Studies investigating the factors which contribute to learner autonomy in CALL have identified both feedback and interactivity as key elements (e.g. Alm, 2006; Figura and Jarvis, 2007), as they allow learners to take stock of their progress and at the same time provide them with opportunities to use the language in a meaningful way, thus at the very least these must be considered in designing such materials. Finally, since some learners will have a natural tendency to take charge of their own learning compared with others, finding solutions that can cater to varied learner needs is indeed a challenging undertaking. These solutions may certainly include CALL, but with a realistic expectation of the role that CALL can play within the context in which it is used.

Use of the term "CALL"

There has been quite a lot of discussion recently on the appropriateness of the term "CALL" to describe the use of technology in second language teaching and learning. A number of acronyms have been used in the past several years, including CALL/CELL (computer-assisted/enhanced language learning), CASLA (computer-assisted second language acquisition), TALL/TELL (technology-assisted/enhanced language learning), NBLT (network-based language teaching), and, more recently, MALL (mobile-assisted language learning), to name a few. Why, then, has "CALL" been used for this book?

Deciding on an appropriate name for the field is hardly new, and periodically there have been attempts to rationalize the terms that are currently in use to determine what is best. One of the most convincing discussions on this topic is provided by Levy and Hubbard (2005), who give three main arguments in favor of using "CALL." Firstly, they argue that "CALL" may be used as an encompassing term, but point out that it does not mean that other terms cannot coexist. Due to the fact that, for the most part, other acronyms generally point to more specific areas or represent alternative perspectives to the field (such as CASLA, NBLT, and MALL), these can quite feasibly be used as sub-terms under the umbrella term of "CALL." The second argument that they raise is that the computer is a specific technology that has had an enormous impact on the language learning process, enabling learners to engage in activities and communication for the enhancement of all language skills and language areas, which sets it aside from other, less sophisticated, technologies. Levy and Hubbard's third point is that the term "CALL" has been the most enduring of all of the other terms which have been used. CALL has been used now for well over two decades, and has been incorporated in the titles of leading academic journals in the field, including *Computer Assisted Language Learning* and *ReCALL*, both of which have been around since the late 1980s, as well as in the titles of several influential books. While TELL may be considered as being broader in scope than CALL at first glance (for some reason, the term "TALL" did not seem to catch on when compared with "TELL," presumably because of the dual meaning of "conveying something" that might be included in TELL), this is not necessarily the case. It could be argued that almost any electronic device that may be used as a part of the language learning process must have a computer of some shape or form at its heart. Many modern mobile phones have more processing power than desktop computers did when CALL was first being established, and even tools such as electronic dictionaries, interactive whiteboards, and MP3 players contain computers that enable them to function as they do. Although the term "technology" is commonly used in a way that is largely synonymous with computers these days, it can in fact be applied to a far wider range of situations than "computer," such as the software that runs on computers or other devices. However, software cannot run without a computer, be it a desktop computer or a computer embedded in some other device, so to this end, the use of the term "computer" removes the potential for ambiguity that may arise as a result of using "technology."

According to Levy and Hubbard, in a Google search conducted on May 29, 2005, "computer-assisted language learning" yielded 99,100 hits in contrast to "technology-enhanced language learning," which produced only 6,550 hits. Five years later, the same search conducted on December 11, 2010, gave 165,000 hits for "computer-assisted language learning" and 23,900 hits for "technology-enhanced language learning." While the percentage of TELL compared to CALL has gone up from 6.6 percent to 14.5 percent over this time, it is still quite clear that CALL is convincingly favored over TELL as a term to describe the field. Thus, given the durability and inclusiveness of the term, CALL has been adopted throughout this book in the belief that it will remain as the encompassing term for the use of technologies in the language teaching and learning process.

Overview of the book

The purpose of the book is to bring together the diverse complexities that are continuing to emerge in the field, and to help readers to understand diversity as opposed to being threatened or intimidated by it. The book seeks to not only describe the various aspects of the field of CALL, but also to maintain a strongly practical tone by drawing relationships between these aspects and actual practice itself. It takes a descriptive standpoint, where readers may see the potential advantages and limitations of the diverse options available to them. These options are presented in a manner that is founded squarely on existing research in the field, thus enabling readers to make informed decisions regarding their own research and practice in CALL. While it is not intended to be a "how-to" book, a practical tone has been adopted to allow readers to consider how the diverse options presented to them may be of immediate use in their own settings.

The theme of diversity in this book is approached from eight overlapping perspectives which make up the discussion in Chapters 2 through 9. Each of these chapters has been written in a consistent format, starting with an overview and discussion of the general issues related to the theme of diversity covered in the chapter. This is followed by one or more practical examples, which illustrate the issues raised in the chapter, either based on authors' actual experiences or on studies from the literature. Potential implications from the general issues and the examples are then put forward so that readers may have an idea of what needs to be kept in mind when undertaking the use of CALL in their own learning contexts.

The starting point for CALL should always be the learners, and for this reason the book starts with three chapters that discuss very different aspects of the learners. As described earlier, learners will often use CALL materials differently from what teachers expect, and Chapter 2 describes how to examine learners to get a better understanding of the ways learners engage with CALL materials to get an idea of what they do to provide suitable training to assist them in becoming more effective users of CALL. This leads into Chapter 3, which describes learner training in terms of both the learning process and the learners who undergo the training themselves, and a three-part training model distinguishing technical, strategic, and pedagogical training. Chapter 4 then looks at the issue of learner support, specifically at how it can be designed in order to contribute to development of learner autonomy, and the advantages of CALL for providing this support. This is followed by Chapter 5 which provides an overview of some of the possible different types of environments that might be seen using CALL, including face-to-face, blended, distance, and virtual, examining them from both a technical perspective and their individual pedagogical implications. Chapter 6 moves into ways in which the availability of open educational resources allows new approaches to organizing, presenting, and using content from the Internet. The next chapter, Chapter 7, discusses the issue of modality, which has become increasingly important as the affordances of technology allow different modes of communication, and how multiple modes have the potential to contribute to learning in varying ways. Given the difficulties in making future predictions about technology (c.f. Levy and Stockwell, 2006), Chapter 8 looks at some of the emerging technological possibilities, divided up into the type of hardware, including multiple and single server technologies, single computer technologies, and mobile technologies. Finally, though it has been argued that research in CALL sits on the margins of mainstream fields from which many of its foundations have been built (Coleman, 2005), Chapter 9 argues that research in CALL has started to assume its own identity, and there is a solid relationship between research, practice, and technology. The conclusion, Chapter 10, looks at the existence of diversity in CALL contexts at an individual, institutional, and societal level.

While it is not possible to cover the entire range of diversities that may be encountered when using technology for language teaching and learning, this book seeks to provide an overview of at least some of the main areas where diversity can contribute to decisions made about the technological options, the pedagogical options, and the organizational options. Knowledge of these options may not make the decisions any easier, but it is hoped that this book can at least help teachers to make more informed decisions based on a holistic view of their individual language teaching and learning context.

2 Diversity in learner usage patterns

Robert Fischer

Introduction

In many parts of the world, it is difficult to think of a foreign or second language (L2) program that does not make use of some form of computer-assisted language learning (CALL). After even just a moment's reflection, many questions of how students actually use CALL materials quickly arise. Do students use CALL materials in similar ways? Do they use them as the software developers intended them to be used? How do we know how students use CALL materials? Why is it important to understand the ways in which they do? These and several other questions have been addressed by researchers who have studied what is commonly called "tracking data."[1] By analyzing what students do as they use CALL software (e.g. enter text in fields, click on buttons, choose a particular kind of help device associated with hyperactive text), we can begin to understand the kinds of strategies students use (or lack thereof) as they work their way through CALL programs. What has emerged from tracking data analysis is a remarkably wide variability in student usage patterns, a variability that ultimately leads to the conclusion that there is a pervasive need for learner training in order for students to become effective users of CALL software.

Overview and general issues

The study of tracking data gives us a clear and discrete view of students' actions as they engage in language learning tasks. It allows direct observation of students' actions, which in turn can provide evidence to confirm or disconfirm language learning principles. While other methods of observation are, of course, possible (see below), tracking student actions via the computer is the most discrete form of observation because students are not immediately aware that their actions are being tracked. Studying students' behavior in CALL environments can be challenged on ecological grounds (van Lier,

---

[1] Chapelle (2003) has noted that tracking data have often been referred to by various names: for example, tracking data, computer logs, CALL texts, process data, and working style data.

1996, 2000) since CALL environments are normally restricted environments and cannot encompass the totality of students' learning. Nevertheless, CALL environments constitute closely controlled environments in which students' actions are clearly visible and less subject to external forces than in the typical classroom environment.

Since the early 1990s, several prominent figures in the field have called for the collection and analysis of tracking data, notably Nina Garrett and Carol Chapelle (Garrett, 1991, 1998; Liddell and Garrett, 2004; Chapelle, 1997, 2001, 2007, 2009). Although interest in tracking data has a long history, relatively few researchers have actively pursued projects in the area. Analysis of tracking data can be an arduous and time-consuming undertaking, requiring careful planning and preparation, anticipating and resolving technical problems in the software itself, storing student information in safe and secure sites, coding learner data appropriately, and finally trying to make sense of the potentially massive amounts of data. Computer logs are not always easy to interpret; they often do not offer straightforward evidence of students' learning. For example, as Chapelle (2003) has questioned, if students click on a hyperactive word in a reading program that also helps them acquire vocabulary items, does that action mean that the students did not know the meaning of the word and that they then learned its meaning by viewing its translation in a pop-up window? Other corroborating evidence (e.g. results on pre- and posttests) is needed to ensure that students did not know the meaning of the word and in fact learned its meaning by using the program. In other kinds of CALL programs such as those used in computer-mediated communication (CMC), computer logs can provide more direct evidence of students' use of communicative strategies and language learning strategies because researchers can see the words that students explicitly use to communicate with their partner in chat transcripts. However, even here, reviewing students' chat transcripts is time-consuming and requires careful attention to details in their utterances over time to uncover clear evidence showing systemic progress in language learning.

Observation methods other than tracking students' actions within the CALL program itself are available to researchers. Some researchers have used video recording software to track students' actions on the computer (Pujolà, 2002; Glendenning and Howard, 2003; De Ridder, 2003). Packages like ScreenCam, HyperCam, and SnapzProX record all the actions taken by students that are visibly displayed on the computer monitor, and make a digital movie of those actions. Other researchers have set up a video camera by the computer and recorded the actions that students take as they use the software (Ganderton, 1999). Yet other researchers have directly observed students using software and taken notes on their actions. However, using video recording software or logging students' actions in the CALL program is a much less intrusive means of capturing students' actions than setting up a video camera near the computer, and also provides a more complete and objective record of students' actions than researchers' direct observation.

Regardless how the data are collected, analysis of those data reveals the ways in which students use the learning materials in the program and the paths they follow as they navigate through the program. For the purposes of this chapter, it is convenient to distinguish between (a) human–human interactions via the computer (e.g. CMC) and (b) human–computer interactions (e.g. clicking on hyperactive text) because these two categories provide different kinds of information in computer logs. Chat logs from human–human interactions in CMC sessions provide interesting language learning data, and analysis of those data shows reasonably consistent results for second language acquisition (e.g. the use of the L1 versus the L2 in communicating with others, the primacy of lexical concerns over grammatical matters in communication, and the value of the use of written language for focus on form).[2] Computer logs of human–computer interactions include much more varied data. When students confront the task of learning a specific aspect of the L2 in a program designed for that purpose (e.g. multimedia programs on reading and listening), analysis of tracking data shows a wide range in the use of the tools and resources included in the program. The rest of this chapter will focus on learner usage patterns in human–computer interactions.

Examples

This section presents a series of studies that show the diversity of student usage patterns in CALL software. These studies are representative of the kind of studies on tracking data, and were chosen because their findings reveal the basic parameters of the variability in students' use of CALL software and illustrate the extent of that variability.

Organized and disorganized learner behavior

Desmarais *et al.* (1998) designed the Vi-Conte multimedia program based on a short Canadian film and analyzed students' use of the program. The project involved three groups of students: (a) students who followed their normal classroom routine (i.e. did not watch the video or use the computer program);

---

[2] There is an extensive literature on CMC and language learning, especially with respect to sociocultural dimensions of second language acquisition. For more information, interested readers may wish to consult Abrams, 2003a, 2008; Belz, 2007; Belz and Thorne, 2006; Blake, 2000, 2007, 2009; Darhower, 2002, 2008; Kern, 1995; Lai *et al.*, 2008; Lee, 2001; Pellettieri, 2000; Smith, 2003; Thorne *et al.*, 2009; Warschauer and Kern, 2000.

(b) students who watched the video by itself; and (c) students who watched the video in the Vi-Conte program replete with ancillary components. The computer program contained procedures for watching the video with a music background, watching the video with a narrative track, and viewing scenes of modern-day Quebec. The program also included comprehension checks and fill-in-the-blanks exercises. The three groups of students were further subdivided by age (adult versus college age) and by proficiency level (intermediate level versus elementary level).

As the students worked with the computer program, the researchers asked the students to describe aloud the actions they were taking, and they also recorded the students as they navigated through the program. The researchers then transcribed the videotapes and analyzed the transcripts to investigate the ways in which the students used the various components of the program. The results of their analysis revealed a very wide range of patterns. At one extreme, the researchers characterized the actions of some students as following a linear schema in which the students moved through the program's components in the sequence of activities prescribed by the software's developers. At the other extreme, they labelled the actions of some students as "chaotic," in which "activities are often interrupted and the learner moves across the program menus. In many cases, the navigation appears so disorganized that it is almost impossible to relate the schedule to any coherent or sensible planning" (Desmarais *et al.*, 1998, pp. 332–334). The researchers were able to determine that as the students became familiar with the program their actions tended to become more linear, suggesting perhaps that at the beginning the students were simply exploring the various features of the program and then later started to use more effective language learning strategies. The researchers also found that the college-age students tended to engage in more chaotic behaviors than the adult students, and that the elementary-level students similarly engaged in more disorganized behaviors than the intermediate-level students. Some of the elementary-level students even abandoned some of the learning activities in the program apparently because they felt overwhelmed by the complexity of the authentic language used in the program.

The researchers hypothesized that all of the students in the project used problem-solving strategies as they worked with the software, and that the elementary-level students were not as adept at using problem-solving strategies as the intermediate-level students because of their lack of proficiency in the language. It may well be that learner experience and knowledge were the overriding factors in the project; the greater the experience and knowledge the students had (whether in terms of age, computer use, or language proficiency), the more they were able to make effective use of CALL software.

*Overuse of a single ancillary component and underuse
of other ancillary components*

One of the consistent findings in the analysis of tracking data in a variety of
CALL programs is that students often overuse a single basic component that
they believe to be the most directly helpful to the task at hand, and underuse
other components that they find less immediately relevant. Noblitt and Bland
(1991) described students' use of the features in Système-D, a French writing-
assistant program designed to facilitate students' writing compositions (see
also Bland *et al.*, 1990). The Système-D program contained a variety of ancillary components: a bilingual dictionary, a verb morphology component on
conjugations and tenses, a component displaying illustrative samples of functional language use, and other components providing information on sentence
structure, word families, and so on. Noblitt and Bland's analysis of student
use of the various components showed that the students used the bilingual dictionary 80 percent of the time. Further, the students adopted a literal approach
to looking words up in the dictionary to the extent of searching for inflected
forms of words rather than the base form (e.g. plants [plural] instead of plant
[singular]), leading Bland *et al.* to describe students' approach to learning as
the "naïve lexical hypothesis."

Davis and Lyman-Hager (1997) logged students' use of components in a
lesson on a Camerounian novel written in French. Using the glossing authentic
language texts (GALT) authoring system, the researchers developed seven help
functions for students to use in the lesson: pronunciation, English definitions,
French definitions, cultural references, grammar notes, explanations of struc-
tural relations in the text (e.g. antecedents) and relationships among characters,
and pictures of vocabulary items. Their analysis of students' use of the help
functions revealed that students used the English definition function 85 percent
of the time.[3]

Pujolà (2002) developed a web-based ESL program, ImPRESSions, focusing on listening and reading comprehension for Spanish-speaking students.
The program presented the content of the same news stories in both written and
video formats within the software, and students had virtually complete control
over their learning in the program. The program had two major kinds of help
devices: learner assistance features (e.g. dictionary, cultural notes, transcripts,
subtitles, buttons to rewind/replay video clips, and feedback/explanations) and
guidance features (e.g. advice on how to use appropriate learning strategies).
Pujolà recorded students' actions with ScreenCam as they used the program.
He found extensive variability in the ways in which students navigated through

---

[3] Ercetin (2003) found similar patterns of student use in an English as a second language (ESL)
reading program.

the program and accessed its help devices. He hypothesized that students with lower levels of proficiency in English would make more use of the transcripts and subtitles for the video clips than students with higher levels of proficiency, but he discovered that "students within each group behaved in varied, idiosyncratic ways" (p. 253). Pujolà was able to derive two categories of usage patterns: a "global approach" in which students infrequently sought help of any kind and "compulsive consultors" in which students repeatedly clicked on various buttons, especially the rewind/replay buttons for the video clips, because they thought they had to understand every little detail of the material to be learned.[4] Finally, corroborating the findings of Bland *et al.* (1990) and Davis and Lyman-Hager (1997), Pujolà noted that students primarily used the learner assistance features, those which they thought provided the most direct help to the task before them, rather than the learner guidance features on how to use appropriate learning strategies.

The four studies described above clearly indicate that many students use CALL software in ways that differ substantially from those intended by the developers of the programs. Many students adopt highly idiosyncratic approaches to using software, some of which do not seem to suggest even a modicum of planning or metacognitive control. A substantial part of the learning approaches noted by the studies above involves students' overuse of the basic components they believe to be most directly beneficial to their completing the task at hand and their underuse of other components designed to strengthen the ways in which they go about completing that task.

Levels of learners and individual variability

Although students adopt highly idiosyncratic approaches to using CALL software, students at lower proficiency levels in the L2 generally seem to make greater use of resources in software, but we still witness considerable variability in the use of these resources by individual students. As Desmarais *et al.* (1998) determined, elementary-level students in their project exhibited more disorganized behaviors than intermediate-level students and, in addition, some elementary-level students abandoned exercises that they found too difficult. In one of the earliest tracking studies, Chapelle and Mizuno (1989) found that lower-level students made significantly greater use of help functions in an ESL lesson than higher-level students, but noted that some lower-level students simply looked at the help functions and quickly exited the lesson without doing any of the exercises.

Brandl (1995) designed a program on the passive voice construction in German for American students. He divided third-semester German students

[4] Roby (1999, p. 98) called this kind of behavior "click-happy behavior."

into a low-achievement group and a high-achievement group, and had students in both groups use the program. Brandl tracked students' choice of four different types of feedback as they worked on grammatical exercises: (a) right–wrong feedback; (b) feedback on the location of the error; (c) feedback explaining why the answer was wrong; and (d) feedback simply showing the correct answer. Brandl investigated the combination of students' initial choice of feedback type and their follow-up choice of feedback type after they attempted to correct their errors. His analysis revealed that students' initial choice of feedback type did not vary significantly between the groups; most students in both groups chose right–wrong feedback. However, students' subsequent choice of feedback type differed appreciably between the groups. The students in the low-achievement group chose a narrower range of feedback types than the students in the high-achievement group. Students in the low-achievement group also chose feedback types that suggested they were less willing to correct errors in their answers than students in the high-achievement group. For example, after receiving initial feedback, low-achievement students chose to see the correct answer more often than the high-achievement students. Further, low-achievement students "made numerous incorrect changes to their answers as well as less intelligent guesses" (p. 206) than the high-achievement students.

Ercetin (2003) studied the degree to which intermediate-level students and advanced-level students accessed various types of annotations in a multimedia ESL reading lesson. She found that intermediate-level students accessed a significantly greater number of annotations than the advanced-level students but that they did not spend any more time reading the content of the annotations than the advanced-level students. Ercetin hypothesized that they were not able to take as much advantage of the information presented in the annotations as the advanced-level students in the same period of time due to their lower level of proficiency in English. In addition, within each group of students, analysis showed wide variation in students' individual use of annotations. Ercetin computed the mean number of times that students consulted the annotations and the standard deviations associated with these means. The standard deviations for each mean were very large, indicating wide distributions in the number of times individual students accessed the annotations.

In a similar vein, the data collected for the project described in Fischer (2004a) included information on the frequency with which students accessed annotations in a multimedia French reading program. This program contained annotations for most words in the text, including twenty-six words that were marked in blue. Students in second- and fourth-semester classes used the program, and Fischer analyzed the number of times the students accessed the annotations for the marked and unmarked words. He examined students' behaviors by level, second- versus fourth-semester, and by extreme thirds (i.e. top third

Table 2.1 *Means and standard deviations of the number of clicks on hyperactive words by level of general proficiency and achievement*

| | Second semester | | | | Fourth semester | | | |
| | Bottom third | | Top third | | Bottom third | | Top third | |
	Marked words	Unmarked words	Marked words	Unmarked words	Marked words	Unmarked words	Marked words	Unmarked words
Mean	20.58	144.00	28.25	86.08	30.89	31.22	29.33	64.11
SD	11.32	116.82	5.48	84.35	12.55	30.37	10.77	41.27

and bottom third of the students as measured by class grades) at each level. This investigation yielded a detailed view of student behaviors by two levels of general proficiency in the language and by specific level of achievement within each level. Table 2.1 lists the means and standard deviations of the number of times students accessed the annotations. The figures in Table 2.1 show some general patterns of student use as indicated by the means of the various groups of students, but the degree of variability for the unmarked words, as indicated by the large standard deviations within each group, attenuate the results of the analysis.

Focusing first on the marked words, the mean number of clicks on the marked words shows that the students at the lower level of achievement in the second-semester group – the lowest level of achievement and general proficiency – clicked much less often on the marked words than the students at the other three levels. Students at the other three levels clicked on marked words with approximately the same frequency. This pattern suggests that the students at the lowest level were simply not up to the task presented to them and in effect did not seriously engage in its completion, even though the appearance of the words was clearly enhanced by the blue color, and that the students at the higher levels took more or less equal advantage of the availability of the annotations.

Now focusing on the unmarked words, the mean number of clicks on these words show a progression of decreasing frequency of clicks from the lowest level to the higher levels (144.00 > 86.08 > 31.22), but then an increasing frequency to 64.11 for the students at the highest level. This general decrease in clicking behavior for unmarked words is what we would expect for students as they gain knowledge of the language. The higher mean (64.11) for the students at the highest level requires some comment. At first glance, it would appear that these students' actions run contrary to the trend of decreasing frequency. However, removing the third mean from the series (31.22) – the lowest third

Table 2.2 *Minimum and maximum number of clicks on marked and unmarked words by level of general proficiency and achievement*

	Second semester				Fourth semester			
	Bottom third		Top third		Bottom third		Top third	
	Marked words	Unmarked words	Marked words	Unmarked words	Marked words	Unmarked words	Marked words	Unmarked words
Minimum	0	0	24	0	19	0	18	0
Maximum	33	280	42	295	60	80	52	115

of the fourth-semester students – leaves the trend of decreasing frequency of clicks intact as students advance in their knowledge of the language (144.00 > 86.08 > 64.11). In fact, the explanation for this situation lies in the third group of students; closer inspection of the data revealed that several students in this group did not click on any of the unmarked words at all, substantially reducing the mean for this group.

Perhaps of greater importance, the standard deviations of the means for the unmarked clicked words show very large distributions in the number of clicks on these words by individual students.[5] Table 2.2 lists the minimum and maximum number of clicks on marked and unmarked words for the four groups of students.

The range of the number of clicks on unmarked words is much greater than that on the marked words and shows the extent of the variability among students in the various groups.[6] This individual variability effectively overshadows patterns of student use based on level of general proficiency or specific achievement, and makes generalizations based on such categories difficult to establish with any degree of certainty.

Individual learner variability and material learned

Since so much variation in the use of program components is attributable to individual student differences, we might expect to see a positive relationship between the degree to which students use program components and the degree

---

[5] Hulstijn (1993) found similar degrees of individual variability in his analysis of Dutch students using an English as a Foreign Language (EFL) reading program.

[6] For the marked words, there were a total of twenty-six words marked in blue in the text. The maximum number of clicks in Table 2.2 show that at least some students clicked more than once on specific marked words. De Ridder (2000, 2002, 2003) demonstrated in very clear terms that marking induces students to click on marked words much more often than on unmarked words.

to which they learn the material presented in the program. Unfortunately, studies that have addressed this issue have yielded results that are far from clear.

Knight (1994) studied students' use of a dictionary in a program on reading authentic texts in Spanish. As part of her study, Knight divided intermediate-level students into high-verbal ability and low-verbal ability groups and investigated the effect of students' use of the dictionary on incidental vocabulary learning in immediate and delayed post-tests containing both vocabulary recognition questions and vocabulary production questions. She also examined the effect of students' dictionary use on their recall of information presented in the texts. Knight found moderate correlations between students' dictionary use and vocabulary recognition questions in the post-tests for students in both groups but not between dictionary use and vocabulary production items, a result that should not be unexpected since students were engaged in reading – not writing – Spanish. She also found a moderately high correlation between the low-verbal ability students' dictionary use and their recall of information presented in the texts, but not for the high-verbal ability students. (This finding is curious given the fact that the low-verbal ability students actually looked up fewer words than the high-verbal ability students.)[7] In sum, Knight's analysis showed the low-verbal ability students seemed to benefit more from dictionary use than the high-verbal ability students, but the relationship between dictionary use and various aspects of learning was not consistent across groups.

Chun and Plass (1996) studied students' use of different types of annotations (text, picture, and movie) in a multimedia reading program designed for second-year German students. For questions that students answered correctly on a post-test (vocabulary recognition items and vocabulary production items), Chun and Plass examined the students' look-up behaviors with respect to types of annotations they consulted. In addition to tracking students' use of the various annotation types, they interviewed students at the end of the project and asked the students which annotation types they consulted. They found weak correlations between the types of annotations students said they consulted and the types of annotations they actually consulted in the program. That is, for vocabulary items that students correctly answered on the post-test, they were able to remember what types of annotations they used, but only minimally so. Most important, Chun and Plass found no correlation between the combined total of all annotation types that the students said they consulted and their performance on the post-test.

Laufer and Hill (2000) investigated the use of annotations for marked words in an EFL reading program by Hong Kong and Israeli students. Their analysis of tracking data revealed that all students in both groups clicked on all

---

[7] Chun (2001) found no relationship between dictionary use and recall of information in a reading program designed for second-year German students.

of the marked words, some students multiple times, and accessed a variety of annotation types: L1 definitions (Chinese or Hebrew), L2 definitions (English) with contextualized samples, supplementary information (e.g. phonetic transcriptions and information on levels of linguistic formality), and lexical roots (base word forms). Laufer and Hill then analyzed the relationship between the number of times students clicked on the individual words – means ranging from 1.0 to 3.2 times – and their performance on a vocabulary post-test. They found only a weak correlation between students' clicking behaviors and their post-test scores.

The three studies above identify some partial or minimal relationships between what students do as they use software and what they have learned after they use the software, but it must be admitted that there seems to be little overall relationship between program use and achievement. Students' use of resources in programs does not seem to relate in any substantial way to the degree to which they learn the material presented in the programs.

Students' self-reports on the use of program components
and their actual use of program components

Students' self-reports, primarily in the form of questionnaires and surveys, have a long tradition in CALL as a way to evaluate CALL software in general and to collect data on student usage in particular. In a series of projects, Fischer (1999, 2000, 2004b, 2004c) investigated the relationship between what students say they do and what they actually do by comparing individual students' responses to questionnaire items focusing on the use of components in programs and their actual use of those components. For the French multimedia program described earlier, Fischer (2004a, see also 2007) examined the relationship between students' self-reported use of program components as indicated by their questionnaire responses and their actual use of those components as shown in tracking data. Immediately after the second- and fourth-semester students used the program in a lab environment, they completed a questionnaire on their use of the program's components and their perception of the instructional value of those components. Fischer then correlated students' responses on the questionnaire and their use of the program's features. The analysis yielded mixed results; Table 2.3 and Table 2.4 give a schematic overview of the results of the correlation analysis.

Table 2.3 shows that students were, at best, not consistently aware of what they did as they used the program, which calls into question the reliability of their perceptions of the value of the program's components. If students' self-reports on the use of program features are unreliable, then their judgments of the instructional value of those features must be considered suspect, as

Table 2.3 *Schematic overview of correlation analysis of students'*
self-reported use and their actual use of program features

Actual use	Self-reported use		
	Marked word annotations	Unmarked word annotations	Dictionary use
Second-semester students	0	+	+
Fourth-semester students	0	–	0

Note: 0 = no relationship; + = significant positive correlation; – = significant negative correlation;
significant correlations only weak or moderate

Table 2.4 *Schematic overview of correlation analysis of students' perception*
of the instructional value of features and their actual use of program features

Actual use	Perception of instructional value		
	Marked word annotations	Unmarked word annotations	Dictionary use
Second-semester students	0	0	0
Fourth-semester students	0	0	0

Note: 0 = no relationship.

evidenced by the absence of any relationship between perceptions of value and
component use shown in Table 2.4.

In a tutorial program for third-year American students studying Spanish on
indirect speech (e.g. *he is going* versus *he said he would go*), Collentine (2000)
measured the impact of specific program components on student learning. The
program contained: (a) video clips illustrating speech acts; (b) exemplars of
indirect speech enhanced by color coding and audio files; (c) consciousness-
raising questions in which students typed in answers to questions on various
aspects of indirect speech samples; and (d) comprehension checks with feedback. Collentine tracked the number of times students accessed the various
components while using the program and the amount of time they spent on
each. He then used regression analysis to estimate the contribution of the
amount of time spent on each component to students' post-test scores. On the
one hand, his analysis revealed that students' use of the audio component contributed significantly to their post-test performance but that they underutilized
this component as they navigated through the program. On the other hand,

students' use of the video component did not contribute to their post-test performance even though they overutilized it. In addition, the students did not use the exemplar component a great deal, but their use of this component proved to contribute significantly to one aspect of their post-test performance – the verb form in the subordinate clause (e.g. *would go*). Students' use of the consciousness-raising component seemed to contribute to their post-test performance, but further analysis revealed that some students did not provide substantial answers to the questions in this component and thus did not benefit from its use. Finally, students' use of the comprehension checks contributed significantly to their post-test performance.

At the end of his discussion of the analysis, Collentine concluded that the key factor in students' performance on the post-test was their use of two multimedia features in the program: audio support for sentences that they read on the screen and color enhancements emphasizing critical features of the indirect speech construction. Of relevance to the discussion here, Collentine's study suggests that the number of times students consult specific components, whether very frequently or very infrequently, is less important for their learning than the pedagogical value of the content of the components and students' active use of that content.

Summary

The above survey of studies covers a variety of languages (e.g. French, German, Spanish, and ESL/EFL) in different kinds of CALL programs (e.g. reading, listening, and grammar) with a wide spectrum of resources made available in the programs (e.g. L1 glosses, L2 explanations, pictures, movies, and dictionaries) used by learners at various levels of L2 proficiency (e.g. beginning, intermediate, and advanced).[8] Some general parameters emerge from these studies. Students clearly use software in unexpected ways, often in ways that differ substantially from those envisioned by the software developers. Lower-level students, whether defined in terms of general L2 proficiency, specific L2 achievement, experience using technology, or simply age, seem to engage in less well organized approaches to using software resources than higher-level students.

Students at all levels tend to overuse a single component in a program that they believe is the most directly helpful to completing the task they are asked to complete and underuse other components that they perceive to be less

---

[8] This survey does not include tracking data for students using intelligent CALL (ICALL) software based on natural language processing. While the analysis of tracking data in ICALL holds a great deal of interest, describing that analysis goes well beyond the scope of this chapter. Readers interested in tracking in ICALL may wish to consult Nagata (1993, 1995, 1996), Heift (2001, 2002, 2004, 2007, 2008, 2010), and Heift and Schulze (2007).

immediately helpful. Although the reasons underlying such a single-focused approach are not at all clear, we can wonder whether one of these reasons is what we might call the principle of "expedient lesson completion," a pragmatic orientation to task completion in which minimal (or perhaps simplistic) effort is made to achieve an objective in the shortest period of time (see Wesche and Paribakht, 2000). Students at all levels also exhibit a wide range of behaviors which can often obscure more general patterns of student usage. The extent of individual variation in the use of program components makes it difficult to identify patterns essential to support generalizations about software use based on student categories such as levels of proficiency, achievement, and experience. It would seem that other kinds of categories are necessary to capture generalizations about student usage, but it is not clear at this time what kinds of taxonomies are appropriate for this purpose.[9] Desmarais *et al.* (1998) attempted to relate student usage patterns to the Myers Briggs type indicator, but the student patterns were so diffuse that the analysis did not produce any results. Felix (2001) tried to do the same with Oxford's (1990) inventory of learning strategies, based on students' responses on a questionnaire, but without success.[10] Finally, comparisons of student self-reports and tracking data have shown that the use of student questionnaires alone is not a reliable source of information about student use of software and should be avoided as a single source of information.

Implications

As shown by the analysis of tracking data, the variability in student usage patterns of CALL software is highly individualistic in nature. This variability has several implications for issues in CALL such as instructional design, the implementation of second language acquisition principles in CALL materials,

[9] As Pujolà (2002) tried to apply the labels of "global approach" and "compulsive consultor" to characterize general student categories, others have also proposed various kinds of labels: De Ridder (2003) – internal regulator versus external regulator; Nelson *et al.* (1999) – browsing, linear, channel surfing, and tentative; Van der Linden (1993) – go on until you get it right, drill, once is enough, and browsing; Heift (2002) – browsers, peekers, and adamants. As useful as these labels are, in the final analysis they may prove to represent only preliminary attempts to characterize student interactions with software; they do not seem to relate directly to underlying learner constructs in a meaningful way.

[10] Plass *et al.* (1998), Jones and Plass (2002), and Jones (2009) have shown that allowing students to choose the kind of annotation they prefer to use (picture or text) has a measurable effect on students' learning of vocabulary. Chun and Payne (2004) were able to relate students' clicking behavior to the working memory. They found that students with shorter working memory clicked more often on words than students with longer working memory as a compensatory learning strategy. Cognitively oriented research and student usage patterns would seem to be an especially fruitful area of inquiry.

and the extent of the real impact of CALL software on learning, especially in less controlled environments such as the web.

The question of carefully developed instructional design quickly arises as a way to guide learners' use of software by appropriately structuring the learning environment for them. Instructional design, which should be understood to mean not only the general appearance of the learning environment for learners but also the ways in which second language acquisition principles are to be implemented and help options are to be made available to learners, figured prominently in the early development of tutorial CALL programs. In stand-alone programs, that is, programs stored and used by learners on local computers, the program designer closely controlled the learning environment by choosing which learning features to make available at specific points in the learning process. As tutorial CALL progressed and learner autonomy came to the fore, learner-centered instructional design became the norm in which students were able to choose which resource(s) to use from among a variety of resources. Finally, as stand-alone programs have given way to web-based programs (Garrett, 2009; Lafford, 2009; Otto and Pusack, 2009), instructional design seems to have lost much of its meaning because learners have a virtually endless supply of resources at their immediate disposal on the web.

Perhaps it is time to reconsider the inherent openness of the web for selected language learning purposes and design learning environments that have a clear focus on specific learning objectives and in addition provide guidance to learners by structuring the learning process and including only help options relevant to their individual learning needs (see Cárdenas-Claros and Gruba, 2009). To this end, browserless learning environments, programs that run on the Internet without a browser (e.g. iTunes), hold considerable promise because they can provide this kind of pedagogical structure. Browserless programs have the same advantages as web-based programs – always being available to learners on the Internet – but, because they do not run in a browser, they can be designed to include only the learning features (e.g. sequenced screen displays and help options) that are pertinent to the learning task at hand.

Regardless of how language learning programs are delivered to students, the survey of studies above shows the pervasive need for learner training. Training learners to be intelligent users of CALL programs will go a long way in addressing questions of student usage, but training learners to use CALL programs effectively – which is a particular case of the general principle of training learners to use language learning strategies effectively – can be a long and difficult undertaking. Learner training in CALL entails not only guiding learners to make good pedagogical decisions to facilitate their learning, but also instructing them how to use technological resources in support of those pedagogical decisions.

Hubbard (2004), Levy and Stockwell (2006), Kolaitis *et al.* (2006), Kassen and Lavine (2007), Winke and Goertler (2008a), and others have underscored the need for learner training in CALL. While some (e.g. Winke and Goertler) have argued for the need to train learners in the use of specialized hardware and software (e.g. microphones and Wimba voice tools), others (e.g. Hubbard) have advocated for more general pedagogical and technical training in the use of the tools and resources included in CALL programs (see also Chapter 3).

Hubbard (2004) has proposed the following five principles for learner training:

(1) Experience CALL yourself. Teachers should experience first-hand the use of a CALL program to learn a language themselves.
(2) Give learners teacher training. Learners should be taught language learning principles that are "necessary for any kind of coherent language teaching" (p. 52).
(3) Use a cyclic approach. Learners should receive instruction in training principles, use those principles in actual learning situations, and then review them in a continuous cyclic approach.
(4) Use collaborative debriefings. Because learners use most CALL software by themselves outside the classroom, it is useful for them to share their experiences with other learners in order that learners can learn from each other's experiences.
(5) Teach general exploitation strategies. Learners should be shown how to get the most out of the software they are using in order to derive maximum benefit from the materials and resources included in the software.[11]

Of these principles, (2) – "give learners teacher training" and (5) – "teach general exploitation strategies" seem the most beneficial to address the problems of students' disorganized actions and "expedient lesson completion" evident in the tracking data above. If students understand the importance of using software in principled ways and of taking advantage of what is made available in the software, they should be able to become much more effective technology users and language learners.

"Give learners teacher training," analogous to learning strategy training, focuses on what may well be the most intractable problem for some language learners. As many classroom teachers have noticed, some students lack even basic notions – or have highly folkloric notions – of how to go about learning a second language. They approach language learning much in the same way as they approach learning in other disciplines and can become frustrated when they discover that their approach does not lead to success. While few educators

---

[11] O'Bryan (2008) applied most of these principles to a group of ESL students with partial success.

would argue against encouraging students to use individualized learning strategies that work well for them, nevertheless many students stand in need of understanding and applying appropriate language learning strategies as they engage in learning tasks. Finally, in CALL, the effect of the learning strategy problem is compounded by the fact that since almost all CALL programs are used outside the classroom, learners do not have the benefit of a teacher who can guide their learning efforts on a daily basis.

"Teach general exploitation strategies" addresses the problem of "expedient lesson completion" and the single-focused approach to using CALL software. The underlying problem may well be that some students are not willing to go beyond minimally meeting explicitly stated objectives or cannot make a sustained commitment to learning, whether in the classroom or in a CALL environment. While motivation of course plays a central role here, helping students to acquire and use effective learning strategies should enhance their willingness to explore lesson components that they initially perceive to be less immediately helpful to completing the task at hand. If students understand the value of ancillary components as devices to facilitate and reinforce their learning, they should be able to know how to make greater use of them, leading ultimately to improvement in their learning.

To implement the two principles above, CALL programs should include not only a clear statement of learning objectives but also an explanation of how to achieve these objectives. They should provide a demonstration on how to use the tools and resources made available in the program, followed by a tutorial guiding students in their actual use in practice exercises in order to give the students first-hand experience in their use. It is also advisable to include prompts at various points throughout programs to remind students of the availability of the tools and resources in the program and to encourage students to make use of them.

The inclusion of explanations, demonstrations, tutorials, and prompts in software will probably not be sufficient to inculcate these principles in students. Simply including strategy training in software alone does not mean that students will heed such advice (Pujolà, 2002). Successful implementation of the principles will likely require a live demonstration by a teacher or tutor on the use of the program, explanation of the pedagogical purpose of the program's components, and instructional guidance in their use, all within the immediate environment in which the software is to be used. While this kind of human intervention is relatively easy in a face-to-face environment such as a language lab, it becomes much more problematic in distance education in which person-to-person communication can be difficult to establish and maintain. In distance education, the use of audio-conferencing, video-conferencing, chat, and perhaps even remote desktop access may offer viable solutions to working with at-distance students. Despite the potential difficulties, human contact with students is critical for effective learner training.

It will also likely not be sufficient to implement these principles only at the beginning of the instructional process; Hubbard's (2004) (3) – "use a cyclic approach" principle is a crucial element. Cobb and Stevens (1996) reported that one of the authors trained learners to use a certain feature in his program in a practice session and that students directly saw how much their use of the feature led to improvement in their learning. However, when the students subsequently used the program on their own, their use of this feature was virtually non-existent. The author was able to solve this problem only by making the feature so prominent in the program that students could not easily overlook it. Effective learner training clearly needs to be carried out in a cyclic fashion over time, much in the same way as training in the use of general language learning strategies needs to be continuously reinforced.

In summary, although learner training procedures such as those proposed by Hubbard (2004) can be difficult to implement in CALL environments, especially at-distance environments, and require active pedagogical intervention over the course of the learning process, doing so may well be worth the effort in the long term. Helping students to organize their interactions with CALL software into well-reasoned approaches to using the software will enable them to take greater advantage of its features and derive greater benefit from its use than in the situations revealed by the analysis of tracking data in the studies above.

Conclusion

Tracking student use of CALL software has a long history, virtually from the beginning of CALL as a discipline. Although the analysis of tracking data is time-consuming, it is nevertheless important to understand how students use software because not understanding can seriously impede progress in our profession. Student usage patterns have direct relevance to questions of instructional design (how to design software to encourage its appropriate use) and learner autonomy (the ability of students to use learning materials more or less removed from sustained contact with an expert – a critically important factor in distance education).

This chapter has focused on students' interactions with materials, tools, and resources in what are commonly called tutorial CALL programs, programs designed specifically to facilitate learning in specific areas of second language acquisition. It has presented evidence on the ways in which students use the tools and resources made available in tutorial programs as they complete language learning tasks. The general results of the analysis of tracking data have shown the remarkable diversity of students' approaches to using CALL soft-ware. Students follow highly individualistic and idiosyncratic paths to task completion that are not easily amenable to standard classifications of types of learner and make generalizations difficult to establish. The key implication stemming from this analysis is that the majority of students stand in clear need of learner training to become effective software users.

More than twenty-five years ago, Clark (1983) described instructional media as a delivery truck and made the analogy that media are to student achieve-ment as the delivery truck is to the grocery store (see also Witte, 2007). That is, media merely deliver content to students in the same way that the delivery truck delivers food to the grocery store. To extend Clark's analogy, language learners need to make intelligent decisions about how to use components in CALL programs to advance the cause of their learning in the same way that shoppers need to make intelligent decisions about which foods to purchase to advance the cause of their nutrition. Learner training should play a leading role in helping learners make those decisions.

3 Diversity in learner training

Philip Hubbard and Kenneth Romeo

Introduction

Learner training for computer-assisted language learning (CALL) is a process aimed at promoting the development of technology competence specifically for the purpose of second language acquisition.[1] As evidence of its growing recognition in language teaching, the recent framework document for the TESOL technology standards (Healey *et al.*, 2009) lays out a set of performance indicators for language learners, with the implicit assumption that teachers are responsible for training the students to achieve them. Beyond that general competence, though, is the more specific competence needed to use technology successfully within a given environment, task, or software program. Since this is a more widely, though still quite inadequately, studied area, it will be the focus of the remainder of this chapter. It should be noted, however, that many of the points discussed here are also relevant for developing general competence for using technology in language learning.

In line with the theme of this edited volume, the purpose of the present chapter is to explore diversity in learner training for CALL. Specifically, we will look at two distinct dimensions: diversity in the training process and diversity in the individuals and groups undergoing the training. By combining these two in a single work, we hope to achieve the goal of providing a broad overview of the possibilities for learner training along with a description of some of the issues that remain to be resolved in accommodating the diversity inherent in groups and individuals. From our experiences with CALL learner training over the past few years, it is clear that both the collective and the individual perspectives need to be addressed to improve the effectiveness of this endeavor.

---

[1] The term "learner training" is used here because of its wide recognition in both CALL and general language teaching literature. One could argue that the goal often goes beyond training to "education," implying the ability to make independent informed choices, rather than mechanically following directions. This is analogous to the shift from the term "teacher training" to "teacher education" in recent decades. In the present work we will continue with "learner training" for ease of exposition but the terminology is an issue which is worth revisiting as this subdomain of CALL – and language learning in general – grows. See Sinclair (2006) for an interesting discussion.

Overview and general issues

Diversity in the learner training process

Background Although a few articles previously mentioned the importance of training language learners for general technology competence (e.g. Beller-Kenner, 1999), Barrette (2001) was perhaps the first to recognize the need for training those already considered "computer literate" – university students in the US. Her paper began with a focused review of fourteen CALL research articles appearing in the *CALICO Journal* and *Foreign Language Annals* from 1997 and 1998, noting that there was little explicit evidence either of participants' previous computer literacy or of training them with the applications being studied. At the outset of her own study, she surveyed her students' familiarity and comfort level with nine applications ranging from word processing to building web pages. She then provided technical training in the use of these applications along with tasks for employing them in foreign language learning contexts. Her results showed impressive gains in students' self-reported comfort levels with these applications, and she concluded that profiling students' computer literacy and providing training are important steps in effective use of CALL. More recently, Winke and Goertler (2008b) conducted a wide-ranging survey expanding on Barrette's work, involving 911 first- and second-year foreign language students at Michigan State University. They discovered that many students did not have access to or proficiency with the specialized tools needed for CALL.

Hubbard (2004) approached learner training for CALL explicitly, suggesting that it should take a prominent place in the field. That paper offered five practice-based principles for CALL learner training consistent with much of the literature on other types of learner training. Kolaitis and a group of colleagues (Kolaitis *et al.*, 2006) conducted a three-year project based on applying Hubbard's model to a set of courses within a community college ESL program and concluded that it not only influenced student interaction with CALL materials positively but also had a noticeable washback effect on the participating instructors' classroom teaching. Adopting the same model, O'Bryan (2008) demonstrated that even a small amount of training (three ten-minute sessions) led to measurable, though not quite statistically significant, distinctions in student use of help options in online reading materials, as well as clearly increased awareness of their value.

A review of subject characteristics in CALL literature across seventy-eight research studies in four major technology and language learning journals from 2000–2004 noted that only 31 percent of those studies included any kind of learner training (Hubbard, 2005). When training was provided, it was typically only basic training at the beginning of the study to insure that students knew how the application functioned. Evidence of research involving any training on how to link the application or activity to language learning objectives or of training beyond the beginning stage of the study was rare. Yet, somewhat surprisingly, twenty-two of the studies (29 percent) mentioned in the discussion section that additional training was warranted and could have led to more favorable results. More interestingly, fourteen of these had not mentioned any training prior to the study and three others had explicitly specified that no training was provided as part of the research design.

The literature to date thus suggests that it is common practice to offer little if any learner training before turning students loose on a CALL software application, task, or activity. However, it also suggests that providing such training can result in improved performance. In the remainder of this section, we explore the options in doing so.

Three-part framework This section addresses diversity by looking at the different types of learner training available to a teacher or developer. It reviews a three-part training model (Romeo and Hubbard, 2010) distinguishing technical, strategic, and pedagogical training, and discusses issues in the type of training that may be useful depending on the proficiency level and readiness for self-directed learning of the language students.

For students to be effective users of a computer tool or learning application, they must first understand how to operate it and then become comfortable with its operation. Although there is often a general sense that today's "digital natives" (Prensky, 2001) need no such training, there is evidence to the contrary. As noted previously, Barrette (2001) and Winke and Goertler (2008b) have provided strong support for the contention that many students are not sufficiently prepared to engage in effective use of computers for language learning and that technical training is therefore needed. Such training is not limited to basic "computer literacy" but crucially encompasses three additional areas. One is the use of general applications, such as audio and video recording, speed controls in media players, and advanced searching with Google and other search engines, that many learners may not have proficiency in from their non-CALL uses of computers. A second is the use of language-specific applications, such as keyboarding skills necessary for foreign character sets. The third and perhaps most overlooked is an understanding of the options and controls in a particular dedicated CALL application. Even if the courseware itself offers tutorials and help options, as many commercial products do, students may forget or fail to discover useful functions provided by the program without sufficient training (Kolaitis *et al.*, 2006).

While technical issues are specific to CALL learner training, the concept of strategy training is already familiar to most in the language teaching community. In fact, strategic training for CALL is an extension of the strategy instruction that blossomed in the 1980s as exemplified in the work of Oxford (1990) and others. A certain portion of CALL strategic training involves strategies analogous to those in non-CALL environments, such as preparing for listening or reading by previewing and reflecting on the likely content of a text. Others, however, are more specific to CALL, such as opening a separate text window for a transcript of a web-based video and placing it beside the video for easy reference (Figure 3.1). To clarify, to know how to open, move, and resize multiple windows on a computer desktop is a technical skill; to use that knowledge deliberately to aid comprehension and vocabulary development when needed is a strategy.

It is well established that there are differences in the effective use of various support features in CALL applications, such as clicking on hypertext links in digital readings to get L1 translations, L2 definitions, graphic support, or cultural notes (e.g. Chun and Plass, 1996) and responding to computer-generated feedback (e.g. Pujolà, 2001; Heift, 2002). These differences in effective use could be lessened if more learner training infusing such features strategically were provided.

A full discussion of learner strategies available for CALL is beyond the scope of this chapter, although it is clear that there are ones that transfer from non-CALL settings as well as those specific to CALL settings (e.g. monitoring the ongoing transcript during an online chat, slowing recorded speech using media player controls, and hypertext linking to comprehension supports of various types in an online reading). It is also clear that there is potential for training that impacts strategy use of the four widely cited types: cognitive, metacognitive, social, and affective strategies (Oxford, 1990). In particular, in online settings where the learner is more independent than in a traditional class, expansion of metacognitive strategies seems warranted.

The final type of learner training, pedagogical, involves giving learners some of the knowledge and skills provided in the education of a language teacher. An example of pedagogical training would be to introduce students to the concepts and supporting research underlying the distinctions between top-down, bottom-up, and interactive processing in listening and reading (Peterson, 2001). This is an extension of the principle from Hubbard (2004) "Give learners teacher training," and it is based on the assumption that CALL environments generally provide learners with more choices and thus more potential control over their learning paths than other environments. Therefore, the decisions a learner makes when using CALL materials and tools should be informed by an adequate knowledge base. Pedagogical training is sometimes integrated with strategic training, providing the foundation for students to determine when and how to use known strategies as well as to devise new ones.

To summarize, technical training provides learners with expertise in *how* to use the options and controls of both general and specific applications on the

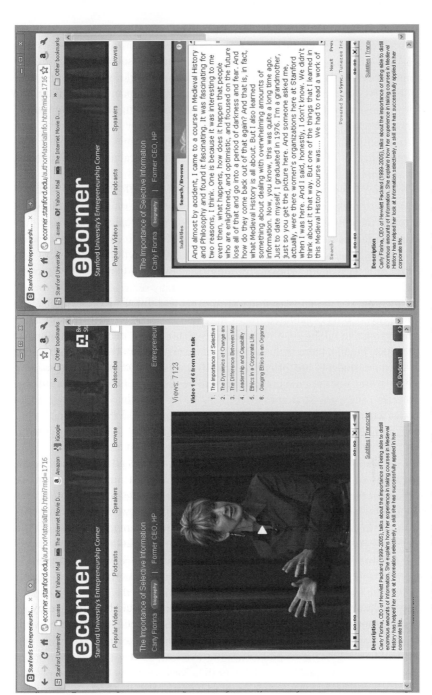

Figure 3.1 Using multiple windows to facilitate listening comprehension and vocabulary development

computer for language learning purposes. Strategic training focuses on *what* to do to support certain task and learning objectives, including how to link sequences of strategies or techniques into coherent procedures. Pedagogical training provides the foundation for helping learners determine specific learning objectives and understand *why* to use certain techniques and procedures to achieve those objectives. The relative weight given to these three provides a range of diversity for environments with learner training.

Determining an effective balance of these training areas in a given setting is a challenge. It is not enough to focus on technical training alone with the tacit assumption that once students understand the operation of the application that they are using, they will be able to use it appropriately for their language learning purposes. It is important to integrate strategic training so that learners can make the connection between what the technology has to offer and how those affordances can be manipulated in an effective manner. The area of pedagogical training is somewhat more problematic. As we will see in the next section, there is an issue of time: all training takes time away from other learning activities, and pedagogical training in particular may seem far enough removed from the goals of the class to not warrant that additional time. Further, when cultural diversity is considered, there may be resistance among students from certain groups to taking on a responsibility that they believe should belong to the teacher. Finally, there is the question of diversity in motivation to consider: just because students are provided with foundational knowledge about language learning does not mean that they will be able to connect that knowledge to selecting and using strategies effectively. These factors need to be taken into account when deciding what the proper balance among the three types of training should be for a given class or individual.

Timing and other options In addition to the diversity provided by the three types of learner training above, there are several other dimensions of diversity in the training process to consider. These include the timing of the training, the form of the training, and the intensity of the training.

Timing. In settings where learner training has been provided, there is a tendency to begin with a preliminary tutorial session and then follow it by allowing the learners to proceed on their own with little if any additional assistance. This may work well in situations where the training needed is relatively simple or when the training builds on areas already familiar to the students. In many cases, however, it is unlikely that a single round of training will have the continued impact, especially before students have familiarized themselves with a particular application or learning task. One of the learner training principles from Hubbard (2004) is to make training cyclical, so that technical information, strategies, and pedagogical generalizations are recycled and expanded upon in a natural spiral. An extension of that principle is that both technical and strategic training may be more efficient if learners are first given the opportunity to explore a new application or learning environment. In fact, rather than overwhelming students with information at the beginning in a single intensive tutorial session, they may be encouraged to explore the CALL application or environment on their own. Xie (2002), for example, showed how allowing students to use a Chinese chat program anonymously and casually first helped them build familiarity with operating the character sets before engaging in target language activities that would be assessed. It is also possible to allow use of the first language to familiarize students with computer-mediated communication (CMC) activities and novel learning tools such as concordancers. Finally, an alternative to the timing in the types of training above, or even a natural complement, is to take an interventionist approach. In this case, training is offered when problems are noted, either at the request of the learner or because of observations from the instructor.

Form. There is also diversity in the form of training. As with other areas of language instruction, teachers may take either an inductive or deductive approach to learner training, or a combination of the two. In an inductive or exploratory approach, learners are presented with an opportunity to discover an application's controls, help options, and so on along with useful paths through the task or activity, either on their own or collaboratively with peers. This is then followed by checking to see if their interactions are in line with the teacher's expectations, followed by hints or other forms of guidance if they are not. In a deductive approach to learner training, students are provided with clear instructions, sometimes through modeling, and then given either structured practice or the opportunity to directly make use of the instruction in using the CALL application or engaging in the CALL task. Because of their more organized structure, deductive approaches are often seen as being more efficient than inductive ones. However, they are not necessarily as memorable or engaging.

Regardless of whether one takes an inductive or deductive approach or some combination of the two, a related question is whether students are internalizing the training primarily on an individual level or whether collaborative learning is occurring. In inductive approaches in particular, the ability to discuss one's insights and interactions with the CALL application or activity with peers can have a positive effect. In lab situations, this can be supported by having students work in pairs in front of a single computer. In settings where students work independently, individual experiences can be posted onto a discussion board or class time can be taken for small group collaborative debriefings (Hubbard, 2004).

Intensity. As was the case historically with strategy training in areas such as reading and listening, one of the barriers facing teachers who want to incorporate CALL learner training into their classes is that it takes time. Another area where diversity comes into play, then, is determining how much time a teacher or a student can spend working independently to provide sufficient benefit, without impacting too much on other class and homework activities. As O'Bryan (2008) showed, even a small amount of time could have a measurable impact in student interaction with materials and awareness of learning supports provided by the software. At the other end of the spectrum is what we have called "pervasive" learner training (Romeo and Hubbard, 2010), where learner training is integrated into virtually every class session and students demonstrate through reports and individual meetings what they have and have not clearly understood with respect to the training.

Diversity in the realm of intensity is not solely a factor of available time but is also related to diversity issues in the learners. Some learners are prepared to make profitable use of the fruits of training, while others may consider training time to be of little value. Kolaitis *et al.* (2006) noted that providing CALL training where learners were expected to reflect on their learning processes did not work as well for students with lower language proficiency. Boling and Soo (1999) and Brandl (1995) similarly note that advanced students are able to make more effective use of the range of controls in language learning software than those with lower proficiency. Research on cognitive resource limitations suggests an answer, namely that less complex and more familiar strategies would be easier for students at lower levels of language proficiency to implement because their attention is focused so heavily on conscious manipulation of the language itself.

To summarize, we have seen that there are a number of dimensions that can be controlled to yield a range of diversity in learner training processes. These include selecting a balance among the three main types of training – technical, strategic, and pedagogical – as well as determining the timing, form, and intensity of the training. Given the limited research to date, it is not yet possible to identify what an optimal training process would be. However, recognizing the range of options, reflecting on the potential costs and benefits of various combinations of alternatives, and collecting data on what does and does not yield desired results, should allow for continuing progress to be made in understanding what is worthwhile. In order to understand the process more fully, however, we need to take into account the diversity of the learners themselves at both the group and individual levels.

Learner diversity

Much of language teaching methodology and second language acquisition (SLA) research aims at capturing similarities. In the case of teaching, this is for pragmatic reasons because teachers work with collections of individuals and in many cases with collections of sub-groups as well, as happens in the multicultural English as a second language (ESL) classrooms common to intensive

English programs. Similarly, for much SLA research, a primary objective is to capture the common elements of second language learning so as to characterize its connections to cognitive processes and social interaction adequately. However, both teachers and learners have long recognized that there are differences across individuals and groups in language learning, and that understanding these variations can be critical in determining what leads to successful language learning. Various aspects of diversity in learners with respect to technology are covered elsewhere in this volume – see Chapters 2 and 4. Here we concentrate on viewing that diversity from the perspective of the process and progress of learner training.

Skehan (1989) was perhaps the first to offer a book-length overview of language learner diversity. He identifies four SLA models relevant to the topic: the monitor model (Krashen, 1981), the good language learner model, Carroll's model of school learning, and a disjunctive model. For most of his work, Skehan builds on the Naiman *et al.* (1978) "good language learner" model, giving particular attention to the construct of *aptitude*, which he says "still generates the most consistent correlations with language learning success" (p. 8). Since Skehan, others have looked at various individual or group factors in an attempt to account for degrees of success and failure of language learning. Lightbown and Spada (2006), for instance, devote an entire chapter to the topic. Among other factors they mention differences in learner beliefs (though mainly at the group rather than the individual level) as important, especially where those beliefs are in conflict with the teaching methodology, even when that methodology may represent "best practices" elsewhere. Another area of diversity is gender: Oxford and Nyikos (1989, p. 295), for example, note "profoundly significant sex differences in strategy choice" in three of the five factors they studied in 1,200 university-level language students.

A relatively comprehensive list of major categories of diversity can be drawn from the keywords in the chapter titles of Griffith's (2008) edited volume, *Lessons from Good Language Learners*. Contributions to this volume cite research that variation across particular categories separates the "good language learner" from the rest. The categories mentioned there under the label of "learner variables," which can also be seen as a checklist for evaluating diversity for our purposes, include the following:

- motivation
- age
- learning style
- personality
- gender
- strategies (strategy use)
- metacognition

- autonomy
- beliefs
- culture
- aptitude.

Complementing these characteristics, a primary area of diversity in language classrooms is that of second language proficiency. Some classes are designed for beginners, some for intermediate students, and some for advanced, with various gradations in between. Proficiency has a connection with some of the elements above: more advanced learners, for example, tend to be more autonomous (Boling and Soo, 1999), engage in more metacognition, and use more strategies than beginners.

Diversity can also be seen in the way individuals and groups interact with computer-based material or with one another in online tasks. A few examples are illustrative of the range. Heift (2002) noted that students using an intelligent tutoring system for German varied in using the correct answer feedback provided by the program. Some checked the correct answer before inputting anything (browsers), some checked the answer after attempting and getting an error message (peekers), and others (18 percent) never looked at the correct answer but continued trying to get it on their own (adamants). Grgurovic and Hegelheimer (2007) studied students who were given the opportunity to select either transcripts or subtitles as help options in a listening activity. When surveyed at the end, the majority preferred subtitles, but five of eighteen preferred transcripts. Looking at small groups rather than individuals in collaborative tandem-learning sessions with students from the US and Germany, Belz (2001) showed diversity in terms of high- and low-group functionality. She identified several factors including differences in language level, cultural expectations, and access to the Internet that influenced the relative success or failure of the groups.

Finally, in any learning environment employing computers, differences in underlying technical proficiency provide another important area of diversity. This can have an influence at the whole class level, where all or most of the students may have limited expertise in some area, or at an individual level, where a specific student or students may be foundering due to lack of the needed technical skill and knowledge, perhaps because of a general technophobia (Robb, 2006). As mentioned previously, Winke and Goertler (2008b) provide a wealth of data demonstrating that contemporary university language students are not, despite their "digital nativeness," prepared to utilize digital technology effectively for language learning. Students may also differ greatly in their overall "eLearning" experience and proficiency, an area that falls between general technology proficiency and proficiency specific to CALL applications and tasks.

Example

Diversity in an ESL listening class

As an example of some of the preceding concepts, we look at a study of learner training in an advanced ESL listening class at Stanford University taught by one of the authors in the fall of 2008. The course was built around online audio and video materials for both whole class and individual assignments, so it was important for students to be able to use them effectively. As this course was the final one in our listening sequence, some attention was also paid to learner training to provide students with the skills and knowledge for continuing language development on their own once the course ended. The overall results have been reported on in detail elsewhere (Romeo and Hubbard, 2010) – here we concentrate on those that relate to issues in diversity discussed above.

The fifteen students from two sections were from Korea, China, Taiwan, Japan, and the Philippines, with the majority in their third quarter of full-time graduate study at Stanford. There were three parts to the course: in-class listening practice, discussion, and learner training; class homework; and individual projects. The projects, explicitly included to accommodate individual diversity, were negotiated with each student to allow them to pick objectives and material types in line with their needs and interests. They were required to do a minimum of two hours per week, ideally divided into three forty-minute sessions, though they were allowed flexibility as long as they met the minimum total time. They submitted weekly reports specifying the objective, materials, time spent, procedures, and reflective comments. Data for the overall study were collected from pre-/post-surveys of technology proficiency, pre-/post-listening tests, notes, and videos from individual tutorial sessions (five per student), weekly student reports, class notes, and an end of course interview. The data reported below are primarily from the class notes and student reports, which turned out to have the richest and most detailed material.

In terms of diversity in the training process, all three types of learner training (technical, strategic, and pedagogical) were integrated into the course and the intensity of the learner training was pervasive. Training on various aspects of computer-based listening was introduced in each class, sometimes deductively by advance demonstration, and sometimes inductively by asking students to try on their own to figure out an effective way of meeting a particular objective and then discussing it subsequently in small groups or individual tutorials. Key techniques and strategies were reviewed regularly both in class and in the tutorial sessions.

The course introduced a number of strategies for improving listening comprehension, and these strategies were often supported by pedagogical training as described above. The goal was to move students towards a state of autonomy where they would be able to make informed decisions regarding the learning objectives of each homework session, the materials used, and the strategies chosen in working with them. Some of the more prominent technology-focused strategies were pausing and rewinding the media, slowing the play-back speed, setting the graphic equalizer on the media player to be optimized for speech, expanding the player size for greater control, using subtitles and online transcripts, linking to online dictionaries, doing background research for pre-listening (e.g. linking to Wikipedia), and listening to materials multiple times with different objectives for each pass. Other techniques were introduced for students to work specifically to build their language proficiency, such as creating personal vocabulary lists, reviewing vocabulary with an online pro-gram using spaced repetition, written dictation to link form to meaning and improve chunking in processing, and oral summarization to connect listening and speaking.[2] Reflecting on the learning experience to enhance metacogni-tive awareness was encouraged in class, the weekly reports, and individual meetings.

Our goal was to observe how much the techniques helped students improve their listening, or at least positively change the way they interacted with online listening materials. On the surface, the students were relatively homogeneous, coming from similar educational and language learning backgrounds in Asia, all having proficiency advanced enough to be admitted to full-time graduate study (most in engineering or science) and all showing high levels of general computer proficiency. The results for the group overall were quite positive (see Romeo and Hubbard, 2010), and we have continued to develop the training component of the course.

However, it was clear that there was also diversity among the learners in a number of areas, especially with respect to the independent listening pro-ject that was a hallmark of the course. For this project, which lasted for seven weeks during the ten-week quarter, students determined which online materi-als they would use, what their learning objectives were, what strategies and procedures they would use to accomplish those objectives, and how they would time the sessions. Below, we discuss a few of the more prominent areas where diversity was observed.

Scheduling was one major area of diversity among learners. Some students arranged a schedule and stuck closely to it, others attempted a schedule but often failed to adhere to it, while a few claimed that sticking with a schedule did not fit their graduate lifestyle, preferring to work on their projects after all the homework for their major classes was done (often on weekends). During week seven, they also experimented with changes in the frequency and length of listening sessions, after the instructor specifically asked them to attempt

---

[2] See the class notes at www.stanford.edu/~efs/693b-08 for additional details.

study sessions of twenty minutes (one each day for six days) and compare the experience with the previously recommended three sessions of forty minutes each. The majority reported that they preferred shorter, more frequent sessions, because they felt that they learned more and were able to form better study habits. However, there were three students (20 percent) who felt that twenty minutes was just too short to cover the material in any satisfactory way, and two of the other students actually offered that six longer study sessions of forty minutes each would have been optimal.

Diversity among students could be seen quite clearly in students' goals. There were many cases of individuals who were ultimately looking for ways to improve their spoken English and would therefore gravitate to media which contained naturalistic native speech, such as TV shows. However, others who were more focused on listening comprehension, especially as it related to academic English, found that news and other informational media was a much more useful resource. One example of this was an interesting contrast which was noted between Chuck and Joe (pseudonyms are provided to preserve student anonymity). Chuck reported experimenting on a variety of strategies such as listening to one clip multiple times (multiple listening), reading the transcript, researching background information, shadowing (see below), and dictation. He focused on vocabulary many times in his reports and reported moving from entertainment TV shows to online news because he found the latter more effective for his comprehension goals. Joe reported experimenting with most of the same techniques, except for pre-listening research, but added written summarization as a comprehension check and an opportunity to engage in language production. In the end he reported preferring to use entertainment to informational media, linked to his interest in everyday conversational English. For these two students, their individual goals played an important role in determining what strategies and materials were effective for them.

While some subjects were quite adventurous with their projects, most of them stuck with a relatively small set of favored strategies, although these sometimes changed in response to discussions during the individual meetings. Besides the strategies presented to students, other techniques were already familiar to them from prior study overseas, but often they had not questioned their effectiveness. An example of one such popular strategy was "shadowing," which entails listening to pre-recorded media (news, or some other entertainment media) and simply following along, repeating the words and sentences as they are heard. Despite its popularity, particularly in Korea and Japan, its effectiveness has not been well documented. However, Tamai (2002) found that a program which focused on shadowing produced a significant positive effect in overall listening scores, though not in other areas such as vocabulary and word span with numbers. Two students in particular explored this technique in their weekly listening activities. Over the course of several weeks,

Nathan reported a greater awareness of the processes involved in shadowing, and, while he did not stop using it, did use it less frequently. More interestingly, he tried adding dictation as a way of increasing his involvement with the media following pedagogical training that explained the relationship between dictation and awareness of language forms.

Nathan's case can perhaps shed some light on students' gravitation to certain strategies. He had a new MP3 player and was in the habit of downloading podcasts and listening to them during the day. His personal situation also had an influence on this study technique; he lived with his wife and new-born daughter and reported difficulty finding time to focus on listening outside of the early morning hours. In the end, he found that increasing the frequency of study times while reducing the length was the most productive plan for him. This shows how some characteristics of group diversity develop: aspects of personal situations and commonalities in available equipment can lead to a natural grouping. Although an instructor could dismiss such trends, saying familial status or purchasing habits should not be allowed to influence academic achievement, it could be argued that finding ways to accommodate such diversity is a more effective means of reaching a larger number of students.

During the training process, students seemed to go through three stages, although we did not have a sufficient number of subjects to make a strong case for this claim. First, they began to realize exactly what made certain media difficult. Many were not exactly aware that characteristics such as the speech rate, content familiarity, and personal interest could be the source of not being able to understand. This realization was reflected in early reports and meetings of almost every subject. At the next stage, they were able to implement strategies to make listening easier and interact more with the material. Finally, these strategies were internalized and used when the need arose, often without a lot of conscious effort, for example, toggling subtitles on and off as needed relative to the task objective rather than leaving them on or off throughout the whole listening activity. This last step is important and students showed diversity here – some failed to demonstrate in their reports and tutorial sessions that they had reached that last stage. An example of one who apparently had was Sam. He reported reviewing media multiple times, recognizing the value in a second or third listening, and was observed hiding subtitles when they were not needed to keep them from distracting him. However, when asked about techniques he consciously used to improve listening comprehension or proficiency, he did not include these, presumably because he no longer considered them "special."

Finally, the topic of subtitles was a very important one for many subjects, especially given the widespread view among both teachers and students that they are more of a hindrance than a help to developing comprehension skills and increasing proficiency. Based on their experience both in class and with their projects, many concluded that listening without them at least once but then using them to confirm meaning and to identify new vocabulary was the most effective strategy. One interesting case was Oliver, who found that the subtitles in the media he was using were not accurate, so he abandoned using them altogether. Previous research in the use of subtitles has largely concluded that they can serve a purpose both for improving comprehension and building vocabulary (Danan, 2004) and even for increasing the amount and quality of subsequent speech (Borras and Lafayette, 1994). However, others caution against their use, arguing that reliance on them may hamper comprehension of real-world speech (Vandergrift, 2004). Our findings indicate that, rather than ignoring them or using them constantly, it would serve both instructors and students well to identify methods of using (and not using) them to scaffold learning. Clearly, this is an area ripe for more targeted research.

Implications

Essentially, the main implication of this chapter is that to the extent that learner training for CALL is worthwhile, it is itself a form of teaching, and like other teaching it can be done with more or less effectiveness depending on a variety of factors. These include not only diversity in the students' readiness and motivation, but also how well the training curriculum fits the students and is executed by the instructor. We have also noted that training takes time away from other class and homework activities that instructors may feel are equally or even more critical to the success of the course.

Our research on learner training in an advanced listening class has led to recognizing some areas for further study and development relevant to the theme of diversity. As noted, the learner training process used in the example class can be characterized as pervasive, with significant elements of all three types of training: technical, strategic, and pedagogical. To a large extent, students were encouraged to experiment with a variety of materials, strategies, and procedures to find those that suited them best. These students were given a lot of independence fairly quickly. Even considering their relatively advanced language proficiency and maturity compared to most language students, for some that independence may have been excessive. They might have profited from a more guided approach, perhaps led by a set of integrated strategies and procedures representing a sort of "best practice." Once they had become familiar with this foundation, they might have found it much easier to select from among those candidates and then adjust them to fit their individual needs.

Given the fact that we are well into the third decade of CALL as a professional field with its own dedicated conferences and journals, learner training for CALL is a remarkably understudied area. Nevertheless, the absence of a solid research base is not a suitable argument for ignoring it in practice. We have increasing evidence that learners do not, automatically, know how to util-ize digital materials and tools effectively for language learning just because they have familiarity with other uses of computers. There is a tendency in any new domain to oversimplify it – our goal in this chapter has been to show that monolithic approaches to training, however elegant in appearance, will not accommodate the range of diversity discussed herein, and that further explor-ation is called for.

Conclusions

This chapter has discussed diversity in learner training for computer-assisted language learning applications across two major dimensions – diversity in the training process and diversity in the learners themselves – with an eye to understanding how the processes and the learner diversity can be reconciled effectively. Given the limited research to date, it is not possible to determine what an optimal process would be, either in general or for a specific group or individual. Additionally, though not a part of the present chapter, there is the rather critical question of what the actual *content* of the training should be. Determining that will require continued experimentation based on our best hypotheses of what is likely to work coupled with collection and analysis of learner data to help us confirm, reject, or refine those hypotheses. We can also predict with some confidence that diversity in both general and application-specific strategies in using technology for language learning will continue to grow as the technology changes.

Irrespective of these daunting challenges, CALL learner training is a very important topic for the future. As we continue taking early steps towards understanding and integrating it into language teaching, we need to recognize the rich range of diversity available in the training process in addition to the well-established diversity within individuals and groups of learners to which technology use only adds further variables.

4   Diversity in learner support

Hayo Reinders and Pornapit Darasawang

Introduction

This chapter deals with language support, or resources and systems for facilitating language learning outside the classroom. Language support encompasses institutional support mechanisms such as self-access facilities and online materials provision, but also refers to a pedagogical approach to learning that places the individual at the center of a lifelong learning process with the aim of developing learner autonomy. In this way, language support lies at the heart of the notion of diversity. In this chapter we will discuss the rationale for language support and show how technology has played a key role in the development and implementation of a pedagogy for out-of-class language learning. Next, we will describe a case study from a university in Thailand to show how online language support can be used in practice and draw implications from this for future development in this field.

Overview and general issues

Language support is a term that describes efforts on the part of teachers or institutions to help students develop their language ability and their language learning skills. This usually involves out-of-class opportunities for language (self-)study, such as self-access, language advising, informal opportunities for language practice, the provision of (online) resources, as well as links with more formal language education. The provision of language support is based on the idea that classroom teaching alone is not sufficient to develop lifelong learning skills, or simply not practically feasible due to the enormity of the task (as a case in point, a recent study at the University of Auckland in New Zealand established that approximately 12,000 of its students needed some form of language help; clearly, this would be at the very least a major challenge to provide through traditional teaching [Reinders, 2007].

Language support aims to build on learners' ability to learn independently, alone or from each other. It usually includes deliberate efforts to develop learner autonomy and thus to give learners the necessary skills to take control over their own learning to allow them to set their own objectives, choose appropriate learning strategies, and monitor and assess their own learning (Dam, 1995; Littlewood, 1996; Breen and Mann, 1997). Language teachers have always attempted to find ways to reconcile the collective nature of most teaching environments with the (inevitably) individual aspects of learning. The development of learner autonomy, or learners' ability to take control over their own learning (Holec, 1981), has been one way in which teachers have tried to make links with learners at a more individualized level, and to connect classroom learning with out-of-class language use.

The theoretical and pedagogical rationale for the implementation of more learner-centered approaches to teaching is well developed and goes back many decades. Starting from the 1950s, and influenced by the work of George Kelly (Kelly, 1955) and others in psychology, there emerged an increased recognition of the importance of the learner as an active individual who brings previous experiences, beliefs, and preferences to the classroom. Rather than seeing the learner as a passive container to be filled with the teacher's ideas, these humanist approaches considered the learner as someone who actively shapes his or her learning experiences with the purpose of self-development and fulfillment (Stevick, 1980).

In addition to the learning aspect, however, autonomy also includes a more political element, relating to the idea of individual freedom of choice. As applied to education, learners are unable to "take control" or make choices about their learning, unless they are free to do so. At a practical level, this means that economic and other disadvantages of certain groups in the wider population, state-led education policies, school curricula, and the prescribed use of textbooks are all examples of ways in which the development of autonomy may be hindered.

More recent developments in education, both as an extension of the work done in the area of autonomy, and separate from it, have seen a greater understanding of the role of the individual in the learning process, where, as Fotos and Browne argue, "most researchers agree that a major shift is taking place … in education away from the teacher-centred classroom toward a learner-centred system where the learner is in control of the lesson content and the learning process" (2004, p. 7).

This shift requires that learners are prepared for and supported in assuming this responsibility. Learner support comprises this preparation and support. The most successful language support systems are those that integrate classroom with out-of-class language learning (Lázaro and Reinders, 2007). Teachers provide preparation in class for independent learning, and perhaps ongoing support in the form of encouragement and feedback and work together with other support providers inside (and sometimes outside) the institution to ensure a seamless learning experience for the students.

One of the most common forms of out-of-class language support is through self-access. A self-access learning center (SALC) is a facility that offers opportunities for self-study, a wide range of language materials, activities, and staff support. Crabbe (1999) has described the role of self-access as providing a "bridge" between public domain (e.g. the classroom) and private domain (e.g. using the language outside the classroom) learning, where learners can move from the sheltered classroom to the "real world" while receiving support in this process. Benson (2001, p. 8) views the relationship between learner autonomy and the SALC as autonomy representing the goal, self-directed learning the means to achieve it, and the SALC the environment where it can be achieved. The term self-access centers used to predominantly refer to a physical space, or center; however, self-access learning can also be, and is increasingly these days, offered online in blended form.

Although self-access is a common and important type of support, it only forms one part of an institution's language support *system*. Other elements include the original entrance (language) requirements, language needs analyses (as carried out at some universities *after* students have enrolled), language across the curriculum, courses taught in English, exit tests, and any other form of language program, support, or requirement that directly or indirectly affects the type and amount of interaction students have with the language and the help that is available to them.

The potential of CALL for language support

The successful implementation of a language support system at the institutional level is in many cases a major and long-term undertaking. On the one hand, this is because for language support to be successful, it needs to be integrated across the institution. This means that, especially with large universities, a uniform policy needs to be developed that involves all stakeholders, and that establishes clear and open communication lines between them. Keeping track of learners, their needs, and their progress across multiple departments and faculties, and between different language providers, can be a major pedagogical challenge and a potential administrative nightmare. Technology has been used to facilitate the development and provision of language support in such cases. The (potential) advantages of technology have been extensively discussed in previous studies and synthesized by Reinders and White (2008) who distinguish between organizational and pedagogical advantages. The results of their study are summarized in Table 4.1.

We will now briefly describe those features that we feel are particularly helpful in implementing language support.

Table 4.1 *The potential advantages of CALL*

Organizational advantages	Access
	Storage and retrieval of learning behavior records and outcomes
	Sharing and recycling of materials
	Cost efficiency
Pedagogical advantages	Authenticity
	Interaction
	Situated learning
	Multimedia
	New types of activities
	Non-linearity
	Feedback
	Monitoring and recording of learning behavior and progress
	Control
	Empowerment

Access CALL materials can be offered to learners independently of time and place. This is a frequently cited advantage especially for online materials. For materials developers this has offered opportunities to provide materials to learners for use outside the classroom and to learners who are otherwise unable to attend classes. In the case of this project, providing easy access to all of the thousands of students who take compulsory English courses to language learning opportunities and support was crucial and an online support system was deemed the only practical option.

Although "anytime–anywhere" access has offered many practical opportunities, recent studies have especially shown the importance of support where learners access materials without the direct intervention of a teacher, whether in a self-access context (Reinders, 2005; Ulitsky, 2000) or in distance education (Hampel, 2006; White, 2006; Wang, 2007). Without such support, learners tend to use fewer or inefficient learning strategies, motivation levels tend to be low, and dropout rates high. It was thus paramount that the system we developed would offer the necessary help and would not leave the students unsupported.

Storage and retrieval of learning behavior records and outcomes Learner progress and test results can be stored electronically (and potentially automatically) and retrieved at any time. This is an organizational benefit for teachers and administrators but also potentially a pedagogical benefit for students.

Sharing and recycling of materials CALL materials can easily be shared and updated. For materials developers, learning *objects* that meet certain international standards such as the sharable content object reference model (SCORM) are interoperable and can reduce development time as they can be employed in different contexts. Changes to online resources are immediately available to users and learners can thus be given new materials without having to return to class.

Interaction A major advantage of CALL materials is said to be that they facilitate interaction and language *use*. Chapelle (2005) refers to "interaction" as "any two-way exchanges." This can be between two people, or between a person and the computer, as well as within the person's mind. Swain's output hypothesis (1995) claims that by producing the language, learners can become aware of gaps in their interlanguage, and others (e.g. Ellis, 1996) have argued that language production can act as a form or practice, thereby strengthening existing connections in the mind. Sociocultural theory emphasizes the importance of interaction in a meaningful context (Lantolf, 2000) and various popular CALL programs aim to create this context and opportunities for language use through email or chat communication, or through language exchanges between learners (where a learner with a specific L1 is partnered with someone who wants to learn that language as a second language). More recent examples of interaction-based activities include building on the popularity of social networking sites such as Facebook and MySpace to create materials and activities in or around online environments in which L2 learners are likely to spend considerable amounts of time (see Chapter 5 for a discussion of social networking sites). Some researchers, however, have pointed out that the comprehensible input from the interaction alone is not sufficient to result in the development of accuracy and that some type of attention to form is necessary. In computer-mediated communication (CMC), materials and instructions would thus have to include some direction as to what learners are expected to do and what aspects of the language they are required to use.

Multimedia The ability of CALL materials to integrate different modes of presentation is an improvement over traditional materials. The support of different modalities has been shown to result in vastly different processing on the part of the learner (see Chapter 7; Leow, 1995) and the ability for the teacher to "repackage" materials to emphasize one modality over the other can be of benefit. Learners, too, can choose on the basis of their preferences or to request more help (for example, by turning on or off the subtitles on a DVD). The ability to use multimedia thus results in an enriched learning environment.

Feedback CALL allows immediate feedback, dependent on the user's input and a whole range of other factors (past input, timing). A variety of feedback forms is possible, such as those using sound, movement, text, etc. or a combination of them. Also, it is possible to implement forms of feedback such as modeling, coaching, and scaffolding that are hard or impossible to implement in traditional learning environments.

Monitoring and recording of learning behavior and progress CALL programs can record and monitor learners' behavior and progress and dynamically alter input, or make suggestions to the learner. They can also compare learners' progress with their own goals and other learners. The records can be made accessible to the student to encourage reflection on the learning process. Part of the rationale behind initiatives such as the European Union's e-portfolio project, which encourage the keeping of personal records to support ongoing study and planning, is to develop learners' metacognitive awareness and to engage their metacognitive strategies. Metacognitive awareness helps learners to prioritize their learning and helps learners select the most appropriate study plan and learning strategies. This, in turn, gives learners a sense of control over their learning and may help them to self-motivate (Ushioda, 1996). Metacognitive strategies also help learners develop autonomy by allowing them to self-monitor and self-assess. In practice, however, it has proven to be particularly difficult to encourage learners to keep records or to plan their learning. Reinders (2006) found, for example, that many learners did not respond to computer prompts to create or revise learning plans, and concluded that more training and staff intervention was necessary.

Control As an extension of monitoring, learners potentially have more control over how they use CALL materials as they can often be accessed randomly or adapted to suit individual needs in level of difficulty of the input, or in the amount of support available (e.g. with or without glossaries, spell checkers, etc.).

Empowerment An important benefit of the characteristics of CALL materials discussed above is that together they have the potential to *empower* learners by offering easier access to materials, greater control to learners, and more opportunities for the development of metacognitive skills and learner autonomy (c.f. Shetzer and Warschauer, 2000).

Of course, an additional potential advantage of CALL is that it can help to integrate the above elements into a cohesive program and facilitate its delivery. We now turn to an example of this in the form of an online support program called "My English."

Example

Online language support in practice

In this section we will describe the main features of a language support program developed at a university in Thailand. We will show how it addresses the language needs in the institution and how it draws on technology to facilitate the delivery and integration of the different support elements discussed above. From this example we will draw some implications for the development of language support programs and the use of technology to facilitate out-of-class learning in other contexts.

Educational background King Mongkut's University (KMUTT) is a leading technical university in Thailand. It has gradually moved towards increasing the amount of classes taught in English over the years, and has implemented compulsory English courses for all students. It has also operated a nationally recognized SALC for several decades now, which offers a wide range of language learning materials and short courses on how to improve language learning skills. Despite these measures, the English proficiency of graduates was not satisfactory. One of the reasons was the small uptake of learning opportunities outside the formal courses. Students did not make use of the self-access facilities much and did not actively seek out other opportunities to improve their language. Surveys and interviews had shown that part of the reason was to do with a lack of easy access to facilities. With three campuses and many buildings located far from one another, visiting the SALC was not an option for many students. Also, the lack of integration between formal courses and additional learning resources did not help to encourage students to perceive English learning as an ongoing process that was part of their lives, both within and outside the classroom. For these reasons it was decided to design and implement an online language support system, with the following objectives:

- to provide easier access to resources for students and staff in the three university campuses;
- to facilitate supporting students while they study English by making it easier for them to contact teachers, and for teachers to monitor students' work;
- to develop learner autonomy by encouraging reflection and by giving students support in their independent learning;
- to provide more resources for the students taking compulsory English courses to practice, as the classroom materials were not able to cater for their individual needs;
- to offer more motivating materials that drew on the benefits of technology to improve learning opportunities;

• to centralize the different elements of the university language support and to make it easier for students to find out where to go for help.

Description of the online language support program In order to ensure the greatest possible uptake, the My English program can be accessed online from both within and outside the university. It has a student, a teacher, and an administrator interface. Figure 4.1 shows the student interface. Students have to log in before they can use the program and use their institutional usernames and passwords for this (in other words, no additional registration is necessary). The login process allows the program to record progress and allows teachers to search for students by their ID number.

The student interface shows nine different learning and support modules, each of which shows a summary of key information specific to the student currently logged in. Clicking on any of these enlarges the module and gives additional information. The modules can be accessed randomly but are numbered from top left to bottom right in an order roughly corresponding to the different stages in the self-directed learning process (Knowles, 1975). Below we describe these modules and their functionality one by one.

Your learning plan The first module (top left) is a crucial step in the self-directed learning process. Learners need to know what their language needs are and then plan their learning around those needs. To this end, the program gives students access to an online needs analysis which can be completed in less than half an hour. It gives students a broad indication of their level and weaknesses in the areas of vocabulary, grammar, listening, and reading. For speaking and writing students are asked to self-assess their level (see Figure 4.2). Many students, however, will get this information from their teachers and can either type in their scores directly or use it to complement the results of the needs analysis.

The results from the needs analysis are used by the computer to recommend (1) a list of priority skills in the order they should be worked on, and (2) a list of recommended resources suitable for the student's level. The student is then asked to write down their personal goals, the difficulties they have in achieving those goals, and any ideas they have to work on them (see Figure 4.3).

Find resources This module acts as an online catalogue specifically for language learning materials (see Figure 4.4). These materials include both online and print materials, commercial and in-house produced materials. In order to make the system as flexible as possible, and in order to accommodate the needs of different faculties and departments, My English was designed as a "shell," or an application without pre-determined content. Individual teachers

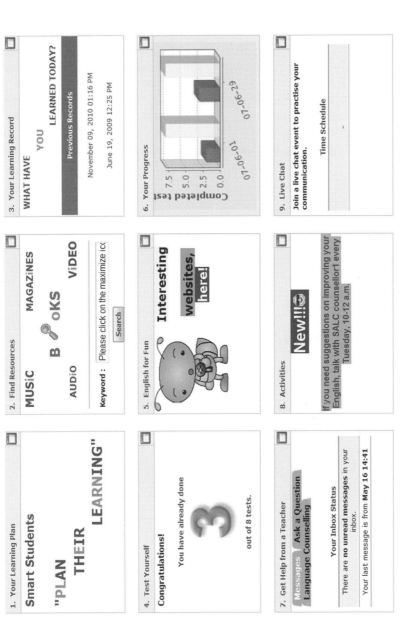

Figure 4.1 The nine modules designed to support the self-directed learning process

1. Your Learning Plan

One of the most important steps in your language learning is to decide what you need to learn first. You can take a short test that will show your level in reading, listening, writing, and vocabulary. Click on the button below to start. When you finish the test write down or select them in below. You do not have to do the test if you think you know your level or if your teacher has already told you. In that case you can select your results below straight away.

Click to start the placement test

You can take the test again and change your scores below. Or you can go directly to your learning plan by clicking | here |

Skill	Result
Vocabulary	11-20 : Pre-intermediate ▸
Grammar	11-20 : Pre-intermediate ▸
Listening	0-10 : Elementary ▸
Reading	11-20 : Pre-intermediate ▸

For the skills below you can choose you level. If you are not sure talk to a teacher.

Speaking	0-10 : Elementary ▸
Writing	0-10 : Elementary ▸

OK

Figure 4.2 The "your learning plan" module

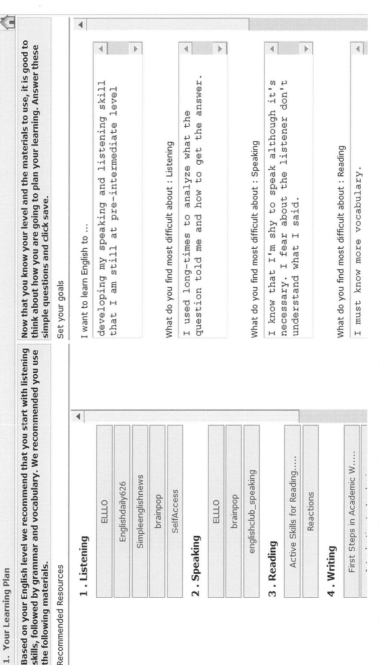

1. Your Learning Plan

Based on your English level we recommend that you start with listening skills, followed by grammar and vocabulary. We recommended you use the following materials.

Recommended Resources

1 . Listening

ELLLO
Englishdaily626
Simpleenglishnews
brainpop
SelfAccess

2 . Speaking

ELLLO
brainpop
englishclub_speaking

3 . Reading

Active Skills for Reading.....
Reactions

4 . Writing

First Steps in Academic W......

Now that you know your level and the materials to use, it is good to think about how you are going to plan your learning. Answer these simple questions and click save.

Set your goals

I want to learn English to ...

developing my speaking and listening skill
that I am still at pre-intermediate level

What do you find most difficult about : Listening

I used long-times to analyze what the
question told me and how to get the answer.

What do you find most difficult about : Speaking

I know that I'm shy to speak although it's
necessary. I fear about the listener don't
understand what I said.

What do you find most difficult about : Reading

I must know more vocabulary.

Figure 4.3 Sample of a completed "your learning plan" module

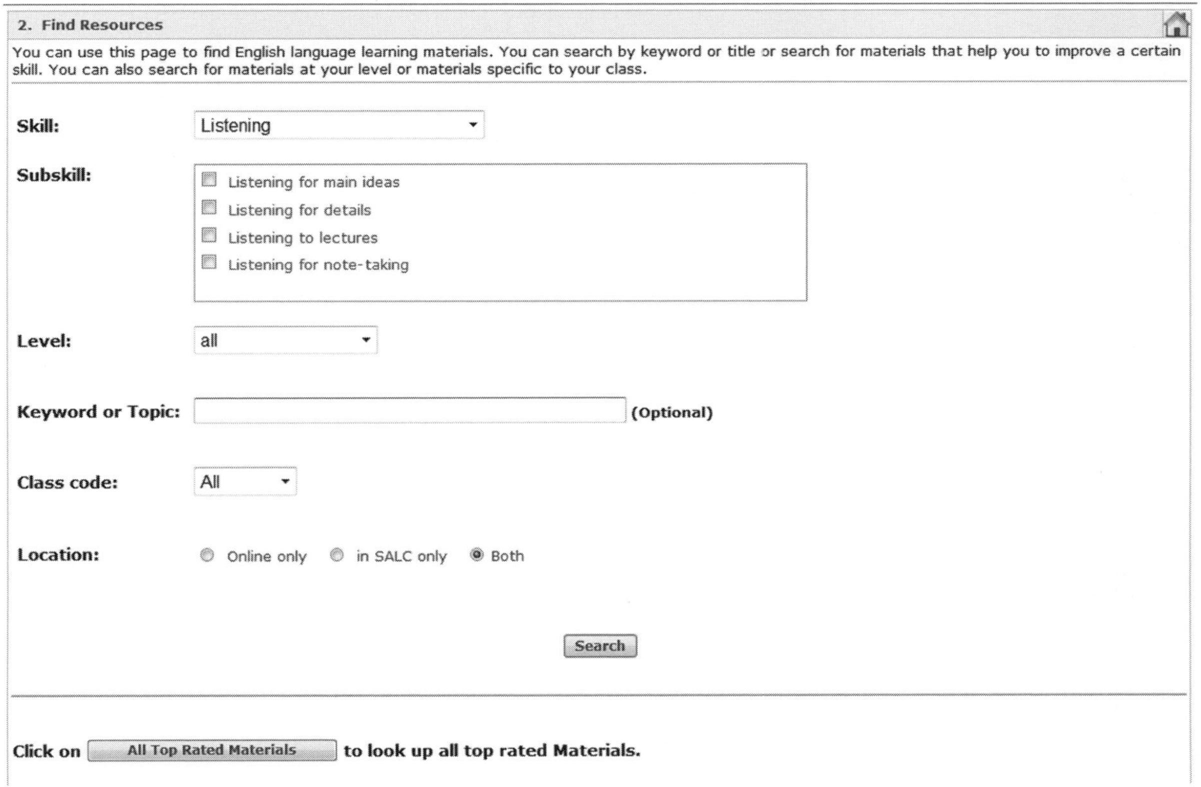

2. Find Resources

You can use this page to find English language learning materials. You can search by keyword or title or search for materials that help you to improve a certain skill. You can also search for materials at your level or materials specific to your class.

Skill: Listening ▸

Subskill:
- ☐ Listening for main ideas
- ☐ Listening for details
- ☐ Listening to lectures
- ☐ Listening for note-taking

Level: all ▸

Keyword or Topic: _____ (Optional)

Class code: All ▸

Location: ◯ Online only ◯ in SALC only ◉ Both

[Search]

Click on [All Top Rated Materials] **to look up all top rated Materials.**

Figure 4.4 The "find resources" module

and departments can add their own (purchased or created) resources, based on local student language needs and levels. The materials are pooled and are stored and accessible centrally, available to anyone.

The catalogue helps students find materials by language skill and by sub-skill (the list of sub-skills appears after students have selected the skill they want to work on). They can also search by level of difficulty, by keyword or title (search results will bring up any resource that has the search term in the title or description), or by class code. This last feature was specifically requested by language teachers in the institution who wanted to be able to make available to students materials that were relevant to their classes. By searching for a particular class code, students can quickly find all the materials uploaded and/or recommended by their teacher. Finally, students can search for materials that are available online only (for example, when working from home), those that are available in the self-access learning center only (i.e. print or copyright-restricted materials), or both.

There is also an option to display a list of "top rated resources." These are the suggested resources for each of the language skills, as selected by the program designers and the SALC staff. This feature was included to help students who do not yet have a clear idea about their learning needs or preferences and do not know where to start.

If students search for specific sub-skills or levels, the results include so-called "recommended resources" (and "all other resources"). These are the resources, matching the search query, that the staff think are the best available. Students can click on the search results to read a description and to access the resource directly (in the case of online materials).

Your learning record My English automatically keeps a record of students' work and specifically stores for each learning episode (login) how long the student worked and what materials they used. Students are encouraged to provide further information (see Figure 4.5) about what they learned and what difficulties they had. There is also an opportunity for teachers to provide comments on these records, which students can read on the same screen.

Test yourself In the Thai context many students expect to be tested and like to get feedback on their progress. In a self-access environment (whether online or not) this is difficult to achieve as every student works with different materials, at different levels, and for different purposes. One partial solution was to create a number of general language tests (although they are specific to the level and interests of the [mainly] engineering students at this university) that students can complete individually (see Figure 4.6). The tests are completed online and comprise multiple choice, gap-fill, and other closed

Date: December 01, 2008 01:50 PM

Today I worked on the following skills (for example 'listening') and subskills (for example 'listening for specific information'):

today I worked on listening for specific information

I used the following materials and/or joined the following activities:

I used ello.

Today I learned:

new vocabulary and different accents

What I found difficult was:

the accent of some people

Next time I will:

test listening

I would like a teacher to help me with:

vocabulary when I can''t guess from listening.

Figure 4.5 Sample of a completed "your learning record" module

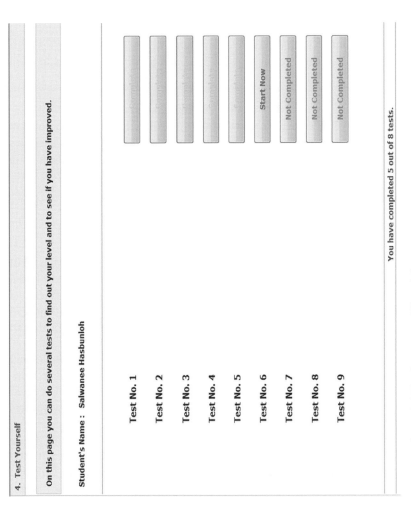

Figure 4.6 The "test yourself" module

questions. After completing eight tests, students are then allowed to complete a final, offline test. This final test has been developed independently by a different department and is intended as a type of exit test to determine students' readiness (in terms of their English skills) for entering the marketplace.

English for fun Many students at the university see learning English as a chore. By collecting tips and materials that are more fun-oriented it is hoped that students will find ways to enjoy their learning. This module includes tips on how to use films, music, computer games, and mobile phones to learn English.

Your progress In this module students can get an overview of their learning progress. They can see how many times they have used My English and for how long, as well as how much time they spend in the various modules and the number of tests (see Figure 4.7) they have completed. This information is also particularly interesting for teachers who can comment and give feedback to individual students.

Getting help from a teacher The next module (see Figure 4.8) allows students to contact teachers in a number of ways:

(1) Students can post messages via chat. When a teacher is on duty they will get a reply straight away. Questions could be practical (where can I find a copy of the Oxford Advanced Learners dictionary?) or learning-related (I need to improve my academic vocabulary. Where do I start?). Students can send attachments (as can staff) and the intention is to use this facility to send examples of their writing.
(2) If no teacher is available, the question is sent to the helpdesk via email and students will get a reply when a staff member is back on duty. The helpdesk is made up of staff from the university's self-access learning center, but it is envisaged that in future also other language teachers on the various courses around the university will take turns to provide support.
(3) Book an advisory session. Students can book an advisory session with a teacher. An advisory (or counseling) session is a meeting usually between one student and an advisor (usually a language teacher trained in language advising). Typically, the student and the advisor discuss the student's language needs and work out a study plan. In follow-up sessions the advisor and student discuss progress and the advisor gives feedback, and recommends learning strategies and language learning resources. In My English, students can request such a session and can choose to have it online (using chat), or in the university's self-access learning center.

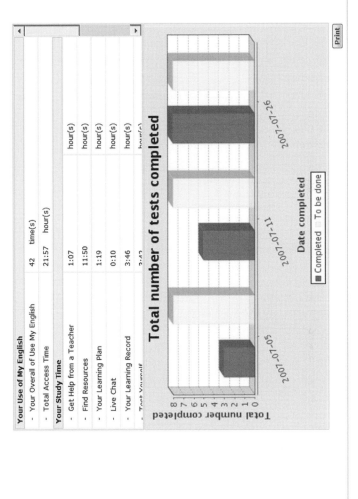

Figure 4.7 Sample of the "your progress" module

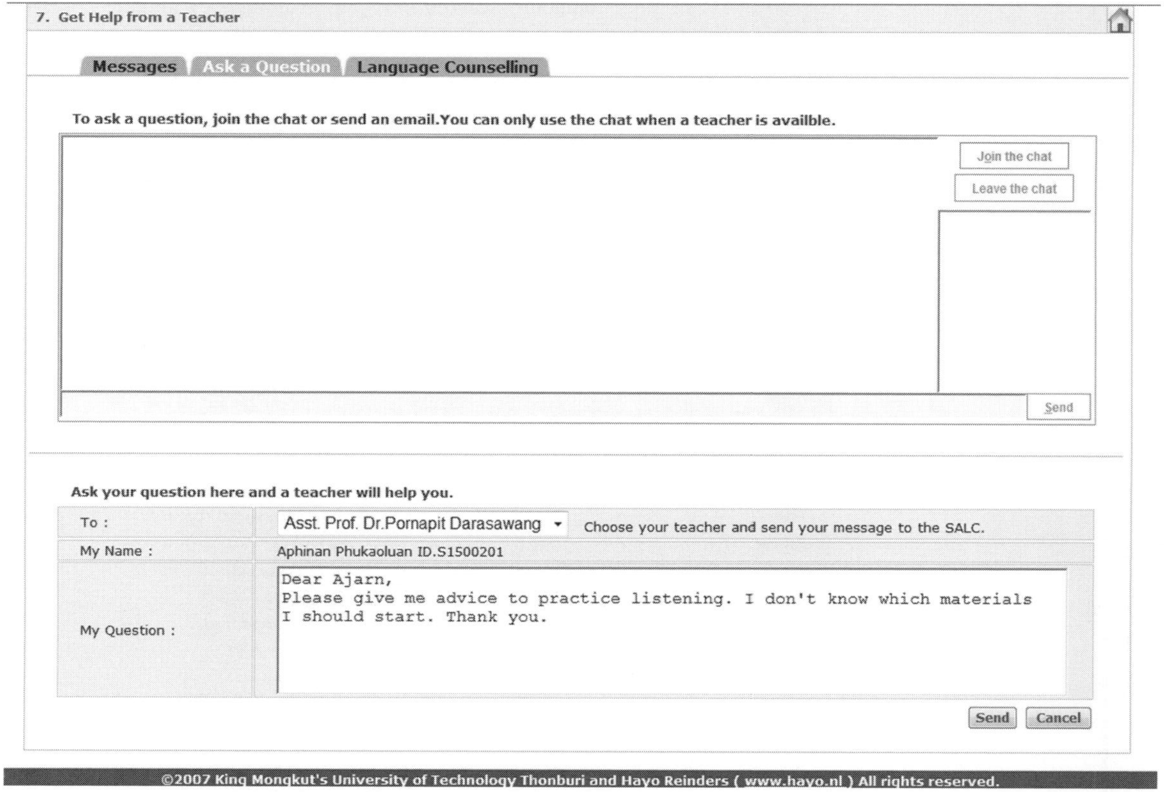

7. Get Help from a Teacher

| Messages | Ask a Question | Language Counselling |

To ask a question, join the chat or send an email. You can only use the chat when a teacher is availble.

[Join the chat]
[Leave the chat]

Send

Ask your question here and a teacher will help you.

To :   Asst. Prof. Dr.Pornapit Darasawang ▾   Choose your teacher and send your message to the SALC.

My Name :   Aphinan Phukaoluan ID.S1500201

My Question :
```
Dear Ajarn,
Please give me advice to practice listening. I don't know which materials
I should start. Thank you.
```

[Send] [Cancel]

Figure 4.8 Sample of the "get help from a teacher" module

Activities On this page the self-access learning center advertises online and face-to-face activities and news. These could include debating groups, academic writing seminars, movie screenings, or even karaoke sessions.

Implications

Implementing language support

The type of program described above has great potential to encourage language learning outside the classroom and to develop students' ability to self-direct their learning. However, the success of such programs depends to a large extent on their implementation and subsequent use. In the case of My English, and following an initial pilot phase and the working out of some smaller technical issues, the reactions from students were generally positive. Students were grateful for the anytime–anywhere access to materials and support. Upon completion of the project, the Department of Language Studies made it a requirement for all language teachers to introduce My English in class. In addition, a self-study component was introduced in the first compulsory English course offered to all undergraduate students. These decisions are likely to positively affect the long-term contribution of the program.

However, in the case of My English, although students were required during the compulsory courses to use the program to plan their self-study, they did not need to use any of the online materials available there. For all other courses there were no guidelines on how much work teachers were supposed to ask students to do with My English, nor how it should be assessed, especially in relation to class work. Also, teachers were not required to make themselves available for help online or provide materials for inclusion, and the level of participation among teachers was highly variable. Some students expressed dissatisfaction with the level of engagement from some of the staff in offering support through the online program. In other words, there was a lack of uniformity in how the program was used across the institution. Such issues are known to negatively impact the eventual integration of CALL use (cf. Reinders, 2007), and indeed of any educational innovation.

Some guidelines for implementing language support

Some of the experiences in the development and implementation of My English, and those reported by previous research on out-of-class learning (Conacher and Kelly-Holmes, 2007, Alford and Pachler, 2007), offer lessons for those interested in integrating online language support. The first of these concerns is the issue of guidelines for implementation mentioned above. Although top-down implementation may not be desirable for a number of reasons, perhaps a requirement for staff to *experiment* and share one's experiences in using the new program may be more feasible. Teachers, both in this university and in other contexts (c.f. Hubbard and Levy, 2006), benefit from specific and detailed instructions or suggestions for using CALL programs. Opportunities for exploration and extended practice need to be built into the implementation process. This applies even more in the case of language support. For many practitioners the technical element is a challenge, but perhaps even more importantly, language support involves a different pedagogical approach whereby the focus is on the individual learner and *facilitating* the self-directed learning process, rather than teaching pre-determined courses. These are skills that not all teachers can be assumed to have.

A second recommendation is to allocate sufficient time for preparation and implementation of language support. All change processes are time-consuming and require careful planning and monitoring (DeLano *et al.*, 1994). In the case of My English, funding issues meant that the program had to be developed in a short period of time and ready for use by the start of the academic year. This put undue pressure on the designers and programmers and left less time than was desirable for obtaining feedback from students and other stakeholders.

Related to the issue of time is the need for broad consultation with teaching staff and administrators from all departments involved, either directly or indirectly, in the use of the support program. By its very nature, language support is not tied to one individual department or school but instead operates at an institutional level and even extends beyond the institution. It therefore requires the support from all staff. Again, and largely because of the limited available time for the project, with My English not enough staff consultation was carried out. Because the project was initiated in collaboration with (and funded by) central university administration through a so-called learning innovation scheme, the project may have been seen by some as an external imposition. Initially, some thought that My English would replace the SALC, as an attempt by the university to take control over the English support and away from the School of Liberal Arts (the faculty that provides almost all of the language teaching and support at the university). Staff sessions have probably taken away most of those fears but a greater buy-in could have probably resulted from more extensive staff consultation and preparation. Related to this is the issue of ownership. With institution-wide resources, such as in language support, there is always a question of who is responsible for the maintenance and the delivery of the resources and who has control over them. The earlier such issues can be worked out, the better.

Teaching with CALL requires a partially different skill set and thus a considerable investment on the part of teachers (Chapelle, 2001). Hampel and Stickler (2005) identify various phases teachers go through in adopting and become comfortable with a technology, as shown in Figure 4.9.

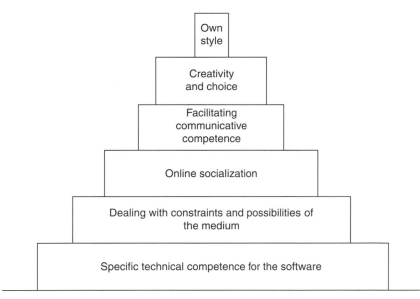

Figure 4.9 Skills for online teaching (from Hampel and Stickler, 2005; reprinted by permission of the publisher: Taylor and Francis Group, www.informaworld.com)

Jones (2001, p. 361) quotes Burston (1996, p. 33) who claims that one reason for the failure of CALL to meet its potential is the "lack of involvement of language teaching professionals." This indirectly also affects if and how students become active participants in the innovation or not; the effectiveness of CALL "undoubtedly requires more learner training and supervision than other self-access pursuits, and such training and supervision would have to be carried out by teachers" (Jones, 2001, p. 361). In the case of My English, this "training and supervision" is a long-term commitment and it will probably take considerably more time for My English to realize its full potential. Future projects should take account of this (lengthy) part of the development process.

This also applies not only to the preparation of teachers but also to that of learners. A great deal of literature exists that has shown that learners need ample preparation and ongoing support to be successful in self-directed learning (Hurd, 2005). This involves both a technical preparation as well as the development of an understanding of the need for learning outside the classroom and without a teacher. Some universities have experimented with formally recognizing students' informal learning (for example, by giving credit for self-study).

Conclusion

Language support is increasingly recognized as a key element in language education. The use of technology has major potential to enable and facilitate the delivery of resources and support to students, not just in terms of immediate language gains, but also, and perhaps more importantly, in terms of the development of lifelong learning skills. The case study above has given one example of what language support looks like in practice and the different components that it includes.

The experiences from that project and previous research have shown that for language support to be successful, it requires careful planning and preparation to ensure that it is integrated into the wider language teaching environment. If this happens, then language support has the potential to have a positive and substantial washback effect on language education as a whole. The focus in language support on the individual learner and on developing learning skills rather than the transmission of content sits well with the current interest in learner autonomy. Due to its distributed and individual nature, a pedagogy for language support benefits greatly from the use of technology, and especially recent developments (such as social networking and location-aware services) are likely, in future, to greatly facilitate the ability for institutions and educators to deliver personalized learning resources and to offer support in the self-directed learning process, and in this way to truly encourage diversity in education.

5   Diversity in environments

Glenn Stockwell and Nobue Tanaka-Ellis

Introduction

The environments in which computers are used these days have changed dramatically compared with the early days of computer-assisted language learning (CALL), where learners were usually expected to complete stand-alone activities in a fixed computer room. These sometimes occurred under the supervision of a teacher, but they could also be undertaken in self-learning situations if required. Recent developments in technologies have meant that learners no longer need to be bound to the computer room, and CALL has undergone a major change in terms of location and time. This chapter looks at the range of CALL environments that have emerged with these new technologies, and divides these into four main categories; face-to-face environments, blended environments, distance environments, and virtual environments. This is followed by an example of a face-to-face environment, to show how even an environment that may be perceived as relatively simple at face value can involve a wide range of complexities. The chapter concludes with a discussion of how the affordances of various environments can play a large role in the way in which language learning that occurs within them takes place, and some suggestions for what must be kept in mind when deciding how technology fits into a language teaching and learning environment.

Overview and general issues

The term "environment" when it comes to CALL is extremely broad, and it includes not only the technological artifacts, but also, among other things, the curriculum, the classroom (or lack thereof), the learners and teachers, and the skills and backgrounds that they bring with them. There are many reasons why varied environments come into being. In some cases, teachers may feel that their learners lack sufficient experience to work with technology completely without teacher intervention and, as a result, they opt to set up a face-to-face environment where they can play an active role in overseeing learner output and identify any technological difficulties that may arise. In other cases, the teacher may wish to keep a large proportion of the class online, but blend in technology to carry out certain aspects of a course which, due to time constraints or specific affordances of the technology, mean that the teacher does not need to be present. There are still other cases where students cannot be physically present in the language classroom, and need to take the course in a distance learning environment. Finally, with new developments in technology, it is becoming possible for students to interact with other students or with native speakers through virtual environments, where participants can be virtually present in a classroom or other situation, irrelevant of their physical location. This section will look at each of these environments, outlining some of the features specific to each.

Face-to-face environments

In face-to-face environments, learners may interact directly with the computer individually, or work together in pairs or small groups at a single computer to orally discuss any information that they read from or input into the computer. When learners interact individually with the computer, much of what the learner does is controlled by the design of the software, and the teacher's primary role is expected to be to oversee and provide support as necessary. Oral interaction would be likely be minimal, apart from what occurs between the teacher and the learner. If learners work at a single computer in small groups, they must interact with one another to achieve the set goals, while the teacher is still present to provide advice and support if required. There have been a small number of studies examining interactions between multiple learners using a computer in this way. One such example is by Jeon-Ellis *et al.* (2005), who investigated Australian students enrolled in a university French class. Students created websites on French culture in small groups using a single laptop computer per group. In her study, she showed that while students were engaged in collaborative dialogs in order to develop their linguistic skills, the social context of these interactions is mediated by personal relationships, preferences, and motivations which have the potential to be either conducive or a hindrance to the interactions.

In another study, Leahy (2004) examined advanced learners of German participating in a collaborative role-play project over a four-week period. The students were divided into five small groups where each group had a specific role: a British company, a German market research company, and three other research groups that provided information retrieved from the Internet and fed it to the British company, either on demand or of their own accord. The scenario of the role-play was that the British company was to launch a new product in Eastern Germany. Communication between each group took place only by email, whereas interactions within each group were carried out orally in front of the computer. She found that when learners communicated in their groups, they did not verbalize all information, but rather the screen itself became an integral part of the communication process to fill in any unspoken blanks. It is also important to ensure that learners are provided with sufficient support to navigate with the new context of the technology. This is illustrated by Meskill (2005), who found that young children learning English as a second language working on computers in small groups benefitted from scaffolding that involved both the language and the technology.

Using CALL in a face-to-face environment is quite complex, dependent upon the learners, the technology, the task or activities, and, of course, the teacher. Learner differences play an important role in many aspects regarding technology (see, for example, Chapter 2; Raby, 2005), and this would be expected to carry over to face-to-face CALL environments as well. This type of environment makes it possible to look first-hand at how learners interact with one another and the technology. In computer-mediated communication (CMC) interactions – particularly of a textual nature – we are only left with the final product as the only clues into the process that took place to bring about this product. In a face-to-face environment where the teacher is present, it is possible to observe the interactions that occur, and to judge from learner behavior when assistance is necessary.

Blended environments

This is an area that has attracted a great deal of attention in recent years, but a clear definition of to what it refers has remained elusive. It is generally used to describe an environment in which technology is used as a part of the curriculum in conjunction with face-to-face activities, but there is a large degree of variation in how the role of technology is described. The Sloan Consortium has advocated very specific figures dictating the degree to which technology should be incorporated into a course in order to be considered as a blended environment (sometimes known as a hybrid environment). It suggests that courses are considered as being *traditional* if there is no online content used whatsoever, *web-facilitated* if technology comprises 1 to 29 percent of the course content delivery, *blended* if technology makes up 30 to 79 percent of the course content delivery, typically with both online discussions and face-to-face meetings, and *online* if technology is used for more than 80 percent of the course delivery, typically with no face-to-face meetings (Allen *et al.*, 2007). While this distinction is theoretically useful, it does not appear to be heavily supported in the literature, with the general consensus appearing to be that when technological and face-to-face aspects appear within a single learning environment it is called blended, with little if any restrictions on the amount or the way that technology is used. Garrison and Vaughan, for instance, refer to blended learning as having as its foundation "face-to-face oral communication and online written communication [that] are optimally integrated such that the strengths of each are blended into a unique learning experience congruent with the context and intended educational purpose" (2008, p. 5). They argue that blended learning should not be an addition to a course but rather represent a restructuring of the course such that both face-to-face and online elements interweave with one another to provide a better outcome than could be achieved through using only one element or the other.

In contrast to this, in lieu of a definition, Littlejohn and Pegler (2007) provide a wide range of examples of what they term as constituting blended learning, the list including tablet personal computers (PCs) with wireless connections to take and share notes in class, text messaging to receive course updates while on the move, and learning management systems, to name a few. These examples reflect a far more liberal view of blended learning than the description provided by Garrison and Vaughan (2008) above, in that in many cases the technology does not *necessarily* constitute a central and integral part of the course in which it is used, but rather, although readily accessible, can play a relatively peripheral role instead. This more liberal definition also appears to be closer to how a blended environment is viewed in literature pertaining to language learning. Sharma and Barrett (2007, p. 7), for example, describe blended environments as "a language course which combines a face-to-face (F2F) classroom component with an appropriate use of technology," involving technologies ranging from the Internet and CMC technologies through to CD-ROMs and interactive whiteboards. In the majority of cases where the term "blended" is used in the CALL literature, very little attention is actually given to what blended learning is beyond being a mixture of both online and offline elements within a single course or program. This has resulted in a rather vague perception of what blended learning is, and in essence any environment where technology has been used in some way within a predominantly face-to-face context has come to be termed as blended, which does not seem to be in line with the original concept when it was first conceived.

How, then, can we define blended learning in CALL? Defining it in terms of percentages such as those prescribed by the Sloan Consortium does not seem to take into consideration the complexities involved in distinguishing between online and face-to-face elements. For example, if students use mobile devices to access content during face-to-face classes, does this constitute online or face-to-face? Similarly, Garrison and Vaughan's (2008) assertion that online communication must be written is also problematic in that it excludes online content that could be provided in video or audio form, yet may still play a central role in the overall structure of the course. When considering the developments of mobile technologies where the line between face-to-face and online has the potential to become blurred, it is perhaps advisable to take a more liberal view of defining blended learning without placing overly restrictive boundaries. In saying this, however, as Garrison and Vaughan rightly point out, the technological aspects in a blended environment should be integral to the overall goals of the curriculum, and technology should be incorporated such that it capitalizes upon the strengths of both the technological and the face-to-face elements.

Blended learning should not only be limited to course delivery, but also include the full range of activities that one would expect to take place in a language learning class, including note-taking, communication with teachers and other students, and in-class and out-of-class activities. Within this broader definition, it becomes clear that there are various ways in which technology may be blended into the learning environment. The first of these is at a *task or activity* level, which is where a task or activity in a class may be completed using technology, whereas other tasks or activities within the same class do not require technology. This may occur either during class time (e.g. Bloch, 2007) or out of class, using computers (e.g. Yates, 2008), mobile phones (e.g. Kennedy and Levy, 2008), or a combination of the two (e.g. Stockwell, 2008). Secondly, it may occur at the *class* level, where one or more classes may be dedicated primarily to using technology on a regular basis as a part of the over-all syllabus for the subject (e.g. Lin and Chiu, 2009). Finally, it may be blended at the *subject* level where one subject out of a list of subjects that learners are required to take in a curriculum is carried out using technology for all or part of each class with technology not being used (or used very minimally) in other subjects (e.g. Nozawa, 2008). It is also feasible, of course, for blended learning to occur in any combination of these three ways.

It is important to note that the complexities in designing a blended learning environment should not be underestimated. While technology may be central at times, it may indeed have a more peripheral role at others, but this is not to understate the importance that it should have in achieving the learner goals. As we enter an era where technology is something considered as natural for many learners to have with them or around them at almost all times, serious consideration needs to be given on how the language learning environment in its entirety can best capitalize on this technology such that it supplements, complements, and enhances face-to-face elements.

Distance learning environments

The development of new technologies has dramatically changed the face of language learning through distance education. While once distance education entailed the sending of teaching materials and cassettes to learners with very little opportunity for oral interaction, this has evolved with the Internet's capability to include multimedia and multimodality (see Chapter 7 for a discussion of modality). The affordances of technologies used in distance learning (i.e. what can be achieved as a result of using these technologies; see Chapter 1) has opened up a range of possibilities that were not possible before this time. Web 2.0, which facilitates communication and collaboration between users (see Chapter 6; Thomas, 2009), has made formats of interaction and instruction possible in distance learning that previously could not be achieved with the affordances of earlier technologies.

The very nature of teaching languages in distance education using technology has become the focus of a number of studies (e.g. Son, 2002; Doughty and Long, 2003), which is a clear indication of the importance that has come to be placed on it. Distance environments will generally rely on a system that operates as the foundation for the delivery of course content, facilitating of interactions between learners and the teacher, administration and grading of assessment, and so forth. In most cases, this takes the form of a learning management system (LMS), which may be commercially produced, such as WebCT (Möllering, 2000) or developed in-house, such as Lyceum (e.g. Rosell-Aguilar, 2007a). These individual systems vary quite significantly in their capabilities, and this will obviously have an effect on what content can be provided and how teachers and learners interact. Systems that inherently include components that facilitate audio or video communication are very limited, with one such exception being Lyceum which was developed by the Open University (see Hampel and Hauck, 2004). In other cases, teachers must rely on software outside of the system itself, such as NetMeeting (Wang, 2004).

There are several challenges associated with distance learning through technology. First and foremost, and this is relevant to any distance learning environment regardless of whether technology is used or not, it is difficult to sustain learners' positive attitudes and motivation, and maintain high levels of interaction in the face of limited personal contact (Strambi and Bouvet, 2003). Obviously, where there is little or no actual direct contact between teachers and learners, it is difficult for teachers to have a clear image of the motivation levels and individual needs of learners, which would be thought to lead to a drop in motivation. As Sampson (2003) points out, learners feel the need for sufficient and timely feedback, and it is possible that they will view a program poorly if they do not receive feedback as they expect.

There are also potential difficulties that may be encountered by learners who are less competent with using technology. It is difficult to provide assistance if learners experience technical problems when they are located remotely. If learners are particularly challenged with technology, then it may be difficult for them to explain exactly what the problem is, let alone find a solution for it, so suitable support from experienced staff is essential in overcoming this. This problem can be magnified if different software is necessary to achieve different goals within the learning environment. In addition, much of the learning that occurs at a distance does so asynchronously. This may be as a result of different time zones or just because learners have commitments which prevent them from being online for synchronous online discussions such as those used by Hampel and Hauck (2004) and by Wang (2004). When there is a speaking element in the course but learners cannot be online at the same time, there is a need to consider other alternatives of an asynchronous nature through tools such as voice email (Volle, 2005), where learners can record their voice and send it by email at a time that is convenient to them.

Social networking environments

Blogs and wikis It may seem unusual to include blogs and wikis in a section on social networking, but if we consider the nature of each of these tools, we can see that they are, in many ways, forerunners to the social networking sites that are in extensive use today. Weblogs, or blogs as they are more commonly known, are popular cyber arenas for self-expression. In essence, a blog is a personal online journal which can be set up and maintained with little technical expertise, and which can include pictures and videos along with textual entries. Blogs also make it possible for other people to post comments regarding what has been written by the owner of the blog or people who posted comments earlier. In this sense, blogs have typically been used by family, friends, and people who share similar ideas or hobbies to interact with one another, thus creating a kind of *de facto* network. It is interesting to note that most of the major networking sites in use today still incorporate blogs within their functionality; however, it is possible to control who is able to see the content and who can comment on it. In language learning environments, one of the most commonly cited benefits of blogs is that they provide an authentic audience to learners when they write in the target language, where their writing can be read by a wider audience rather than just the teacher for assessment purposes. There have been a number of studies carried out on blogs, incorporating tasks that enable learners to study and write about the target culture where feedback is provided by peers (Dippold, 2009) or by native speakers of the target culture (Lee, 2009). Reactions from learners regarding publicizing their blogs have been varied, with some learners opting to keep their blogs private between themselves and the teacher (Murray and Hourigan, 2008), and others welcoming feedback from the wider community, even when it was less than positive (e.g. Pinkman, 2005).

Wikis are very different in nature from blogs, in that they are used predominantly for collaboratively composing online documents rather than as a journal. One key point of a wiki is that, externally, at the very least, it is difficult to know who contributed to what part of a document as any person who has editing rights can add to, delete, or alter any information which is contained within it. Records are kept of changes and it is generally possible to "roll back" to a previous version should editing be carried out that is not appropriate or desired. Perhaps the best known example of a wiki is Wikipedia, the online wiki-based encyclopedia. Information is provided by people all around the world in an essentially anonymous manner (although it is possible to check contributors' handle names) to create a massive reference resource. The anonymous collaborative nature of wikis makes it an attractive tool to use in language learning environments as well (Lund, 2008; Yates, 2008), but there is still surprisingly little written about using wikis in this capacity. Work that has been done has focused on the wiki's appropriateness as a tool for learners to work together to create shared documents (e.g. Kessler, 2009) and participants' editorial behavior in composing a document through a wiki (Kessler and Bikowski, 2010). Feedback regarding using wikis by learners has been mixed. While some learners claim that they feel encouraged by the fact that someone can come back and correct what they have written so that they can focus more on content than on linguistic aspects, others have been more negative with respect to having entries changed or deleted by others even though it was correct (Lund, 2008) and not feeling comfortable in correcting their peers' writing (Lee, 2010).

Social networking sites Social networking systems (SNSs) like Facebook, MySpace, and Twitter have rapidly gained in popularity since their emergence in 2005. Social networking sites are potentially useful for language learning, where learners can choose with whom they interact by viewing their profiles, and then discuss common topics of interest or share photographs or videos with them. In this way, learners can, to a degree, tailor the input that they receive, making it more relevant to their individual needs. One example of investigating SNSs for language learning is by Pasfield-Neofitou (2010), who examined learners of Japanese in their spontaneous personal use of CMC with native speakers. In her study, she found that email still remained by far the most commonly used method of interacting with one another, although a small number of the participants also used Facebook. The Japanese social networking site Mixi, however, was the most commonly used site, undoubtedly due to the fact that the learners were interacting with Japanese native speakers and that the site is well established in Japan. MySpace was hardly used by the participants in the study, but in the case of both Facebook and Mixi, participants sent messages as an alternative to using email, as well as posting photographs and videos. Twitter differs from Facebook and MySpace in that it is intended for sending very short postings and, as Mork (2009) describes, this makes it convenient for sending out small pieces of information either to individual students or to the class, without fear of filling up their mailboxes.

One form of social networking, social bookmarking websites, can be used as a hub for sharing information and opinions. Registered users are able to save links to articles on their personal page, which can be shared by others, and in much the same way as social networking websites, approved visitors can leave notes and comments under each bookmark. In a study investigating the use of social bookmarking sites for language learning, Prichard (2010) used a site called Diigo in an English as a foreign language (EFL) reading class at a university in Japan. The students were asked to read two or more articles they or their classmates found on the Internet every week, add a tag to each article (e.g. sports, health, etc.) and write a short summary and reaction on the social bookmarking site. Other students added extra comments on the bookmarked articles and decided whether they liked the article or not by clicking on the "like" button. In this way, learners were able to share information that they found interesting with one another and read articles that received favorable reviews from other students. It is perhaps this point that is one of the advantages of social networking, where learners have the ability to be selective in the input that they receive in terms of both the areas of interest and with whom they choose to interact.

Virtual environments and online games

Virtual environments Virtual environments for language learning have developed quite dramatically over the past several years. From the early 1990s, multi-user domain object oriented (MOOs) have been used in education due to their potential for learning, teaching, and training (Mateas and Lewis, 1996; Shield, 2003; see Chapter 7). Early MOOs were entirely text-based, and a number of MOOs for language learning purposes were developed, such as SchMOOze University for English learners and LeMOOFrançaise for learners of French. Although these text-based MOOs did receive attention for some time from the mid-1990s, they have all but been replaced by graphic MOOs (now more generally referred to as multi-user virtual environments, or MUVEs), through which users can navigate using an avatar of their choice as their self-manifestation. While most of the currently available virtual environments were developed as a means of social networking rather than for learning purposes, using avatars as these environments does make it possible to maintain anonymity, enabling learners to take risks in communication that they may be less willing to take if their actual identity is known. This means that learners can feel more comfortable about using the target language and thus potentially increases opportunities to communicate.

There are currently two major MUVEs which have been used in second language learning; Active Worlds and Second Life. Active Worlds allows its users to create 3D virtual worlds where they can communicate with each other through text-based chat (Toyoda and Harrison, 2002) although it was later equipped with a real-time voice communication component (Peterson, 2008). Second Life resembles Active Worlds in that it is also a 3D world that can be explored and manipulated by the participants, and contains both text and voice chat. Second Life allows users to also play recordings and slide shows and to teleport to other places or worlds at will (Stevens, 2006). There are examples of both of these environments being used for language learning purposes. Svensson (2003), for instance, used Active Worlds to provide learners with an environment where they could perform presentations in front of other students in a virtual classroom, whereas Toyoda and Harrison (2002) created an online virtual university campus using Active Worlds for Japanese learners to communicate with native speakers of Japanese. Although it was viewed positively by the learners, Toyoda and Harrison found that while actions such as waving, dancing, and fighting were possible in the environment, the program did not allow users to control their avatars to behave in culturally appropriate ways within the context of the target culture (i.e. bowing). Despite communication taking place entirely through text chat, they found that there were multiple instances of negotiation of meaning observed in the interactions as learners carried out conversations with participants in the environment.

With the gradual decline in popularity of Active Worlds (Stevens, 2006), Second Life seems to be taking over the role that it once played, and research on this MUVE is also starting to appear. In one such example, Peterson (2010a) used Second Life in much the same way that Toyoda and Harrison used Active Worlds above, with the learners communicating via text chat in an online virtual university, noting that the interactions were largely learner-centered rather than being led by the teacher. In another study, Deutschmann *et al.* (2009) examined Second Life to determine how learners viewed the virtual environment for learning purposes and whether it could contribute to increased participation. In contrast to the text chat used in the previous examples, learners communicated using real-time voice chat, and while there were technical difficulties in early communication, learners appeared to become gradually more comfortable over time. Some notable results from the study included that many learners felt more comfortable hiding behind their avatar, but that role-play activities learners engaged in relatively easily in a face-to-face environment did not translate as well as expected in the virtual environment, with the technology acting as a hindrance to communication as learners struggled with how to work out the interface. It should also be noted that technical difficulties were cited in the early stages of each of the studies. Both the studies by Deutschmann *et al.* (2009) and Toyoda and Harrison (2002) indicated that learners did not manipulate their avatars very much, and focused their concentration on engaging in the communication rather than on the avatars. Thus, it may be possible to conclude from this that if the technology is overly complicated, it has the potential to detract from the objectives at hand rather than facilitating them.

It is important to note that in virtual worlds the outcomes depend on the participants. This means that, as in any offline environment, there is a need for teachers to have concrete objectives in mind, and to make these objectives clear to the learners. Failure to do this could result in a similar situation as to what would happen in an uncontrolled face-to-face environment (with or without technology) where learners may start engaging in activities that are not relevant to their language learning purposes. In a virtual environment, however, unless there are controls in place to prevent outside interruption, the learners can very easily be distracted by other non-learner participants or even simply teleport away to other distant virtual places.

Online games In much the same way as Active Worlds and Second Life, online games allow learners to experience the target language in a virtual environment, either individually or with other players. In single-player games, learners interact with characters that appear in the game in order to carry out certain activities, whereas massively multiplayer online role-playing games (MMORPGs) allow participants of games to communicate with each other online through text or voice, depending on game consoles and games. In either case, the outcomes of the games are, however, decided by the game, not by the participants. This is an area still very much in its infancy, but there have been a small number of researchers who have explored the possibilities of using online games as a second language (L2) learning tool.

For example, Purushotma (2005) examined affordances of a single-player simulation game called The Sims as a language learning tool, and noted that the three-dimensional (3D) environments provided in the game were similar to what tertiary-level foreign language learners would learn in their classes. By using a foreign language version of The Sims, learners were able to simulate their virtual life in the L2 with the assistance of first language (L1) annotations. Language acquisition may also be possible using simulations, as suggested by Ranalli (2008), who found that learners exhibited gains in vocabulary as a result of using The Sims for studying English. In other gaming environments, Rankin *et al.* (2006a, 2006b) studied Ever Quest II for its capabilities of providing L2 learning opportunities. Rankin *et al.* (2006a) argue that MMORPGs support situated learning to provide immersive learning environments that promote deep and conceptual knowledge of a particular domain. They also claim that MMORPGs provide opportunities to L2 learners to engage in authentic social interaction among native and non-native players. In a pilot study by Rankin *et al.* (2006b) using MMORPGs for language learning, four ESL students played Ever Quest II for four hours a week for four weeks. Like Second Life, learners chose their avatars from a range of races, professions, and classes to complete sixty levels of quests. Players could interact with characters in the game to receive information for completing quests. The students took the part of playing characters (PCs), which were actively involved in the quest, and interacted with non-playing characters (NPCs), which gave directions and provided information but were not involved in the quest. The results indicated all four participants were able to identify 35 percent or more words that appeared only once in the interactions with the NPCs, and 55 percent of the words that appeared more than five times. However, the lower-level students struggled more to adapt to the virtual environment as they needed more support to navigate through the game and comprehend the information on the screen. A detailed overview of the potential of MMORPGs in language learning has been provided by Peterson (2010b).

In both cases above, participants were not required to engage in physical activity in the games, except for a minimal amount of actions such as clicking on objects on a screen with a mouse or typing with a keyboard. The Nintendo Wii game console has had a large influence on the way game participants play virtual games. The Wii game console comes with a wireless game controller that allows the player's avatar to move in the virtual environment of the games in approximately the same way one might move in the real world. This has implications for its use as an educational tool. Through an examination of the affordances of the Wii, Morgan *et al.* (2007) claim that the controller enables the manifestation of behaviorist learning theory, and as learners need to physically engage in the interaction sequences through actually moving their bodies to achieve the goals in the game, the tasks the learners are engaged in can be argued as being more authentic. Although learners can play virtual games individually, as with other interfaces, the multiplayer mode allows learners to work collaboratively.

Example

Using CALL in a face-to-face environment

As described above, the environments in which CALL can be used are extremely broad, making it impossible to give any kind of encompassing examples as to how CALL is used. As a result, just one example of how CALL may be used in a face-to-face environment has been given here. In the example below, learners interacted with native-speaking interlocutors through a bulletin board system (BBS), but at the same time they interacted with each other in the reading and drafting of the messages that they posted on the BBS during class time, meaning that there was both a face-to-face element and an online element.

Learning context The learners were students in an Australian high school with little or no opportunity to interact in Japanese, so an arrangement was made with a high school in Japan so that they could engage in authentic interactions with Japanese native speakers of around their own age. There were twenty-five Australian and thirty-five Japanese students who engaged in posting messages to each other via the BBS in order to create a web page based on cultural issues pertaining to each other's culture. Learners posted messages to the BBS collaboratively, meaning that there was interaction between the Australian and Japanese students through the computer, as well as face-to-face interactions that occurred between participants as they read and drafted the BBS postings for their interlocutors. Learners were required to work in small groups of three or four students at a single computer in order to read and post the messages to the BBS. The students used both English and Japanese to communicate with each other, by completing a few group tasks and one individual task each week. The language used for communication alternated each week. An element of tandem learning (Brammerts, 1996; Calvert, 1992) and reciprocal teaching was also incorporated into this project where the Australian students were to learn Japanese from their Japanese partners, and the Japanese students were to learn English from the Australian students. In other words, they were set to teach each other, and learn from each other as native speakers of one language and learners of the other. The CALL classes were integrated at a class level in that one fifty-minute class per week (out of four classes per week) was dedicated to completing the CALL activities, although the CALL component was not included in their assessment. The Australian students were audio and video recorded in order to examine how they interacted with each other while engaged in the tasks. Interactions from the BBS exchanges were also collected, but were not used in the current study.

Activities completed by the learners The topics of the tasks were carefully selected in advance of the interactions taking place by the teachers of both the Australian and Japanese schools and the researcher, to elicit the students' interest in the target culture and language. The topics of the tasks were related to the issues that the Australian students covered in previous years, so that the students could actually use the vocabulary they had already learned during their classes in communication with the Japanese partners. This view of task arrangement is in line with Skourtou's (2002) view of selecting activities for online communication that promote activation of students' prior knowledge. Themes for the bulletin board discussions were decided by the researcher and the teachers, in both the Australian and Japanese schools. The themes, leisure and sport, shopping, famous people, festivals, and fashion, changed at approximately monthly intervals. The students were to ask at least one question every week to their counterparts, to sustain their interaction on the bulletin board (see Stockwell, 2003). Towards the end of the project, each group of students was required to create a web page based on their bulletin board discussions.

The design and content of the web pages were of their choice, but they needed to include what they had learned from their BBS discussions. The students were asked to choose one or more topics from the themes from their online discussions for web page production. The software for web page production was Macromedia Dreamweaver MX (currently called Adobe Dreamweaver) or Microsoft Word, both of which were already installed on the school computers for other subjects.

Observations Students engaged in two different channels of communication for task completion: group interaction around computers, and written exchanges between the Australian and Japanese students. As the task involved composing and reading postings on the BBS with group members, one channel of communication was the oral interaction among group members as a process task completion, involving computers by forming a "triangular relationship" (Leahy, 2004, p. 133). This triangular relationship made it possible for the students to share thoughts and L2 knowledge, generating a flow of knowledge among students. The example below (Example 1) shows that two students are negotiating the correct spelling of the name of a Japanese athlete written in a L1 message by looking at the words shown on the computer screen.

   Example (1)

[TEXT OUTCOME IN THE L1] The Japanese sports person we know is ai sugiyama [*sic*].
(1) AU4: *Ai, Sugi, ya, ma?*
(2) AU22: Ah, a space between her first name and last name?

AU4 is typing a message in English regarding a Japanese tennis player, Ai Sugiyama (line 1). AU22 is providing the content of the message for AU4 to type. She notices and mentions that AU4 did not insert a space in between *ai*, the first name and *sugiyama*, the last name (line 2, also see the text outcome). Although the sentence is not free of error, even after the correction, because AU4 failed to capitalize the "A" and "S" in "*ai sugiyama*," AU22 guided AU4 to write the Japanese athlete's name more appropriately, by telling AU4 to insert a space between "*ai*" and "*sugiyama*." The computer in this example allowed the students to share their output as they typed. Thus, the computer facilitated peer collaboration, revision, and negotiation on the message that appeared on the screen.

This environment also worked in favor of L2 instruction for the teacher, as the messages on computers served as "anchored referents" (Meskill, 2005), which were used while the teacher was helping students decoding L2 messages posted by the Japanese students and revising their own L2 messages. This face-to-face environment also contributed to producing oral L2 output, individually or together with group members, by reading aloud L2 messages, both composed by themselves and the Japanese partners, during a course of task completion. In the following example (Example 2), three students are reading a L2 message posted by their Japanese counterpart. Their teacher is trying to assist them with decoding the meaning of the text without giving them the translation of the message in focus.

Example (2)

[RECEIVED L2 MESSAGE] ライゴン道でのパレードはいつですか？
[PHONETIC] *Raigon Dori deno pareedo wa itsu desu ka?*
[TRANSLATION] When is the parade on Lygon Street?

(1)   TEACHER: *Dori deno, pareedo wa, itsu desu ka?*
      (On the street, when is the parade?)
(2)   AU1: Have been? *Itsu?*
(3)   TEACHER: *Itsu desu ka? Kurisumasu wa itsu desu ka? Tanjoobi wa itsu desu ka?*
      (When is it? When is Christmas? When is your birthday?)
(4)   AU1: Is it?
(5)   Teacher: *Itsu,* when.
(6)   AU2: Oh.
(7)   AU3: Oh.
(8)   TEACHER: When is it? *Itsu.*

The teacher is reading a sentence on the computer screen aloud (line 1). AU1 asks if "*itsu*" is "have been" (line 2). The teacher provides a recast, by repeating the whole sentence, "*itsu desu ka?*" (line 3). Together with a recast, the teacher provides two different questions that include "*itsu desu ka?*" within the questions, to help AU1 work out the meaning of "*itsu desu ka?*" (line 3). AU1 still is not able to deduce the meaning from the examples provided, and asks if the question means "is it?" (line 4). The teacher reveals that "*itsu*" is "when" (line 5), and "*itsu desu ka?*" is "when is it?" (line 8). The teacher, therefore, used the recast to show it was "*itsu desu ka?*" that the students needed to understand, rather than "*itsu*" only. She highlighted the phrase, by giving the students a few examples of phrases that included "*itsu desu ka?*" to have them deduct the meaning of "*itsu desu ka?*" from the examples, without giving out the answer. After AU1 gave the teacher another erroneous answer (in line 4), she gave the students the correct answer, but only by telling them "*itsu*" meant "when," still not giving out the translation of the entire phrase "*itsu desu ka?*" (line 5). The teacher was, probably, waiting for the students to translate the whole phrase by themselves; however, after the students' interjections (lines 6 and 7) she provided the answer (line 8). In this example, the role of the computer screen is not visible. However, the students and the teacher are all looking at the screen to discuss the meaning of the message.

The computer screen served as a display of the L2 messages, a meeting point of the Australian and the Japanese students' communication, and the source of learning new words and phrases with the help of their teacher. The following example (Example 3), however, shows a clear role of the computer. In this example, two students (AU10 and AU11) are composing a message in their L2 with some help from their teacher. AU10 is invisible in this conversation as she is participating in this activity by sitting next to AU11, looking at the screen, possibly thinking or observing.

Example (3)

[TEXT OUTCOME IN L2] 一番目になったうまです。
[PHONETIC] *Ichibanme ni natta uma desu.*
[TRANSLATION] The horse became number one.

(1) TEACHER: *Ichibanme no uma. Ichiban, ichibanme no uma.* (The first horse. The number one, first horse.)

(2) TEACHER: *Ichiban ni natta uma.* Became number one. (The horse became number one. Became number one.)

(3) TEACHER: *Ichiban, me, ni narimashita. Natta, narimashita.* (Number one, -st, became. Became, became.)

(4) AU11: Double T?

(5) TEACHER: *Natta uma desu.* Yeah, that's good. (*Horse became.* Yeah, that's good.)

The teacher is reading a sentence written by the Australian students, shown on the computer screen (line 1). She then utters a new sentence "*ichiban ni natta uma*" followed by its translation (line 2). She goes on and tries different forms (line 3). AU11 is listening and typing, while the teacher is uttering different forms, and asks if the spelling for "*natta*" has double T (line 4). The teacher reads the sentence that AU11 composed on the screen, and assures that her writing is correct this time (line 5). This example is different from the oral recasts presented in the previous example, as the communication between the students and the teacher is exchanged through what was written on the computer screen. AU11 expressed her thoughts through the screen by ongoing typing, and the teacher provided recasts of the sentence that appeared on the screen as AU11 was typing. The teacher also appears to elucidate the correct form, by providing recasts and repeating a few different forms. However, the teacher's speech seems to have worked as a guide for AU11, to come up with the correct form of the L2 sentence. In this example, the students and the teacher were sharing their thoughts by reading AU11's ongoing typing on the screen, and by speaking out their thoughts. As the screen broadcast AU11's real-time editing process, the participants of the conversation around this computer were able to share the cognitive process of the typist and the people who influenced the typist's thought, which resulted in altering the message on the screen.

Implications

Considering affordances of an environment

It is clear that every environment brings with it a range of affordances (see Chapter 1 for a discussion), in terms of the technologies that are used, the amount of time that learners spend using the technologies, the way in which they interact with the technologies, and how the use of the technologies fits into the larger picture in terms of task, class, and curriculum. In the example listed above, the affordances of the environment, including the bulletin board system (BBS) and the physical arrangement of the computers, allowed interaction to take place between the Australian and Japanese learners, while at the same time the learners in Australia were able to interact with one another face-to-face, seeking assistance from the teacher as necessary. This provided opportunities for learners to interact in different modes: text-based communication through the BBS, and oral communication around the computer (see Chapter 7 for a discussion of modalities).

The example provided here shows the affordances that can occur as a result of a face-to-face environment, but other environments also lend to the affordances of the technologies that are being used. The technology itself will have a lesser or greater effect on what can be done depending on in which environment it is used. Technology is central in distance learning, hence concern must be given to the affordances of the technologies as they will largely determine what can and cannot be taught through this environment. In social networking environments, while the technology allows learners to make information available not only to their classmates and the teacher, it can also be used to interact with the wider community. The technology of both virtual environments and online games provides a means through which learners can interact not only with real people through their avatars, but also with virtual people and objects. In addition, depending on the software, learners can have the option of communicating through text, audio, or a combination of the two. A blended environment, however, combines both CALL and non-CALL aspects, meaning that consideration needs to be given to the CALL element so that it capitalizes upon the non-CALL ones (c.f. Leakey and Ranchoux, 2006). Thus, while technologies bring with them certain affordances, the environment itself will determine the degree to which these technological affordances are applicable.

Language learning in various environments

From the discussion above, it is possible to see that each environment will bring with it varying affordances that vary significantly depending on the technology that is used, the background and experience of the learners, the objectives of the curriculum, subject, class, or task, the experience and teaching philosophy of the teacher, and the physical environment. As Felix (2003) points out, regardless of what technology is used, it is important to keep sight on the pedagogical goals. Egbert *et al.* (1999, p. 4) suggest that for language learning, ideally learners must have opportunities to interact and negotiate meaning, interact with the target language with an authentic audience, be involved in authentic tasks, be exposed to and encouraged to produce varied and creative language, have enough time and feedback, be guided to attend mindfully to the learning process, work in an atmosphere with an ideal stress/anxiety level, and have their autonomy supported.

While these may not necessarily have the same weighting in all teaching and learning situations, they do form a guideline for identifying the essential needs of the learner. The affordances of some environments mean that these may not necessarily be as easy to achieve as other environments, hence time and attention must be given to how they may be provided. It is also important to note here that when technology is involved, that an extra key factor must come into play, that being how to support the learner in the language learning process. This will obviously be completely different, depending on the affordances of the environment. In face-to-face environments, the support may be provided by the teacher or other staff who are present where the technology is located, and can immediately respond to learner questions and problems, as was the case in the example cited above. There is much greater variation in a blended environment, however, as it will depend greatly on the technology and the amount of contact between teachers and learners. Considering that a lack of support has been cited as the major reason why learners drop out of a blended language learning class (see Stracke, 2007), it is important to put in place sufficient procedures to ensure that learners' problems are addressed within a reasonable timeframe. Providing sufficient support in distance environments is probably the most difficult, as there is generally less contact between the teachers and the learners. In this case, support needs to be provided such that learners do not feel abandoned, and at the same time can be offered regardless of differences in time and place. Finally, as research has shown, virtual environments are the most prone to difficulties in the early stages, particularly when new technologies are being introduced. Providing training to make sure that learners are sufficiently familiar with the technology that they are using, and incorporating this training on an ongoing basis (see Chapter 3), can help learners work their way along the learning curve in a more efficient and stable manner.

Conclusion

Technology does not inherently facilitate language learning (Doughty and Long, 2003), but rather, it is how technology is used that dictates whether or not language learning occurs through its use. The learning environment guides how the affordances of technologies can be capitalized upon and thus what can be achieved using technology. CALL environments have evolved dramatically as a direct result of advances in technology, and it is likely that technologies will continue to develop, producing even more diversity in environments.

Regardless of the type of environment in which CALL is used, however, there are certain principles that must be kept in mind, which relate to the importance of knowing the technology, the learners, and the educational goals, and finding a balance between these with regard to the constraints of the particular environment.

6   Diversity in content

E. Marcia Johnson and John Brine

Introduction

The Internet is a source of endless and diverse content that could potentially be used effectively by language teachers for the creation of curricula or other teaching resources. Any cursory search for language learning quizzes, for example, or other types of language-based exercises, will yield millions of hits. However, having access to vast amounts of non-categorized content, much of which has not been evaluated in any systematic manner, is of little benefit to language teachers and does nothing to advance the field of computer-assisted language learning (CALL). Even among software and content-based exercises that do exist, teachers cannot depend on them to remain "as is" for any length of time in the ever-changing web environment. In addition, language on the Internet is "messy"; it can contain factual, grammatical, or syntactical errors and it can reflect cultural biases. And yet, the web is a vast language corpus that contains almost endless examples of language-in-use, and as such its potential as a source of diverse content for language teaching is undeniable.

This chapter will discuss and describe ways in which open educational resources (OER) in conjunction with specific open source software (OSS) tools can provide new approaches to content organization, presentation, and use within English language teaching environments. However, it will also discuss the fact that although OER have the potential to stimulate both teacher and curriculum development initiatives through the provision of diverse content, there are a number of fundamental issues which must be considered explicitly. We have found that the (relatively) easy access to OSS tools and the recent availability of OER can create a mistaken assumption that using them meaningfully within a real instructional context, such as the language classroom, will be straightforward. Rather, new approaches to curriculum design and classroom pedagogy are required, which can illuminate the complex interactions of people, instructional content, and institutional context (Clarebout and Elen, 2008; Cunningham *et al.*, 2001).

The chapter will begin with brief definitions and overviews of four primary developments related to the overall theme of "diversity in content" – general developments in eLearning, the OSS movement, OER, and key issues related to Open License Agreements and copyright. From the authors' development projects in Vietnam, common observations of OSS and OER implementations will be described and discussed, followed by implications for future educational initiatives and research.

Overview and general issues

The growth and expansion of online education (eLearning)

While there is extensive literature documenting the rise and pervasiveness of fully online and blended learning environments, it is not clear to what extent fundamental changes to education are occurring (Felix, 2002; Goodfellow and Lamy, 2009). Crook (2008) in the comprehensive British Educational Communications and Technology Agency (BECTA) report provides an insightful overview of current thinking about the use of Web 2.0 technologies – generally, and in education specifically.

Web 2.0 technologies focus on such tools and activities as trading, media sharing, media manipulation, conversational arenas, online gaming and virtual worlds, social networking, blogging, social bookmarking, wikis, collaborative editing, and really simple syndication (RSS) (Crook, 2008, pp. 9–15). Essential ideas associated with the use of such tools include identity formation and expression – both of which can be considered key components of second language teaching and learning. However, as Crook (2008) makes clear, Web 2.0 tools are being used more frequently within the realm of recreation, as opposed to education. Within education itself, in spite of the ready availability of computers, high-speed Internet access, and the expansion of eLearning possibilities, it remains the case that "most of the new media genres – wikis, blogs, and podcasts, instant messenger (IM) and Facebook, virtual realities and gaming – have emerged from the popular culture, not university culture" (Woolsey, 2008, p. 214). This has led to an interesting debate among educators who extol the capabilities of digital natives, yet often fail to appreciate the personal transformations required to change the "natives" into digital citizens (Woolsey, 2008, p. 216). Integrating the exciting world of popular Web 2.0 tools into higher education and more specifically into CALL environments will require fundamental changes to how learning is conceptualized and organized (Trinder *et al.*, 2008). Gaining deeper understanding of the range of literacies, skills, and experiences needed to shift from the deeply engrained, paper-bound publication environment of higher education to one focused on digital collaboration, sharing, and cultural identity formation will require profound changes to educators' thinking and their academic expectations of students (Convery, 2009). It cannot be assumed that the leap to using

Web 2.0 tools for education and second language learning purposes will occur effortlessly.

In the area of CALL, these issues are particularly salient as students are introduced to the learning of foreign languages within virtual environments. Some Web 2.0 communication tools could be considered better suited to personal communication in their first language with close associates than to other learners in the classroom. In fact, Westberry (personal communication, 2009), in her research into second language learners' use of a learning management system (Moodle within nursing education), found that second language speakers were reluctant to communicate with her in English via Skype. They believed it to be a medium more appropriately suited for personal communication with friends or family than a research tool. All of these points illustrate the need for new research directions within the Web 2.0 environment, including much better understanding of the "cultural dimensions of communication and the negotiation of identities" (Goodfellow and Lamy, 2009) and particularly for the learning of languages (Garrett, 2009).

As part of this overall discussion of the theme diversity in content, we now focus on the availability of powerful, readily available software tools, developed so that teachers can take advantage of new technologies and in affordable ways.

Open source software (OSS)

Since the term OSS was first used in 1998, a variety of new and powerful computing tools have emerged from the open source movement. With OSS, the source code for computer programs is made freely available and software users are also free to redevelop and redistribute the code. There are several key advantages to this approach over the use of proprietary software. First, the cost of obtaining software is significantly reduced or eliminated altogether, although it cannot be assumed that "open source" means "free" – it means that the program's source code can be downloaded and modified (if desired). In some cases, use of OSS does involve payment of a licensing fee, but such fees are typically much lower than those charged for proprietary software. In addition, developers who designate their software "open source" agree to the licensing agreement for GNU General Public License (GPL). In general terms, people who participate in the development or refinement of OSS become part of a global community of authors and users.

Coffin (2006), in her development of a definitional framework for successful open source software communities, identified a number of their common characteristics. These include, for example, the fact that the OSS movement is self-regulated, advanced by collaborating teams of programmers and users from multiple locations around the world, and characterized by online discussion of appropriate uses, bug fixes, and new developments. One might claim that OSS is propelled more by users' enthusiasm and a sense of common good, than by purely economic motivation.

The availability of OSS tools facilitates entry of both large and small educational institutions into an international world of eLearning, without massive investment in the purchase or licensing of proprietary software. In terms of access to and exchange of information, the OSS movement can be truly liberating. However, a variety of constraints can limit the effective integration of even this type of software into teaching. These can include, for example, cost/funding issues, limited access to computers, or restrictions on available staff training and development opportunities. Technological potential does not guarantee successful, or worthwhile, use of computers in educational contexts (Convery, 2009). While there are many OSS systems available for educators, three (Moodle, Greenstone Digital Library, and FLAX) will inform discussion within this chapter. We do not assert that these are the only or necessarily best OSS tools for use in the language classroom, but we include them because of their extensive range of data structuring and management tools.

Moodle, a learning management system (LMS), includes a variety of communication, classroom management, and assessment tools and it supports asynchronous and synchronous communication through different types of discussion fora and chats. In addition, there is a news forum for general information and the Moodle environment supports a wide range of text-based or audio-visual resources. Navigation is by point-and-click with various drop-down boxes or windows listing options or help. Users can download the code and program their own modules; they can install the software on a server and implement modules that others have programmed; or Moodle can be accessed through a managed hosting site. Consistent with Coffin's (2006) framework for a successful OSS community, Moodle's community support is extensive and global, which is a strong feature of the software.

Greenstone Digital Library (DL) software incorporates a straightforward interface so that teachers can create their own library collections styled after existing ones from material on the web or from their own local files (or both). Most text, audio, and video file formats are supported within the Greenstone environment; versions of the software are available for a variety of different operating systems; the user interface and documentation have been translated into numerous natural languages; and there is a strong global network of supporters. Making information available within Greenstone is more than just putting it on the web, however. It involves transforming information into a fully searchable, browsable, and maintainable metadata-driven digital library. Such transformation requires a range of technical and categorization skills on the part of the digital library creator, yet these can become constraints within a language teaching environment where teachers might not possess such necessary background and skills.

FLAX is the third OSS tool that will be discussed and one that is still in development by an expanded Greenstone programming team (see also Chapter 8). The project's aim is to enable language teachers to draw upon existing digital library linguistic and multimedia material, stored and structured within the Greenstone DL environment, so as to automate the production and delivery of practice exercises for English language students. Given that the preparation and administration of high-quality student language learning exercises can be enormously time-consuming, teachers will be able to use existing prose and multimedia content already present in public digital libraries or on the Internet. Much of this material is available under the GPL so that teachers in school systems with limited financial resources are able to freely draw on much-needed content.

What is unique about FLAX is how it defines its metadata. Although formalized metadata schemas have been developed specifically for education and training – the most prominent being learning object metadata (LOM) from the Institute of Electrical and Electronics Engineers (IEEE), and sharable content object reference model (SCORM) from the US Department of Defense – neither suits the purpose of teachers using content resources to generate language lessons. Such metadata needs to include, for example, information about the intended reading level of the text, or descriptions of particular verb tenses being used in sentences. Part of the FLAX research project has been to design a metadata set to help teachers and students locate and manipulate material for particular language learning activities, at both the document and sentence levels. To achieve this aim, FLAX applies automated techniques of language parsing, word collocation detection, identification of reading level, and exercise construction to texts or other file format material. Exercise types include, for example, jumbled sentences, matching words, predicting words, image guessing, word phrases, collocations, and content word guessing. Recently, FLAX has been developed as a Moodle plug-in, with a simple user interface, so that teachers can select from different exercise types and develop language learning tasks tailored to specific classroom needs. Alternatively, FLAX can be downloaded and installed on its own server.

These OSS tools provide a framework within which educational content, activities, and resources can be structured, searched, and manipulated. However, obtaining high-quality educational content is not always a simple or straightforward process. Content can be expensive to produce; its publication is still predominantly in English; and copyright and licensing issues can severely limit or prohibit altogether its use outside of the original venue in which it was created.

Open educational resources (OER)

The OER movement has emerged out of a desire to promote equality of access to resources for teachers and learners in developed and developing economies (Downes, 2007; Gourley and Lane, 2009; Organisation for Economic Co-operation and Development [OECD], 2007). The term "OER" was adopted at a United Nations Educational, Scientific and Cultural Organization (UNESCO) meeting in 2002, and refers to the open provision of educational resources – through information and communication technologies – for consultation, use, and adaptation by a community of users for non-commercial purposes (Atkins *et al.*, 2007; UNESCO, 2002; Wiley, 2006). OER "are digitized materials offered freely and openly for educators, students and self-learners to use and reuse for teaching, learning and research" (OECD, 2007, p. 131) and can include courseware and content, software tools, material for eLearning capacity building of staff, repositories of learning objects, and free educational courses (Hylén, 2006).

Although free and open access to learning materials has been available on the Internet since the mid-1990s (Smith, 2009), it was the decision of the Massachusetts Institute of Technology (MIT) to make available its core academic course content through the OpenCourseWare (OCW) initiative that spurred the development of the OER movement (Abelson, 2008). Between 2000 and 2002, course outlines, lecture notes, assessments, and other digitized course materials were made freely available on the MIT website. The OCW project was followed closely by the Open University's OpenLearn initiative in the UK. A two-year project, beginning in 2006, set about to make the OU's course content openly available to both enrolled and non-enrolled students (Gourley and Lane, 2009). There are also other large-scale OER projects (for example, the Commonwealth of Learning), but our discussion will focus just on the OCW and OpenLearn.

There is a major difference to the approaches taken by the OCW and OpenLearn initiatives. Basically, the OCW is a collection of resources from existing courses, designed as "top-down organized institutional repositories that showcase their institution's curricula" (Baraniuk and Burrus, 2008, p. 31), but which cannot be used easily for self-study. Students wishing to use the OCW materials would need to have very well developed independent learning skills. OpenLearn, on the other hand, has been developed specifically to include stand-alone self-study material, which can be used to supplement other teacher-developed course materials or used "as is" if instructional resources are scarce (Gourley and Lane, 2009, p. 61). It should be noted that most material in both of the massive OCW and the OpenLearn collections has been produced in English.

A common question posed about OER is "why" – why would anyone give away (for free) instructional materials, which are, after all, labor-intensive and expensive to produce. D'Antoni (2009), in her discussion of OER and the free and open source software (FOSS) movement, describes the fundamental principle of both – that being the free sharing of information in the same manner that one understands "free speech" rather than "free beer" (p. 4). Nevertheless, even at the Open University, an institution to which the concept of "open" is embedded within its operational mandate, there was considerable (initial) reluctance to developing and making available OER (Gourley and Lane, 2009). Substantial external funding from the William and Flora Hewlett Foundation during the initial establishment of both the OCW and OpenLearn collections was a strong motivator for the projects' developers and proponents (D'Antoni, 2009).

Finally, and of particular interest in the area of CALL, Lane (2008) questions whether the availability of open educational content is sufficient to promote student learning and concludes that it is not. What are required are multiple opportunities for discussion, both among students and between students and teachers, so that ideas can become integrated into new knowledge formation opportunities (Dazakiria, 2008). Resources alone are insufficient to inspire deep learning. We will return to this idea later in the chapter.

Open License Agreements

The final general issue related to diversity in content concerns copyright. Since the 1920s, the term "copyright" has been increasingly defined by international convention, which has resulted in copyright legislation that is now very similar across different national jurisdictions. According to the OECD, "the default rule is that all uses not expressly permitted by the copyright holder are prohibited" (2007, p. 74). This rule applies to all creative and artistic works, including for example such intellectual property as academic teaching materials, books, or journal articles. In fact, since 1989 any such work created in the US is by default copyrighted – something that many authors might not fully realize (Smith, 2009, p. 91).

Such a constraint places considerable limits on what can be included in publicly accessible OER. In an attempt to address copyright restrictions yet still protect the intellectual property of authors, Smith (2009) describes the development of Creative Commons, "an organization focused on designing easy-to-use licenses for individuals and institutions that allow them to maintain ownership of open content while providing users with selected rights" (www.creativecommons.org). Under Creative Commons licensing regulations, an individual can specify in increasingly restrictive terms, the level of access, reproduction, and use of their materials – ranging from entirely free (no rights reserved) to some rights reserved. Most authors do specify, how-ever, that appropriate citation for their work be ascribed to it. While Creative Commons licensing is a good start to addressing the issue of copyright, it still covers only a relatively small (although increasing) proportion of published material.

Other issues affecting the "diversity in content" theme

Given the availability of OSS, OER, Open License Agreements, and a general interest and expansion internationally in eLearning, what then are the major barriers to OER adoption and use in developing countries and particularly in CALL contexts?

In 2005, UNESCO established the International Institute for Educational Planning (IIEP) to address what D'Antoni (2008) describes as one of the most critical limitations within OER – that being lack of information about OER. In 2007, in an attempt to better understand and elucidate this concern, more than 500 members of the international UNESCO community joined an online forum to discuss and specify OER's key limitations. The result was a list of fourteen overall priorities – five of which were ranked as being the most important, but with a sixth warranting attention. These included:

- *awareness raising and promotion* – the effective distribution of informa-tion about the availability of OER and promotion of their use in educational settings;
- *communities and networking* – the development of interacting and cooper-ating communities of resource developers so that OER can be supplemented and tailored to individual educational needs and contexts;
- *capacity development* – the training and assistance for educators to develop the necessary skills and knowledge to begin to participate in the OER movement;
- *sustainability* – the development of methods to ensure that OER, once imple-mented, can continue to be developed, enhanced, and used;
- *quality assurance* – the development of evaluation frameworks and under-standing of how to ensure overall high quality of OER regardless of where they are produced;
- *copyright and licensing* – the development of ways to ensure that OER that contain copyright materials can be legally distributed and reused (D'Antoni, 2008, p. 11).

Important for this discussion is the fact that approximately half of the forum participants were from developing nations. It is not surprising therefore that the order of priorities differed between developed and developing countries (see Table 6.1).

Table 6.1 *Priority issues for developed and developing country respondents (D'Antoni, 2008, p. 12); used with permission under the Creative Commons license, http://creativecommons.org/licenses/by-sa/3.0*

Developed countries	Developing countries
(1) Awareness raising and promotion	(1) Awareness raising and promotion
(2) Communities and networking	(2) Capacity development
(3) Sustainability	(3) Communities and networking
(4) Quality assurance	(4) Technology tools
(5) Copyright and licensing	(5) Learning support services
(6) Capacity development	(6) Research
(7) Accessibility	(7) Policies
(8) Financing	(8) Quality assurance
(9) Standards	(9) Financing
(10) Learning support services	(10) Sustainability
(11) Research	(11) Accessibility
(12) Policies	(12) Copyright and licensing
(13) Technology tools	(13) Standards
(14) Assessment of learning	(14) Assessment of learning

In addition, more finely tuned priorities were reported depending on participants' regional priorities. For countries in East Asia, which includes Vietnam, the top six rankings were different again (see Table 6.2).

Table 6.2 *Priority issues in East Asia (D'Antoni, 2008, p. 23); used with permission under the Creative Commons license, http://creativecommons .org/licenses/by-sa/3.0*

East Asia
(1) Awareness raising
(2) Copyright
(3) Sustainability
(4) Communities
(5) Quality assurance
(6) Capacity development

One noteworthy feature of these rankings, however, is the lack of explicit reference to pedagogy, which we find curious. While it could be argued that the concept of "pedagogy" is subsumed within the category of capacity development, we believe that the omission of pedagogy as an explicit and ranked category is problematic. We will return to this idea in the implications section of the chapter. Factors identified here, coupled with others identified throughout this section, will inform discussion in the following Vietnam example.

Example

Since 2005 we have been collaborating with colleagues in higher education in Vietnam to develop web-based approaches to the teaching of English as a foreign language (EFL) and more recently to the teaching of computer science concepts through the medium of English (Brine and Johnson, 2008; Johnson *et al.*, 2006). The main focus of these projects has been the implementation of OSS tools and the use of OER specifically for English language teaching and learning.

Vietnam is a dynamic, developing country in which educational and technical reforms, coupled with a keen interest in English language teaching, have emerged strongly over the past several years. Recently, pressure on all levels of education providers in Vietnam has increased due to the Ministry of Education and Training's (MOET) Education Development Strategic Plan, 2001–2010 (Thang and Quang, 2007). The main objectives of the plan are to increase the competitiveness of Vietnamese education and industry and to substantially improve English language education. In order to accomplish these goals, the percentage of government funding for education has increased from 10 percent in 2000 to 15 percent in 2005, and is projected to reach 20 percent by 2010 (Internet World Stats, 2009). Importantly, the MOET intends to develop and introduce new curricula and teaching methodologies at major teacher training colleges and universities, so that English can be used in schools as a means of communication (for example, in the teaching of math or science), rather than just be taught as another school subject. This represents a major shift from how English has been taught in Vietnamese schools until now.

In the area of technology, inexpensive access to computers and high-speed asymmetric digital subscriber line (ADSL; broadband) is available now in most urban centers in Vietnam through Internet cafés and, increasingly, in homes (Internet World Stats, 2009). Between 2000 and 2008, the percentage of the population using the Internet rose from 0.3 percent to 24 percent, with the government committed to an Internet penetration of 35 percent by 2010 (Internet World Stats, 2009). In addition, there is an enthusiasm for eLearning throughout Vietnamese education as is evidenced, for example, by the recent launch of the Vietnam OCW project – a collaboration between Vietnamese educators and the MIT OCW project (VietnamNetBridge, 2007). In this case, localization of OCW materials is occurring through the organization of locally produced Vietnamese language resources and materials. Thus, in many urban centers around the country, access to computers, high-speed telecommunications, OSS tools, and some OER have become a reality. Given this context, the following brief example will be used to illustrate some of the key issues that can affect OSS and OER within the Vietnamese context and, we would conjecture, elsewhere.

The example provided here is based on two government-supported development projects – one funded by Education New Zealand and the other by the Ministry of Education, Culture, Science, and Technology (MEXT) in Japan. The New Zealand project was completed during 2005–2006 while the Japan project is still in process. Both projects involve academics from tertiary institutions (in New Zealand and Japan) working collaboratively with academic colleagues in Vietnam; both involve strategies to introduce and implement OSS and OER, and both projects have encountered similar issues and constraints.

The key goal of the New Zealand-based project was to improve the ability of the partner institution to develop and support its own eLearning initiatives within local English language courses. In this regard, staff in Vietnam and New Zealand were committed to the localization of English language training programs and materials, effectively tailored to meet the academic and professional needs of teachers, students, and educational institutions within Vietnam. The project involved reciprocal staff visits to New Zealand and Vietnam, installation of the Greenstone DL software (but not FLAX as it was not yet in development), and staff familiarization training as regards the use of an LMS. In addition, a team of collaborating teachers was established in the Vietnam institution to plan how an LMS could be used within the local teaching environment. It is worth noting that the face-to-face interactions were of relatively short duration and much of the communication throughout the project was carried out through email or voice over Internet protocol (VoIP) Microsoft network (MSN) video-conferencing. Finally, although this project was not immediately successful in achieving its aims, it did help inform subsequent (ongoing) project work in Vietnam as conceptualized in the second project.

The key goal of the Japan-based project, across a three-year period, is to implement a computer science (Logic Circuit Design) course along with concordancing and language exercises based on Greenstone DL and using FLAX tools (Wu and Witten, 2007). At the partner tertiary institution in Vietnam, the language requirements of this foundational computer science course will be addressed through the creation of language exercises to develop lexical and semantic knowledge in English as students acquire computer science content knowledge. Furthermore, both the Logic Circuit Design course and the corresponding English language support are being prepared for blended learning using Moodle and will be delivered by colleagues in Vietnam, but supported by the project partners in Japan. As with the New Zealand project, researcher visits to Vietnam have occurred, collaborative teams have been established, and the Japanese project holder has run a number of staff training workshops in Vietnam.

Although the issues ranked in the UNESCO project (D'Antoni, 2008; UNESCO, 2009) related specifically to OER, we would suggest that considering OER alone, without reference to how resources can be structured and made available to teachers, presents an incomplete picture. We are therefore shaping our discussion within the UNESCO categories, but are extending it to consider OER within the context of OSS tools and an eLearning framework.

Consistent with the UNESCO project findings (D'Antoni, 2008; UNESCO, 2009), we would identify awareness raising, capacity development, and sustainability as being the most difficult areas to address in both projects. By this we mean the initial up-skilling of staff and the sustained development of technical, pedagogical, and curriculum development skills among teachers. The other difficult issue that we have identified relates to copyright. We believe that some of these issues are intricately related to the developing nation status of Vietnam although, as we will discuss, the issues are by no means exclusive to Vietnam (Wright *et al.*, 2009).

In both authors' studies, we have become aware of the amount of personal pressure and sheer volume of work undertaken by educators in Vietnam as they contribute to their country's economic development. It is not unusual for such staff to work seven days a week and often in more than one job. In addition, and more problematic, we have found in our partner institutions that English language teachers (in particular) tend to be employed on part-time or short-term contracts and overwhelmingly they are women who have other competing family obligations outside of work. Under such conditions, developing appropriate skill levels in the use of Moodle, Greenstone, or FLAX has proved extremely difficult. For example, we have found that attendance at workshop training sessions can vary from day to day as different teaching staff and/or non-teaching clerical staff are available. Given that training materials contain sequenced topics, this has made it difficult for teachers to be presented with, let alone master, prerequisite technical skills.

Even when initial training is successful, helping teachers to actually implement Moodle has been challenging. Using an LMS within a language teaching context requires curriculum redesign, development, and trialing and all of these endeavors are time-consuming. Also, because an OSS tool such as Moodle is relatively straightforward to use (once installed) and courses can be set up in a point-and-click manner, it can appear to teachers that the conversion from paper-based to online-supported teaching is similarly straightforward. Thus, in spite of ample good will and interest in using OSS, the existence of adequate computing facilities within the partner institutions, and competent technical teams on-site, it has remained the case that language teaching staff have found it extremely difficult to obtain enough experience and practice time to develop eLearning expertise.

Another issue when considering capacity development is that although most staff know how to use email, online chat, word processing, and presentation software, their experience with communication tools is restricted mainly to personal interaction with friends and family, not teaching. Thus, although teachers have some experience with computer tools, it cannot be assumed that they know how to use Web 2.0 tools for instructional purposes. And, similar to what was reported earlier (Crook, 2008; Woolsey, 2008), teachers did not imagine that personal communication tools could have a place in the language classroom.

As regards content, staff in the partner institutions were very interested in documenting and maintaining educational resources through the development of digital libraries, but one immediate problem was that they did not have a clear understanding of how copyright restrictions could impinge on the selection of materials. Specifically, and in hindsight, this problem should have been anticipated. Within her own institution Johnson knew that strict observance of copyright was not always a straightforward matter and often required consultation among staff at various levels of the university. Even in relation to Open License Agreements, the issue of copyright is far from being adequately addressed, and within the OER movement itself there is considerable discussion of what constitutes open licensing and consequently what can be considered legitimate OER use.

In addition, although the FLAX OSS language learning tool has been programmed to take advantage of openly available texts on the web (Wu *et al.*, 2009) and has developed collocation tools to help students with their independent language learning, we have found three important issues that constrain its use. One is that it remains a difficult process for teachers to build their own digital library collections as was described earlier; second is that the language learning exercises are decontextualized; and third, some of the more powerful concordancing tools are not easily usable by lower proficiency students. In fact we have found in our own instructional contexts that only highly motivated, senior-level language students can use FLAX effectively in an independent manner.

In spite of these constraints, the interest in eLearning, OSS, and OER (awareness raising) is extremely high in Vietnam and it is noteworthy that when the Southeast Asian Ministers of Education Organization Regional Training Center (SEAMEO RETRAC) co-sponsored the recent Pacific Association for CALL (PacCALL) conference in 2007, it was heavily oversubscribed by interested teachers in the region. However, developing ways to build and sustain capacity as well as developing an understanding of copyright issues remain critical concerns. We would like to stress, however, that it is not just within the context of Vietnam that these issues exist, as can be evidenced in the overall concerns identified by UNESCO across a range of countries (D'Antoni, 2008). For example, within the New Zealand context teachers frequently cite lack of time as the main constraint in implementing CALL, but it is usually other factors that limit innovation (Johnson and Walker, 2007). These include lack of vision, skills, incentives, resources, or planning (Butler, 2006; Garrett, 2009).

Implications

The promise of technology to transform learning, but the reality of its frequent inability to achieve change, has been discussed often in academic literature (Convery, 2009; Goldberg and Riemer, 2006; Johnson and Walker, 2007; Lane, 2008). Rapid technological progress can create the illusion of shifting educational goals, which can only be attained when technology has become sufficiently capable or powerful, and yet consistently, the most significant constraints within eLearning appear to be at the personal, human level (Hernández-Ramos, 2006; Kopyc, 2006; Wright et al., 2009). Not only are abstract or general statements about the need for computers to support education not helpful, they can lead to confusion about expectations and frustration when project goals are not met (Butler, 2006).

According to Witten et al. (2001), "It has often been observed that technological advances in developing countries can leapfrog those in developed ones" (p. 85), yet the fact still remains that until very recently access to a wide range of content-specific, age-, and reading-level-appropriate educational content has been expensive, inconvenient, or in some cases impossible for teachers outside of well-funded teaching contexts (UNESCO, 2002). The implications, then, of teachers and learners having easy access to OER and OSS tools are enormous. In the area of CALL, teachers now have the technical means to construct and manipulate their own collections of language learning materials – specific to the curricular and linguistic needs of their students – and implement them within flexible virtual environments. However, as is clear from our example, well-coordinated, structured, and planned implementations are required if effective computer-supported learning environments are to be developed and used. For this, an understanding and appreciation of pedagogy is essential.

The process of change, both technological and curricular within traditional educational contexts such as Vietnam (or elsewhere, including New Zealand or Japan, for example), presents a range of problems, as we have described. Even among teachers and students who do possess technical skills, a coherent approach to the interaction of technical, curricular, and pedagogical levels of expertise needs to be developed explicitly and in identifiable stages. Insights from practical teaching experiences as well as our development projects have led to strategies for building intellectual and practical capacity and focus on structured, collaborative "learning-by-doing" approaches to developing students' expertise. Our approaches reflect key priorities not only of capacity development, but also awareness raising and promotion, communities and networking, and quality assurance. In short, simply providing access to diverse content, without explicit attention to the holistic nature of the instructional context, will be insufficient to improve language teaching practice.

As discussed in the example, language teachers in our projects not only have a skills deficit in using an LMS; they require training beyond the mechanics of creating exercises. Specifically, they need to understand how an LMS can be used to manage teaching and learning processes and they also need to understand how interesting language learning content can be incorporated into everyday instructional practice. And, they need to be able to accomplish such learning within tight time constraints. The two – technological skills and the ability to locate and use openly accessible content – need to be blended together seamlessly.

Some ideas for addressing the difficulties we have described emerge from the authors' own instructional environments. For example, Johnson's fully online graduate course in CALL in New Zealand has also operated under a variety of constraints, which affected course design and implementation. Because the course is fully online, students can be (and usually are) located anywhere in the world; they never meet face-to-face; and in some rural parts of New Zealand, the only available access to the Internet is via dial-up. All students taking the course are studying to obtain a graduate qualification in English language teaching, although many of them are already employed as language teachers. Consistent with the Vietnam example, most of the students have used a variety of computer tools for personal communication, but few, if any, have attempted to incorporate Web 2.0 tools and diverse openly accessible content into their classroom instruction.

Throughout the CALL course all students participate in online (Moodle) group discussion of ideas, based on academic content provided by Johnson as well as open content resources that they (the students) locate. By completing a series of skills-building tasks students locate, trial, evaluate, and report on other software tools and open content that they identify on the Internet. They then share their insights with other students through online discussion fora. Once students have gained familiarity with a range of resources and have, through multiple discussions with the teacher and with each other, gained understanding of what could be relevant within their instructional contexts, they are required to conceptualize, design, and implement their own language learning course within the Moodle environment. These courses are then evaluated through peer review, and students write a final reflection on their personal journey from novice computer users to CALL course designers, implementers, and educators.

Uniformly, students are anxious about their projects before they begin and virtually everyone assumes that they do not have sufficient technical knowledge to design and develop a Moodle course. However, in every year that the course has been taught, students have successfully developed Moodle courses that have included, for example, really simple syndication (RSS) feeds, links to text-based and audio/visual language teaching resources, and have created student-centered language learning exercises. Moreover, they all report feeling empowered by the project. The provision of multiple opportunities to adopt such tools for personal learning requires students to change their perception of teacher–learner roles and leads to an acknowledgment that their peers can provide valuable insights into teaching and learning processes (Oakley *et al.*, 2004). In short, community and networking help students acquire a range of skills over a relatively short timeframe. What is noteworthy is that there is no particular emphasis on any *single* aspect of developing the CALL approach; students use open source tools, assemble a variety of openly accessible content, and practice team building through peer review and evaluation. It is the development of a coherent and cohesive group of skills that facilitates a successful learning experience.

Through such a structured course-creation activity as this, students' roles have changed from student-learners to student-developers as they have become knowledgeable creators of their own eLearning environments and, importantly, have felt supported throughout their personal journey (Dazakiria, 2008). After becoming language teachers within their own classrooms, they possess the experience and knowledge to find and evaluate OER, to use OSS, and to do so within a collaborative environment. Moreover, such an approach is highly consistent with the open source software model (Coffin, 2006), which has already inspired the open courseware approach to curriculum development and sharing.

More broadly, in a school setting, and if teachers lacked confidence in designing and building their own courses, they could be provided with a pre-specified structure into which they introduced their own content choices. These structures would not be prescriptive about content, but would provide standard organizational approaches that could help teachers manage classroom teaching effectively. Small groups could design interchangeable curriculum modules to be used by other teachers working within the same content area at the same level, but within a different school. The main points here are that regardless of context, there will always be limitations, but reflective, action research types of projects can help raise group awareness of potentially new ways of working together to achieve common goals. The implementation of an innovation, such as OER, needs to parallel the type of globally collaborative work that has emerged in the OSS movement itself. Content without structure and effective pedagogical approaches, even if such content is diverse and easy to locate, will not be of much benefit to CALL teachers.

By using a collaborative courseware model to promote shared development (or idea generation) among teachers irrespective of location, we believe that Moodle and other OSS tools can create stimulating and productive environments for curriculum collaboration. In addition, by creating, sharing, or accessing course content in the form of OER, several teachers could edit and revise

courses or observe other courses in which they are non-editing teacher participants in order to gain new ideas or insights. An evaluation team could then provide feedback or input to the curricular development process. Backups could be
retained by teachers so that if a server were to fail, the course could be quickly
mounted elsewhere and whole courses, or parts of courses, could be backed up
and then used at another site in existing or modified form. Alternatively, entire
courses could be zipped and emailed to colleagues for use elsewhere. In this
distributed approach, open educational resources, tailored to a wider school
district as opposed to a single classroom or school, could ease the curriculum
development burden on teachers and help foster collegiality.

On the technological side, implementing Moodle or FLAX on a server is
straightforward enough and once a group of teachers has become knowledgeable about server setups, they can assist other groups in their area. A standard
installation of Moodle is highly recommended since problems are more likely
to occur if non-core modules are used. In this way, less time will be spent maintaining the system and useful supportable modules will eventually become part
of the core code. The linking of other OSS modules into Moodle can also
prove effective for encouraging collaboration among teachers. Finally, OSS
tools themselves are becoming increasingly straightforward for non-specialist
programmers to install, set up, and maintain, which can help shift the focus
from the technical to the more nuanced human side of being able to use the
tools in "real" instructional contexts. It is essential for teachers to have stable
and easily usable computing environments. Having easy access to content, but
without having corresponding access to a straightforward and stable computing environment, would ensure failure.

In terms of harnessing the potential of OER, vast amounts of text are not
particularly helpful for teachers who want to take such diversity in content
and create motivating and meaningful language learning environments for
their students. Instead, teachers need access to other comprehensive and easily accessible software tools and resources, such as are included in the Open
University's Development Kit (McAndrew and Wilson, 2008), to help them
with the organization and use of OER. McAndrew and Wilson (2008, p. 699)
describe a range of resources from guidelines for the use of community-
building tools to how teachers can transform their own educational materials
into OER. Geser (2008), in his detailed report on OER practices and resources,
describes the need for incentives, recognition, and rewards for participating
teachers, community-building, and clear educational policies for OER implementation and use.

Also required is research of OSS and OER implementations within specific
country contexts and which draw on a range of evidence (Convery, 2009) so as
to develop robust, culturally appropriate approaches to pedagogy (Goodfellow,
2008; Okada, 2008). Such research needs explicitly to seek to understand how

OSS and OER, as computing tools, mediate human activity (Blin, 2004; Brine and Franken, 2006; Johnson, 2008; Lantolf, 2005). The process of *mediation*, that is the use of both conceptual and physical tools within an activity, is central to an activity theory research perspective. As Lantolf (2005) explains, the interactions between tools and tasks are not one-way; the tools affect how and why learning emerges, but also the learners themselves use the tools in "unexpected and creative ways in order to make sense of their own learning activity" (p. 348). Lantolf states that because activity theory focuses on the context of human activity, it seeks to answer such questions as how, where, when, and, importantly, why something is done, which involves uncovering the "motives and goals of human action" (2005, p. 345). Thus, research that is grounded in activity theory focuses on the interactions of people, tasks, and mediating tools, rather than on individual behaviors, performance, or mental models. This paradigm is particularly suited to the activity of complex organizations as it can help identify and explicate multiple perspectives. Of particular importance are research projects that "enable rather than oppress teachers' practices and professional identities" (Convery, 2009, p. 39).

Conclusion

Clearly, it is not the easy availability of OER or OSS *on their own* that is of prime importance in a discussion of diversity in content within CALL, although having access to both is essential. Rather, in order to fully exploit the potential of OER and OSS to transform language teaching practice, there needs to be a shift in thinking about what could potentially be done through technology to what is realistically achievable within local contexts and constraints (Convery, 2009; Iiyoshi *et al.*, 2008). There also needs to be good understanding of institutional change processes within complex, social, educational settings and for this, new approaches to conducting research are critical. As aptly noted by Fullan (2001), "the answer to large-scale reform is not to try to emulate the characteristics of the minority who are getting somewhere *under present conditions* ... Rather, we must change existing conditions so that it is normal and possible for a majority of people to move forward" (p. 268).

The adoption of OER and OSS can facilitate steady development of collaborative skills to help teachers and students prepare for ongoing technical change, but such development must be explicitly planned and introduced in identifiable stages. Iterative cycles of raising awareness of what exists, which tools are most valuable within local settings, and which sites of high-quality OER content exist, can assist this process. Capacity development and sustainability of innovation need to be undertaken through collaborative team-based approaches in which long-term goals, milestones, curriculum design and development projects, implementation, and formative feedback cycles are planned and evaluated (Somekh, 2001). It is only through such structured approaches that institutional change will emerge and can be sustained.

Finally, along with access to and collaborative use of open source computing tools, teachers need opportunities to reflect on and share their experiences of working within a wider, global socially networked environment so as to better mobilize their emerging knowledge and expertise. It is not sufficient to "train" teachers in tool use on an occasional basis, but ongoing, sustained support for the access and exchanges of ideas is required. As for knowledge mobilization more generally, Levin (2004) and Campbell and Fulford (2009) have argued for frequent, targeted, and multimodal communication of research, involving direct and mediated means such as face-to-face, print, electronic, and formal and informal communication. This can include traditional websites, media announcements, journal articles, research networks, and local, national, and international conferences. It can also include specialized CALL language teacher training programs in which OSS and OER play prominent roles.

We now have the tools to structure and support networked collaboration, and we have access to an enormous range of diverse learning materials. We now need to take the next steps of building coherent organizational and collaborative support structures so that such tools are well integrated into every language teacher's expectation and understanding of effective teaching.

7   Diversity in modalities

Marie-Noëlle Lamy

Introduction

Why include a chapter on modality in this book? Computer-assisted language learning (CALL) practitioners do not generally use the word "modality" when instructing their students (for instance, they don't say "make sure you carry out this interview using the audio modality," or "share your thoughts on your partner's ideas using the commenting modality"). On the other hand, researchers do use this word, all too often failing to define what they mean by it, or by the word "mode." The idea of "diversity" in such a context comes close to taking on overtones of "mix" or even "mess." It is my intention, in subjecting the notion of "modality" to a critical examination, to show how lack of clarity about this term is damaging published research in CALL, and to suggest how we can think about "modality" so as to facilitate our understanding of the educational benefits to be expected from CALL, whatever it is that "technology" throws at us next, in its increasing diversity.

In the literature of technology-mediated language learning, the term "modality" is rarely defined (although for a brief overview see Chanier and Vetter, 2006) and it is used inconsistently. For example, the following list contains items that have variously been offered as illustrations of different modalities: "audio," "text," "icons," "webcam," "image," "written," "oral," "video," "voice-only," "voice-image," and "text chat." However, one might equally say that a "video" is a material object or an electronic object; an "icon" is an artifact as well as a sign; a "webcam" is a tool; and "written" is one of the two forms that human language takes. The polysemy and semantic heterogeneity of this list make the word *modality* unusable as an operational concept.

In the field of multimodality research, a neighboring discipline to CALL, a consistent definition is available. Multimodality research seeks to understand how we make meaning through the diversity of communicative forms – language, image, music, sound, gesture, touch, and smell – that surround us. With the exception of smell, these can all be found within the experience of learning and teaching online, which is why I propose to draw some definitions from the work of multimodality research's main theorists, Kress and van Leeuwen, who developed a theory for understanding the meanings communicated to us by objects such as adverts and posters, which use language as one – but not as the main – resource for meaning-making.

Let us start with the notion of "mode." "Words processors," these authors tell us, "must systematize such things as the thickness and positioning of the lines that separate sections of text, and develop a metalanguage, whether visual or verbal, for making these choices explicit" (2001, p. 79). Anyone who has had the opportunity to compare a page from a magazine in the English-speaking press with one from the French press knows that choice of typeface and positioning of headers, annotations, captions, and so forth are systematized differently in these cultures. The culture-dependent systematization of graphic resources amounts to a specific "grammar" of visual communication, which Kress and van Leeuwen call a "mode." The physical tool (a computer) changes the physical media (paper and ink) into a mode (a culturally intelligible page layout). Other, much more immediately obvious, culturally intelligible systems include language (written, spoken), the visual (figurative and non-figurative or coded, such as icons), sound (figurative and non-figurative such as music, or coded such as signals), and body-language. Modes are basic to meaning-making (hence the adjective "semiotic" is frequently used in the rest of the chapter) and they work together in complex ways to bring about our understanding of how objects communicate to us certain ideas or emotions such as "adventure," "authority," "humor," "hope," and hundreds of others. For example, a piece of architecture, an art installation, or an immersive game screen are made up of physical matter fashioned into cultural styles which we recognize as conveyors of the different ideas or emotions in question. "Modality," therefore, is the relationship between modes and the culturally intelligible object that they underpin, and "multi-modality" is:

the use of several semiotic modes in the design of a semiotic product or event, together with the particular ways in which these modes are combined – they may for instance reinforce each other ("say the same thing in different ways"), fulfill complementary roles ... or be hierarchically ordered, as in action films, where action is dominant, with music adding a touch of emotive "color" and synch sound adding a touch of realistic "presence." (Kress and van Leeuwen, 2001, p. 20)

For the purpose of our discussion of CALL, we will in a moment add the notion of "tool" to this definition, adding to the number of elements that can be combined into a particular "modality." For these reasons it has seemed difficult to construct this chapter around a "list" of modalities available in CALL. Rather, the approach will be a discovery-based one, using a corpus of published CALL studies through which I hope to outline the challenges associated with the concept of modality in our field, the risks associated with misunderstanding modality, and an alternative way of addressing these problems.

Overview and general issues

In order to learn a language online and to communicate (including online) in that language, you need to orchestrate a variety of resources. These include natural language in its written and spoken forms and they always also include visual resources. Understanding even a simple written text requires sensitivity to two modes: a linguistic mode (written language) and the visual mode (the choice of fonts and the organization of spaces on the screen). In CALL, many resources are used, such as icons, images, colors, and shapes, in combination with each other. For example, a tool such as a floating tag – the small window that opens as the cursor is floated over specific parts of the screen – can support the written language. But it can also support pictures (as with some online bookshops, where the floating tag reveals an enlarged picture of the book cover) or even a search form (which is a further tool supporting written language). The floating tag tool in itself has no "meaning" of interest to a language learner or teacher. On the other hand, the written text, picture, or search form may convey many meanings, some of which are relevant to the language learning situation. For example, the text facility accessible via a floating tag may be used to support a vocabulary gloss, an image may be used to illustrate a cultural reference, and a search box facility may be exploited as part of a grammatical, lexical, or other type of exercise. On "multimodal" platforms the physical material includes keys to be pressed for text creation, and pads or mouse attachments to be tapped, stroked, or clicked for opening up the audio channel in order to hear or speak. In other words, the learning objective will be jeopardized if the learning design has not fully taken account of the materiality of the tool and of the specific mode or modes involved.

To sum up, then, in the context of CALL semiotic resources are made up of (a) material tools; (b) modes, such as written language, spoken language, or visual language; and (c) language learning objectives materialized through educational designs. The conjunction of these three elements makes up modality, as exemplified in Table 7.1.

Not all technologies that have proved of interest to language learners and teachers are listed in the table. For example, neither blogs, multi-user domain object oriented (MOOs), virtual worlds, nor social networks are featured (see Chapter 5 for a discussion of these technologies). This is because in the terms of this chapter, they are not tools in themselves but rather they are made up of combinations of tools and modes, much like the piece of architecture or art installation mentioned in the Introduction.

The central issue when discussing modes and modality

If there was a one-to-one correspondence between physical tools and the other resources that make up modality, e.g. if synchronous messaging tools were

Table 7.1 *Examples of modality relationships in CALL*

Tools	Modes	Language learning objectives facilitated
Browsers	Multiple modes	Access to authentic material in L2
Word-processors	Written text mode	Productive text-based activities
Photo editing software	Visual modes	Productive image-based activities
3D artifact manipulation	Visual modes	Cultural or geographical learning outcomes
GPS tools (mobile devices)	Visual and iconic modes	Geographical or other location-dependent learning outcomes
Automatic recording and screen capture tools	Multiple modes	Reflective activities (revisiting tutorial sessions)
Hot buttons	Iconic modes	Communication and interaction (e.g. vote button); create telepresence; help with turn-taking (e.g. raised-hand button)
Asynchronous sending/receiving (fora)	Mainly written text mode, may have some element of visual modes	Written work. Peer collaboration; feedback; meta-commenting (extended, reflective commentary)
Synchronous messaging tools (chat)	Mainly written text mode, some element of visual modes	L2 messaging styles. Peer collaboration; feedback. Also group bonding
Voice over Internet (telephony, audio)	Mainly spoken language mode, with textual, visual, and iconic modes	Oral communication and interaction; collaborative work; feedback
Webcam-based video-conferencing	Spoken and visual modes, with iconic mode	As above

only ever used with the written language mode and the only learning objective was to practice informal writing, this chapter would not be necessary: we could then happily talk about "the chat modality." However, it became clear above that a single tool may be associated with more than one mode, and more than one educational meaning. Even a synchronous messaging facility can support several different modes (for instance, meaning can be made within a chat window using smileys, which belong to the iconic mode, or with thumbnail photographs, which partake of the visual modes).

Take the example of how dispersed distance learners used a chat tool in a multimodal platform project (reported in Lamy, 2006) where the task instructions required students to:

- give priority to the audio channel and communicate orally;
- use the chat facility in case of sound breakdown, writing in their mother tongue in order to avoid compounding difficulty.

An analysis of usage showed that students did prioritize the audio channel but that they ignored the instructions constructively, appropriating the chat tool in a range of ways, forming "parallel talk" and "cross-talk" conversations in the target language instead. Conversation patterns included the following:

- parallel talk (i.e. interaction between the oral and the written language) went on in audio and in chat on topics that were:
  - unrelated (e.g. students communicated orally about the task while text-chatting about the possible whereabouts of a latecomer);
  - identical (e.g. students communicated orally about the weather in one of their locations while text-chatting about the weather in another location);
- cross-talk (i.e. interaction between the written and spoken modes) used topics that were:
  - divergent (e.g. the oral talk was about the task but the text-chat box displayed a call for help from a participant with a sound problem, immediately triggering an oral debate about how best to help him out);
  - convergent (e.g. the spoken conversation was about the *Alliance Française* while text-chatters were writing about the British Council, until the group started comparing both organizations orally in the audio channel.

In these parallel and cross-talks, the meaning to which the chat function had been assigned by the task designers rarely came to the fore. Rather, socio-affective discourse and other types of discourse arose, as summarized in Table 7.2.

The issue for our understanding of modality is as follows: we cannot say that we are dealing with one modality ("the chat modality") as this would be a reduction of the diversity that is going on in this chat-based class. The chat software tool alone supports three different modes and a variety of learning interactions, both in terms of content (discourse type) and group dynamics (parallel talk, cross-talk). Increasingly, learners and teachers are working with more than one tool at a time, as do the above with a chat window and an audio tool, which makes it even more difficult to accurately describe the process.

Example

Comparative methods have proved useful in semiotic analysis (Neergaard and Ulhøi, 2007) for identifying the features of an object, by contrasting them with

Table 7.2 *One tool, three modes, and many meanings in text chat*

Discourse type (most frequent first)	Mode	Content of parallel talk and cross-talk
Socio-affective	Linguistic (free, written), iconic (coded: smileys)	Greetings, jokes, compliments, apologies
Cognitive	Linguistic (free, written), linguistic (coded: URLs)	Suggesting ideas, websites, documentation
Methodological	Linguistic (free, written)	Requesting clarification of instructions, or assignments
Linguistic	Linguistic (free, written)	Checking or suggesting vocabulary, requesting corrective feedback
Technological	Linguistic (free, written)	Requesting or offering help

one that is broadly but not entirely similar. Thus Lamy and Hampel (2007) created four meta-studies, each based on comparing two projects that had a tool in common, e.g. pairs of studies that used fora, chats, MOOs, and multimodal platforms. The authors hypothesized that a comparative approach would make it easier to derive a rich understanding of the modality relationships at work through this literature than by examining cases singly. In the following section, I sum up their main findings.

Study pair 1

The first pair of studies in the survey (Savignon and Roithmeier, 2004; Weasenforth *et al.*, 2002) used fora. The starting point for Savignon and Roithmeier's research was learner uptake of form, positioning the study on the cognitive end of online language learning research (the opposite end of the spectrum being more socio-constructivist). Savignon and Roithmeier were looking for evidence that "the collected bulletin board postings on a single subject qualify as a cohesive, coherent text" (2004, p. 269). Their second research question focused on discourse as well: "What discourse features can be identified that reflect participant engagement in terms of sustaining a collaborative dialogue?" (2004, p. 269). The setting for the project was a class of German students of English at a German secondary school, eight years into their study of their second language (L2). Working with them was a class of US students of German enrolled in their third year at a high school. They discussed societal topics (the American Dream, the death penalty, drinking and driving, the Kosovo conflict) over a three-week period. All research questions received a positive answer. Uptake and peer-sharing of lexical items were shown to have occurred "implicitly or explicitly" (2004, p. 272). The issue of the sustaining of a collaborative dialog received an equally positive answer, based on observations about both the use of strategies to mitigate potential conflict and the co-constructing of a coherent and cohesive text: "[t]hrough the incorporation of previously used lexical items, ideas, and even entire postings, participants show they were following the discussion" (2004, p. 284).

The second forum study, by Weasenforth *et al.* (2002), aims to determine under what conditions teachers may be "[r]ealizing constructivist objectives through collaborative technologies." The authors use constructivist principles as a framework, which positions them on the other end of the continuum of pedagogical philosophies compared to Savignon and Roithmeier. They evaluated a three-semester process involving fifty-two advanced-level university reading/writing students of English as a second language (ESL), all international graduates. Course requirements were explicitly oriented to participation patterns (e.g. "[D]uring semester 1, students were required to introduce a new thread each week and to participate in a total of twelve discussions about course content" [2002, p. 61]). The asynchronous nature of the threaded discussions, according to Weasenforth *et al.*, "made [the course assignment] particularly useful for the promotion of coherent discussion. The additional time available for reading and composing postings encourages reviewing and responding to classmates' arguments" (2002, p. 74). The asynchronous nature of the tool was also credited with enhancing the reflective learning style of quiet students, and with introducing flexibility through the possibility of extending assignment preparation time whenever necessary.

Lamy and Hampel's comparison of these two studies shows that the combination of forum as a tool and the written language as a mode afford flexibility of the type that language educators need, facilitating the success of such divergent learning designs. The question then is whether all possible learning designs could be facilitated by forum-based work. If the answer was yes, we could say that we had identified a stable modality.

Study pair 2

Lamy and Hampel also looked at synchronous tools as used in a study by Blake (2000) and compared it with Thorne (2003). Blake, who has written extensively about task types offline, set up networked learner–learner discussions via a synchronous chat program associated with other tools. Fifty intermediate learners of Spanish took part in the study, carrying out a series of online task types: jigsaw, information-gap, and decision-making. Blake's main finding was that well-designed networked tasks "promote learners to notice the gaps in their lexical interlanguage in a manner similar to what has been reported in the literature for oral learner/learner discussion" (2000, p. 132). The only benefit of the online situation compared to the face-to-face one, for this author, is the remote linking of learners, i.e. a "communications" advantage rather than a learning one.

The other paper in this pair, Thorne (2003), is based on telecollaborative exchanges between US and French students via chat facilities. Thorne presents a case study of students of French at Penn State University and engineering students at the Ecole Nationale Supérieure de Télécommunication de Bretagne. The study focused on US students' perception of different tools, and in particular their preference for synchronous communication via instant messenger (IM) rather than email. It showed that although the exchange was supposed to facilitate intercultural communication between these students, the way it was set up did not take account of the "cultures-of-use" of the communicative media. That is, it created a mismatch between how students use these tools in everyday life and how they were supposed to use them in the educational context. In order to talk to their peers outside class, the students tended to use IM rather than email. For them, email was a communication tool to be used with parents and teachers, that is, between power levels and generations, and therefore inappropriate for an exchange with peers in class and for building a relationship with them.

The turning point of Thorne's article, initially an exploration of sociocultural conditions, is the active resistance to email in favor of IM by the US (and some of the French) participants. By re-orienting his research towards a wider socio-historical focus ("cultures-of-use" and their influence on learning), Thorne is able to return his reader to a level of reflection that goes beyond a limited inter-rogation of the possibilities of the tool. Modality, as a relationship, is seen here to include not only the immediate educational context but the socio-historical context within which those in the educational institutions operate. The contrast between the two approaches to modality in study pair 2 is stark: while Thorne contributes a refinement to our understanding of how modality works, on the other hand Blake's results appear to be offered regardless of whether there is an electronic tool involved or none, telling us a lot about task design but nothing about modality in CALL.

Study pair 3

MOOs have characteristics in common with synchronous text-based systems such as chat, which they combine with asynchronous written systems such as fora, but also have distinctive features. Peterson (2004) explains that "these environments are designed around a hierarchy of user privileges that enables the creators of a MOO to structure the environment to meet the needs of a particular learner group … Typically MOOs contain numerous virtual rooms, linked together by entrances and exits … Some MOO environments contain numerous learning objects including virtual projectors, lecture spaces, notes, web pages and recording devices" (Peterson, 2004, pp. 40–44).

Kötter (2003) reports a 1998 project with fourteen German-speaking learners of advanced English at the University of Münster, and fifteen US students of intermediate German at Vassar College, who met for twice-weekly interaction, for seventy-five minutes at a time, in a MOO where they collaborated in a total of eight sub-groups of three or four students, to complete projects of their choice. For example, they created self-profiles and discussed the cultural implications of this experience with their partners. All were asked to present their work to the other groups during the final sessions of the exchange. Kötter researched four questions, one of which directly addresses the specificity of the MOO ("How do students who meet in a MOO rather than in person deal with the apparent 'virtuality' of their encounters, that is, which 'MOO-specific' tools and strategies do they employ to express themselves and exchange information?"). Kötter observed that many participants:

had begun to make themselves at home in the MOO by creating their own rooms even before they met with their tandem partners for the first time. Some learners had fitted these rooms with objects ranging from a sofa or a carpet to a piano or a refrigerator, and several students had additionally composed elaborate descriptions of these purely text-based locales … Equally important, many of the remarks that the students made to each other documented that they conceptualized the MOO as something with a spatial dimension. One learner commented upon arrival in her partner's room that it "looks okay here," while another stated that she preferred her peer's room to the MOO's entrance … Moreover, many learners exploited the notion of space in the MOO by engaging with things they found in these rooms (e.g. Jack settles down in a comfortable chair) to create a pleasant atmosphere for their encounters even if they had no previous experience with MOOs. (Kötter, 2003, p. 152)

However these socio-affective exchanges remained confined to a pre-sessional "settling in" phase and did not sustain as part of the core learning opportunities available when the course itself unfolded. Kötter thus had no opportunity to develop his thinking on these specific MOO modality issues.

The second MOO-based study is by Schneider and von der Emde (2006). Eleven German-speaking learners of English from the University of Münster and fourteen US students of German from Vassar College met twice a week for sixty minutes at a time, for intercultural work in small groups. The cultural content was derived from documents and synchronous discussions about two comparably emotional events: the shootings at a school in Columbine, Colorado in 1999 and at a school in Erfurt, Germany in 2002. Carried out by means of student-created "project rooms," the "project work" phase can claim to specifically exploit the functionalities of the MOO tool. In this phase, students built open-ended and interactive rooms in which to raise questions rather than give answers. These rooms "depict all the conflicting perspectives on the various topics in order to encourage the visitors to the rooms to draw their own conclusions" (2006, p. 191). For instance, one group "explicitly embedded the concept of conflict into the structure of their project by calling one of their rooms *Missverständnisse* 'Misunderstandings'" (2006, p. 192) and posting the following explanation: "This room has information about our discussions but it does not have any answers. Why? Because there aren't any concrete answers" (2006, p. 192). Schneider and von der Emde commented on this use of the environment, but their focus on cultural learning (rather than on educational technology) prevented them asking questions that might bring a better understanding of the modality of MOO-based language work, such as "how did students use the meaning-making resources specific to MOOs; for example, did the creation of the room called *Missverständnisse* support the learning project that the students had in mind when they created it (e.g. facilitating reflection and demonstrating a critical engagement with the cultural agenda of the course)?" Schneider and von der Emde's study touches on these questions, yet it falls short of problematizing the relationship between discourse objectives (critical engagement) and the MOO tool's user-extendable spaces and graphics.

For Lamy and Hampel, what emerged from these two studies of MOOs was Kötter's sole concentration on chat within MOO, and Schneider and von der Emde's strong focus on pedagogy, rather than on the mediation of that pedagogy via the MOO tool. They concluded that insufficient notice has thus far been taken of the work of those who, as early as 1999 (Shield *et al.*) and 2001 (Peterson) were trying to identify the specific modalities that could be associated with the MOO tool. If over the years these have not been perceived as anything other than identical with those of chat tools, it is perhaps no surprise that MOOs have not been widely used in language learning and teaching online.

Study pair 4

Erben (1999) was a pioneer project using a synchronous multimodal platform. Lamy and Hampel contrasted this work with Svensson's multimodal project in 2007. Erben's work is a case study in an immersion context, involving a B.Ed. program at Central Queensland University, in which up to 80 percent of the curriculum is delivered through the medium of Japanese. Erben produces an understanding of participants' behavior, which he expresses as "reduction" and "amplification" of the range of symbolic cues available to them. Amplification and reduction refer to "those classroom discursive practices which, because of the nature of the mediated interaction at a distance, participants need to modify … in order to achieve the same effect as if the equivalent cue, sign or behavior

was produced in a face-to-face classroom" (1999, p. 237). An example of amplification might be an instance of teachers having "to increase question wait time
due to the fact that delayed transmissions from site to site may occur" (1999,
p. 238), while reduction might be "the loss of learning opportunities through
such technical hiccups, where the connection between sites may freeze" (1999,
p. 239). Initially, Erben found that in the online setting teacher-led activities
were amplified; after a while, however, teacher control was reduced. Private
classroom communication was generally amplified.

Modifications of discursive practices occurred, as existing ones did not
suffice to guarantee clarity of meaning in the new environment. Erben called
this phenomenon "reconstruction" (1999, p. 240). An instance of a reconstructed sociocultural practice is that of "bowing in the classroom," a neces-
sity in Japanese culture, leading "to the use of different verbal cues or picture
icons" to replace the bodily bowing in the online setting. The author notes
that "as classroom participants adapted to the use of the platform, instructional
processes came to be increasingly reconstructed in ways which represented
a substantive shift away from how these processes occurred in face-to-face
immersion classrooms" (1999, p. 240).

The final study in Lamy and Hampel's survey is Svensson's (2003) project,
located at Sweden's Umeå University, at Humlab, a then "state-of-the-art" technology laboratory for humanities students and researchers. The project brought
together different language subdisciplines. It involved twenty-two advanced
post-graduate students of English, the majority of whom did not have advanced
computer experience, taking part over three years. The work involved producing a piece for assessment, equivalent in workload to the twenty-five-page
essay required of offline students. However, going far beyond the communication modes used in the essay genre, this assignment involved linguistic
modes ("free" as well as "coded" – such as displayed text) as one part of the
whole rather than as the principal means of communication, combining language with images, movement, and sound. The assignment was therefore truly
multimodal.

The environment used (under the Active Worlds program) combined sound,
text, and graphics. In order to participate, users choose to be represented by an
avatar – a person, an animal, or an object. Students worked in sub-groups to
build a graphical world around themes (e.g. "weddings," "the city," "monstros-
ity"), to link objects in their "world" to web pages, which they created, and to
represent, often in non-linguistic form, the concepts relevant to their theme.

The project is deliberately process- rather than product-oriented, and
Svensson shows how students collaborate and negotiate in building their
"world." He stresses the importance of space: "visual and auditory means of
expressions in *distributed spaces* have a very strong motivating and creative
effect" (2003, p. 139, emphasis added). According to Svensson, such project

work is particularly useful for language learning, which "is about language, immersion in other cultures, communication, media, intercultural meetings and role-play, and virtual areas supply us with a place where all these can come together" (2003, p. 140).

Lamy and Hampel's conclusion is that Erben has helped define some of the new learning practices of the online world (reductions, amplifications, and reconstructions) by mapping them to the known reality of the physical class-room, thus creating a generalizable model, i.e. one that could be interpreted by later researchers as a position from which alternative models could be constructed. In contrast, Svensson has offered a rich description of practice. Each approach has its merits. With Svensson's we gain a "feel" for what the students working in that modality may have experienced. With Erben, our understanding of modality is more theoretical.

What have we learned about modality through the discovery process of contrasting studies? Table 7.3 is an attempt to redevelop and revisit the scheme set out in Table 7.1 to highlight reflections about modality.

Implications

We have seen that in technology-mediated language learning and teaching, modality is at best a misunderstood and at worst an ignored concept. The survey in the preceding section showed that research that ignores it is in danger of missing out on ways of explaining the nuances in the learning process (study pairs 1 and 2), or of failing to exploit learning possibilities to the full (study pair 3). Researchers who integrate modality into their research (even if implicitly, as is the case in the studies surveyed) have been able to improve our understanding of the ecology of learning (e.g. Thorne) and to provide the sort of generalizable framework that is important for ensuring the relevance of local findings to the CALL community at large (e.g. Erben). The comparative survey has also shown how modality is affected by the materiality of the online environments and by the role that "space" (the physical spatial experiences of the user and the represented spaces on the screen) plays in them. In this final section of the chapter, we suggest a framework that may help to make these aspects of modality more visible to research.

Materiality

The materiality of the environment impacts on the dynamics of conversations. In two parallel conversations in chat, for example, it is not accidental that a tutor-initiated discussion is carried out orally while the students' exchange about sound levels is conducted in text chat: if we mentally invert the modal choices and imagine that the tutor led his tutorial via postings in the text-chat

Table 7.3 *Modality: issues emerging from our corpus*

Pairs of studies/tools	Modes	Language objectives	Reflections on modality
Pair 1 Fora	Linguistic – written	Acquisition, collaboration	The success of both pedagogical projects seems to have inhibited the researchers from further investigating the role of modality
Pair 2 Chats	Linguistic – written	Better task design Cultural	Blake: no differences between F2F and online modalities are discussed Thorne: the "mixed" outcomes of the learning project seems to have encouraged the researcher to extend his reflection on modality
Pair 3 MOOs	Linguistic – written, iconic	Cultural	The researchers seem to have experienced difficulty in reflecting on the specific modalities at work in the MOO project, remaining within a discussion of chat modalities instead
Pair 4 Multimodal platforms	Linguistic – written and spoken	Professional development	Erben: the researcher engaged with modality issues and set out a generalizable framework to deal with them
	visual, iconic	Cultural, self-expression	Svensson: the researcher provided a rich description of the modality at work in the project (rather than a framework)

window while students talked about other topics orally, we see that such an arrangement is unlikely. In the next section I explain why.

These authors' accounts of meaning-making in multimodal environments went further than the opening up of non-linguistic modes to analysis that we mentioned earlier. For them discourse is only one of four dimensions of modality, which also includes the design, production, and dissemination of any given multimodal artifact.

The impact of design on meaning-making

The design of an artifact embodies the ergonomic and esthetic reflections of its creator. In our context, the notion of "design" subsumes the choices that have determined what the users see on their screen, such as the architecture of the environment, the choice of colors, and the ergonomic harmony (or disharmony) of the frames, buttons, and icons as they appear on screen. For example, in some audio-synchronous platforms, a loudhailer icon signals the opening of the audio channel. In others, an icon representing a pair of fleshy lips carries out that function. The impact on meaning is not the same in both cases.

A fuller understanding of these meaning-making resources and their impact may be obtained by contrasting the experiences available to users on two platforms that have been used for language learning: Elluminate and Traveler. The metaphor underpinning Traveler is that of a fantasy world bringing together natural, supernatural, and built objects, peopled with avatars, reminiscent of video games. The visual design of Traveler is in complete contrast with the textual-visual design of an educational product like Elluminate, with its square workspaces, its stationery box full of pencils and erasers, and its hierarchy of "rooms" reminiscent of the serious educational purposes of a face-to-face campus. The ergonomics of these two environments are different too: while Traveler users work in three dimensions, using the keyboard's arrows to walk or fly their avatar around, those of Elluminate use text or click icons to create new rooms. A final material difference adds to the contrast: while Traveler users may remain anonymous, Elluminate participants are always identified (via a nametag which appears automatically on log-on). Overall, then, Traveler gives learners opportunities for meaning-making through a playful design that connotes the "cultures-of-use" of the young, and Elluminate does so using the connotations of the academic life. Do these different approaches have a different impact? We have as yet no empirical learner data with which to answer that question, but we can gain a fairly good idea about how educators see the issue by noting that when the Mathematics and Computing Department of the Open University adopted Second Life (which has a ludic design similar to Traveler's) to help its dispersed post-graduate students to collaborate, the decision was made to build an "island" dedicated to this group within Second Life and the design chosen for the island was, significantly, not the fantasy "look" that we mainly associate with Second Life, but one representing an idealized version of a university campus (http://virtualmphil .open.ac.uk; see Chapter 5 for further discussion of virtual environments such as Second Life).

The impact of production on meaning-making

In their notion of modality, Kress and van Leeuwen also included the production aspect of cultural artifacts. A simple example of the differences in meaning resulting from different conditions of production can be taken from the world of art, with such questions as "what different meanings inhere in an original painting as opposed to within its fake?" or "what different meanings inhere in a paper reproduction as opposed to within an electronic image?"

etc. In our context, an example is the extent to which the system has been produced to constrain the user to certain actions or how free the system allows the user to be. At one extreme the user cannot change anything and is dependent on the meaning-making resources produced by the system (a pre-interactive-TV television viewer would be a good example). At the other end of the continuum, the user has a lot of freedom to produce his/her own resources (MOOs, avatar-based worlds, graphic tools). Even in a "free" situation, the system provides many fixed features, so a "semi-constrained" position is what users mainly find themselves encountering, giving rise to creative usage. Here is an example of user creativity: in push-to-talk systems, users must press a button in order to ensure that their voice is heard by others, and one person only will be heard at a time. However, vocalizations from listeners (such as a happy "oh!" or an ironic "ha!" or a sigh) are meaningful resources in conversations. Deprived of these paralinguistic possibilities in one push-to-talk system studied by Lamy (2006), users responded by switching modes, i.e. by co-creating a "library" of custom-build smileys which they input into the text-chat window.

The impact of dissemination on meaning-making

Finally, another dimension of multimodal semiotics for Kress and van Leeuwen relates to differences in meaning resulting from the way in which a cultural artifact is disseminated. Here is an example from a CALL project. In distance or blended educational projects, students participate from their homes. According to the specification and age of the user's monitor, an image may be disseminated to them with higher or lower resolution, and the colors may be more or less true to the original files input by the designers. In the following example, a role-play involved dispersed English learners of intermediate French looking at photographic stimuli on their screens. The group was required to discuss these images of six sea resorts and to decide on the basis of that discussion which resort would be most suitable for a fictitious family with specific needs. Students were to arrive at an agreed choice through oral consensus. One participant, misled (at it was discovered later) by the poor quality of the image on her browser, created confusion by talking about "a multi-storey car park" – which her peers did not recognize (they could see a pretty seaside villa instead). As a result, the negotiation of meaning did take place, but instead of hinging on the carrying out of a pedagogical role-play focused on the vocabulary of houses and seaside resort facilities, the learning objective became the disambiguation of a real-life misunderstanding. The tool and the mode remained unchanged in the planned version of the task and in the actual task that was carried out, but as the learning objective changed, so in our definition the modality can be said to have changed too.

The impact of screen and perceptual spaces on meaning-making

While Scollon and Scollon (2003) acknowledged the importance of Kress and van Leeuwen's design dimension, they reinterpreted and reinforced it in order to account for the role played by spaces, in a way that we have found useful for understanding how our users perform on multimodal platforms. Scollon and Scollon call their framework "geosemiotics" and they define it thus:

Geosemiotics is the study of meaning systems by which language is located in the material world. This includes not just the location of words on the page you are reading now but also the location of the book in your hands and your location as you stand or sit reading this. (Scollon and Scollon, 2003, pp. x–xi)

The authors structure geosemiotics into three sub-sets: the interaction order, visual semiotics (on which we will not elaborate here, as this concept comes close to Kress and van Leeuwen's notion of design mentioned earlier), and space semiotics.

The interaction order provides a way of understanding how individuals perceive the interactional value of the space they choose to use. In their description of the interaction order, the authors include perceptual spaces and interpersonal distances. According to them, in face-to-face situations dominant perceptual spaces are visual and auditory ("less noticed" ones are olfactory, thermal, and tactile). The notion of interpersonal distances allows geosemiotics to ask questions about the relationship between space, sound, and socialization. For example, the auditory space that I perceive, and my perceived intimacy or distance with the individual vocalizing the sound that I am hearing, together form the semiotic resource by which I embody meanings. Applying this framework to multimodal platform users, the question becomes: how do they co-construct interpersonal values (intimate, personal, social, public) into conversations that proceed simultaneously through visual spaces of varying salience and through an auditory space defined by the spatially and tactilely intimate device of an earpiece or headset? Here lies the answer to our earlier question about why an online tutor would not use the chat windows to carry out their teaching, while the students chatted off-topic on the audio channel.

Space semiotics, in Scollon and Scollon's words, is the most fundamental part of geosemiotics, because it asks "Where in the world is the sign or image located?" and because it aims to account for "any aspect of the meaning that is predicated on the placement of the sign in the material world" (2003). For example, if students have a choice of inputting a comment into a narrow chat window at the bottom of the screen or into a whiteboard that occupies most of the screen, what will determine their choice: the visual salience of the space, the type of information to be imparted, and/or the nature of the particular group they are working with? A theory of space semiotics applied to a

CALL situation needs to address these questions, taking into account wider "ecological" issues such as the fact that any user is free to shrink the screen or to open other screens, which makes the visual message received very different from the visual message sent. In terms of multimodal electronic environments, space semiotics provides the basis for asking questions such as "how do users decode and encode meanings in a material situation involving their computer and its various peripherals (keyboard, mouse or keypad, webcam) as well as other stimuli around them (possibly another computer, a video screen, a person physically present in the same room as them)?"

To put this in semiotic (rather than in multitasking) terms, consider the difference in meaning-making between two situations that I recently experienced. One was when I created a blog at home using a template from a website and sheets of paper to help sketch out the blog's design. The other was when I created another blog using a WiFi connection while sitting in the audience at a talk given by a speaker on the subject of creating blogs, then publicly revealed what I had been doing, as part of my contribution to an end-of-lecture debate on the pros and cons of allowing ubiquitous WiFi technology on university campuses. In the first situation, I was understanding instructions and carrying them out to create an artifact. In the second situation, I was creating evidence to support my position in a professional discussion. Although the tools and modes were the same in both activities, the impact of place was different, the objective of the person carrying out the activities was different, and therefore overall the modalities can be said to have been different.

Conclusion

In offering to the CALL domain a reinterpretation of modality which is based on semiotics, I am aware of stepping into a territory that is just beginning to be charted, although pointers have been provided from neighboring educational research. For example, based on his work with virtual games worlds, Lemke (2006) sketches out a research agenda which, I suggest, is applicable to the context of CALL:

[I]t is possible to create real-time, synchronized video and computer log records of monitor display, keystroke and mouse or joystick input, and user speech and action. It is possible in this way to follow user activity in entering the gameworld, acting and moving within the primary gameworld and among various subsidiary "screens" or auxiliary attentional spaces, communicating within and parallel to the gameworld action ... and on leaving the gameworld. Ideally we would also like to observe how people integrate or cumulate in-game meaning-making activity and meanings made with out-of-game life activities and identities ... We would like to understand class, gender/sexuality, cultural and subcultural differences, which games people play, how, and why; the kinds of meanings they make and feelings they experience; and what persistent learning effects result. But we need to take such an ambitious agenda one step at a time. (Lemke, 2006, p. 11)

Providing Lemke's word of caution about a gradual approach is heeded, I see a useful research agenda emerging: to test out, with a large volume of learner interaction data collected from a variety of technological environments, the methodological claims made in this paper according to which what appears to be the bewildering diversity of modality in CALL can be understood in a more systematic way through the synergistic use of social semiotics and geosemiotics. In other words, in this chapter I have been arguing for the development of a cultural approach to understanding the "CA" part of the acronym CALL.

8   Diversity in technologies

Gordon Bateson and Paul Daniels

Introduction

This chapter will examine the diverse technologies that are used in language education today. In a single chapter of a book, it would not be possible to usefully describe all the electronic devices, computer equipment, and software utilized by computer-assisted language learning (CALL) practitioners. Instead, we will highlight what we believe to be the current trends in this field, and present several innovative and emerging technologies, which are not currently in widespread use but which we feel offer some interesting possibilities to language teachers.

Generally speaking, all electronic devices nowadays have some kind of interface to a computer, so this chapter will be framed in terms of computer-based technologies and will consider how these technologies can enhance the teaching and learning of languages. We begin by offering a categorization framework for the technologies based on the computing hardware involved. The four main categories we will look at are:

- multi-server technologies;
- single-server technologies;
- single personal computer (PC) technologies;
- mobile technologies.

For each category, we will describe the kind of technologies that are available, and give examples of web services, websites, and products that can harness the target technologies for language learning. Following this categorization, we present three actual examples of these technologies in use. At the end of the chapter, we consider the implications of the availability of these technologies for the language teacher.

Overview and general issues

In this section we present a categorization for CALL technologies. With so many technologies available, there is inevitably some overlap between the categories listed here. We have put each technology into the category that we feel best reflects the original intention behind the development of the technology.

Multi-server technologies

The advent of extremely large multi-server computing centers, which connect to form an online computer resource comprising massive data storage and web-based applications, referred to collectively as a "cloud," offers exciting possibilities for language instruction. In particular, because the resources of a "cloud" are ubiquitously available, learning materials can be deployed on different devices and in different locations, thereby freeing educators and learners from the boundaries of the traditional classroom. There are many classic web services based on the "cloud" concept, of which the most familiar are likely to be search engines and web-based email services. We also include in this category social networking sites, tools for creating online communities, resource creation and sharing services, tools for online collaboration and conferencing, learning management systems (LMSs) and tutoring services, and large multi-player games and virtual online worlds.

Online groups and communities There are many websites nowadays offering tools to create online communities (see Chapter 5 for a discussion of the pedagogic possibilities of social networking sites). These sites often include storage space and sophisticated tools to store and maintain data owned by the community. They also allow varying levels of access to the community and its data based on the role that users have within the community.

On the most general level, there are several sites where one can set up an online group to interact and share files. One such site is Yahoo! Groups. This service allows teachers to set up a restricted online space, where students can come to interact and share files, photos, and links. This service includes a database functionality, which teachers can use to store information about students, such as contact information and even grades, and a calendar, which can send reminders to students about upcoming events and deadlines. While there are no functions specifically for language teachers, the sharing of resources in this way affords learners opportunities for authentic communication (e.g. Kelly, 2010). Other companies with a major presence on the Internet, including Google and Microsoft, offer similar community-building services. The final decision as to which one to use may well depend as much on the teacher's previous familiarity with the technology provider, as on the details of the service.

The community-building technologies may be combined with other services into a "one-stop shop" for teachers and teaching institutions. For example, Google offers "GoogleApps for Education." It brings together several of Google's online tools into an integrated system for teachers and students to communicate (email, calendar, voice chat), share, and collaborate (documents, web pages, video, groups). It integrates with current email, calendar, and authentication systems. GoogleApps does not itself offer tools to grade student work or compile course grades, but it does integrate with well-known online LMSs, such as Moodle (open source) and Blackboard (commercial). The integration takes the form of allowing users to access and edit Google's mail and document stores from within Moodle.

There are also sites that specialize solely in creating learning communities. Some of these sites offer less cluttered interfaces, such as EdModo for instance, which may make them more appealing in certain situations, for example when the teacher or the students are apprehensive about technical complexity, or when the technology's ease of use is paramount. On other sites, such as EduBlogs, it is possible to set access restrictions so that access is only allowed from computers located on campus.

Online resource sharing The concept of sharing is not new to CALL, for example there have been advocates of shared content (Ward, 2002; Cushion, 2004) and also of shared software (Stockwell, 2007a), but this sharing concept has not yet materialized, although there are a few exceptions (e.g. Hopkins, 2010). As has been argued by Prensky (2001), the modern generation of young digital natives are often much more comfortable than their older teachers with congregating online to communicate, socialize, and share content, and there are tools available that enable them to do that.

Collaborative web-based applications provide auditory and visual tools, which allow learners to interact with global audiences (see Bush, 2009, for a discussion). For example, there are numerous repositories for video clips on the Internet. The undoubted leader in this field is YouTube, with millions of searchable video clips that are ideal for use as language samples for students to study, analyze, and imitate (Berk, 2009). Teachers can upload their own videos to show mini-lectures, short tutorials explaining how to use hardware or software, samples of how to complete tasks, and even verbal feedback on students' work. Of course, students can also create and upload their own work, as in the student video project reported in Alm (2006). Creating user accounts and uploading videos is simple, and access to a video can be restricted to certain users only.

Other sites in the "cloud" allow the sharing of different types of media. For example, Yahoo!, Google, Microsoft, and Apple all have online repositories for creating and viewing digital photo albums. As with the video sharing sites, access to photos on these sites can be restricted to only classmates and teachers. Photos can serve to stimulate ideas, provide examples, or keep a record of students' work. Most photo galleries allow text to be attached to an image. This functionality can be used to invite students to discuss or comment on a photo.

Over time, the collection of photos becomes a valuable resource for current students to view and learn from work by previous students (see Daniels, 2008, for a description of media-enabled blogs in Moodle).

As well as video and photo sharing sites, there are sites for sharing other kinds of files. For example, SlideShare handles presentations, word-processing documents, and PDF files. The privacy settings allow content to be shared only with teachers and classmates. The site allows for commenting on content that has been uploaded, so students can comment on and discuss their peers' work. Another notable document sharing site is Scribd. It allows for documents to be easily inserted into web pages using an "iPaper," which allows documents to be inserted into ordinary web pages. This technology can be used to distribute worksheets produced by the teacher, or view documents created by the students. The great advantage of this technology is that for teachers and students who are familiar with word-processing documents and spreadsheets, there is no need to convert files to web pages, as this is done automatically for them by the iPaper-embedding technology.

Online conferencing Online conferencing refers to technologies that allow a group of two or more people to communicate synchronously via the Internet. The communication may be done using text chat (e.g. Darhower, 2007), audio (e.g. Meskill and Anthony, 2007), video (e.g. Wang, 2007), or combination of the three (e.g. Blake, 2005; Sotillo, 2005; Yamada and Akahori, 2007), and may be enhanced with other features such as the use of a whiteboard to show images, drawings, and notes, the sharing of files, and recording of the conference session. The most popular online conferencing services are based around websites that are ubiquitously and constantly available via the Internet, thereby potentially allowing people from anywhere on the Internet to take part. These sites often have a "free" service and one or more commercial versions of the service, which are generally paid for as a renewable monthly or yearly license, the cost of which varies according to the maximum number of "seats" required at any one time.

Synchronous communication often demonstrates more active discussion on the part of the participants (see Abrams, 2003b), allowing for enhanced interaction and sharing of ideas. However, one must remember that web-based conferencing is vulnerable to technical difficulties (Hara and King, 1999). There can be problems that the individual users have in setting up their audio and video equipment, or there can be problems with network capacity or connectivity. Consequently, web-conferencing systems generally have one user nominated as "presenter," where the others are generally just listening. Any of the "listeners" can raise their hand, and be given permission to control the microphone. Listeners are also able to show appreciation using an animated "clapping" icon, as well as broadcast text messages, in which one can add "emoticons" as a visual way to communicate feelings, to everyone in the group. Some conferencing software allows sessions to be recorded so that they may be used as a reference for students who could not participate in the conference, or inserted into a student portfolio for the teacher to view later.

Probably the most full-featured and well-established conferencing tool is Elluminate. It is a general-purpose conferencing tool that offers video, audio, chat, whiteboard, and recording. However, it is probably prohibitively expensive for teachers operating outside of a well-financed institution. Teachers interested in an open source alternative may like to try Big Blue Button software, and there are numerous cheaper commercially available conferencing tools, such as Adobe Connect Pro, Yugma, Webex, and DimDim, all of which have free versions for small numbers of participants, but require licenses for more than a certain number of students or to enable certain features.

Online collaboration and resource creation Enabling students to collaborate and create resources online brings the benefits promised by constructivism, such as the "real experiential learning in the form of meaningful, process-oriented projects" (Felix, 2002, p. 2), and social constructivism, that is "teaching in contexts that might be personally meaningful to students" (Dougiamas, 1998). Social websites such as Facebook, MySpace, and Mixi have grown up primarily as social sites, where individuals meet, interact, and share images, movies, and links (see Chapter 5 for further discussion). Encouraging the students to communicate on these sites in the target language builds up an online record of text interactions and collections of files and links. Together these constitute simple examples of resources created through online collaboration.

There are also websites that allow groups to share other kinds of media objects, such as diagrams, collages, and presentations. These sites do not simply store and deliver files created on a stand-alone PC, like the sites described earlier in the "Online resource sharing" section. Rather, they allow the object to be created online, via the user's browser, and in some cases several people can work on the same object at once.

For example, to create an image, poster, or collage, a site called Glogster allows you to combine pre-drawn and hand-drawn elements to create a visual image. It is also possible to create new types of media objects, such as the presentations available at Prezi, which allow zooming and panning. These presentations are like a large picture containing many elements, to represent ideas to be expressed. You can zoom in on, and pan across to, different areas of the whole picture. The resulting object can be embedded in any web page. Another site for producing novel media objects that may be interesting to language teachers is Wordle. It allows you to create a "word cloud," in which many words are displayed in a crossword collage. It can act as the focus of a brainstorming session or discussion, or perhaps the theme graphic for a reading.

The resource creation sites mentioned so far have allowed individuals to create and share objects, but there are also sites where students can create objects as a group. One such site that seems tailor-made for language learning is VoiceThread. At this website, registered users are invited to take part in a discussion that takes place around a central stage, which appears as a whiteboard on a web page that all participants have access to. Files, such as an image, a sound file, a video file, a word-processing document, or a PDF file, can be uploaded to the stage, and participants can comment on what is on the stage or on other people's comments. Participants have a number of ways to add comments to the discussion; voice (via microphone), text (via keyboard), or by uploading an existing audio file or video file. Communication can be synchronous or asynchronous, but in the latter case, the discussion proceeds even when all members are not present.

Online LMSs and teaching services There are several sites available that offer an LMS plus content creation tools and even personal tutoring for students. For example, the free site called WiZiQ offers both an LMS and web conferencing. It is intended as a place where teachers can set up classes and attract students from within the WiZiQ community. The classes can be public or private, free or not. Teachers can create content online, upload content created on a PC, create tests online, and enroll and attract students. A similar site that offers an LMS and content creation tools is Udutu. The online content creator creates content that complies with standards for reusable learning objects as set out by the sharable content object reference model (SCORM). This means that the content can be imported into any SCORM-compliant LMS, which includes all the major LMSs. Also of interest are sites such as Smart .fm, where content creators from the site's community contribute short learning objects, which other members of the community can select to study with. This site is based on Ebbinghaus's forgetting curve and the idea of "spaced rehearsal," that is, learning of new items can be optimized by repeatedly presenting the items at progressively larger intervals of time (Schacter, 2001). As well as sites that offer "empty" courses to be filled with content generated by teachers, there are numerous sites that come pre-populated with content, for example ReallyEnglish offers courses filled with activities and content, as well as personal human tutors to encourage students, check their writing and speaking (recorded audio file) assignments, and check up on them via email if they fall behind schedule.

Online virtual worlds and gaming Online virtual worlds are places where individuals appear as avatars and interact with each other and the objects in the world. Because of the immersive and interactive nature of these worlds, they have the potential to create a compelling environment for language learners to use a foreign language in authentic situations (see the section on virtual environments in Chapter 5 for further discussion and examples).

Single-server technologies

Learning management systems Rather than storing content and data on publically accessible servers in "the cloud," many educational institutions prefer to manage their own servers, so that data, particularly student data, are kept securely out of the public domain. A single server can run a website that can support many of the Web 2.0 applications that are available in "the cloud." Web 2.0 applications are those in which users can modify the web content by adding comments or even editing the page itself, using a standard web browser. The most common application is a content management system (CMS). A CMS is a collection of small programs called scripts, which maintain and display the contents of a database, allowing websites to evolve from being predominantly a collection of static hypertext markup language (HTML) pages into content, which can be manipulated by users without sophisticated programming skills. Both the scripts and database reside on a server. There are many general purpose CMSs, some of which, like WordPress, are small and simple enough to enable teachers to quickly set up websites to distribute news and information to their students. A CMS for education can also be known as an LMS, or a virtual learning environment (VLE), and may be commercially produced, such as Blackboard and WebCT, or available as open source, such as Moodle, Sakai, and aTutor. Such systems share features of content creation and distribution with other CMSs, but they place more emphasis on control of access to the content and, in addition, include tools for student assessment.

The open source LMSs are marvelously flexible tools, but this very flexibility poses two major hurdles for teachers who wish to incorporate such technology into their teaching practice. Firstly, the systems have myriad settings, and a multitude of pages with which to interact. In the case of Moodle, the system continues to expand every day as plug-ins are developed for themes, filters, blocks, and activity modules. Secondly, these systems come with no content, so the onus is on institutions and teachers to develop their own materials. Some would say that this is a good thing, because any learning materials could be said to embody the pedagogy of the content creator, which may not always suit the teacher, learners, or environment of a given learning situation. However, with repositories of shared learning objects and the advent of content sharing through the new community hubs feature of Moodle 2.0, perhaps it is possible to have the best of both worlds; that is to say, teachers choose to either make their own material or import ready materials if appropriate.

In contrast to open source LMSs, commercial LMSs offer the security of having someone to call when things go wrong – although the support fora of open source software can also be highly informative – or when wanting to customize a system to meet particular needs. While generic commercial LMSs may be used for language learning purposes, such as Blackboard (e.g. Morris, 2005) and WebCT (e.g. Orsini-Jones, 2004), there are also commercial LMSs designed specifically for language learning. For example, DynEd offers a system for learning English which can be hosted either on a DynEd server or a server of the educational institution. It comes complete with content and a variety of functionalities including speech recognition (see Brown *et al.*, 2008). As the system does not allow teachers to add their own content, another LMS is required in addition to DynEd if a teacher wishes to include content that goes beyond that which is provided in the system. Despite the possible limitations that this type of closed LMS may have, they provide a very useful service in the learning situations for which they were designed.

An LMS can also be used as a portfolio system, which allows students to build up and present collections of their work. These systems typically include a file repository where students can store their files, and fora where students can interact socially or reflect on their learning experiences. In one such system, Mahara, users can select who they share their work with, and can build "views" which define how the work is presented. The content can be shared with everybody, or selected groups of users. Mahara can operate as a stand-alone system, or it can be integrated with other LMSs, such as Moodle. A very useful tool for building content for an LMS is digital library software, such as Greenstone (see Chapter 6 for a discussion). Briefly, this software examines repositories of text and builds searchable indexes of the words and phrases it finds. It can be used on public repositories of non-copyrighted material, such as Wikipedia, or on local digital repositories. The libraries then become accessible to language students to use to find examples of language in authentic use. The software can be used in tandem with LMS content creation software, named FLAX, which guides teachers to selecting text to create cloze activities, multiple choice questions, and other interactive exercises based on the texts.

Versioning systems allow for duplication of files in a central repository. They are potentially most useful for teachers collaborating on content materials. Systems such as CVS, Subversion, and GIT can handle not only written documents but also media files, such as audio, video, and Flash files. The files in the central repository can then be easily reproduced on different servers, or even different courses within the same LMS, which makes it a convenient way to distribute the same learning objects across different LMSs.

Single PC technologies

These technologies require only a single PC, which may or may not be connected to a network. As well as the software for making documents, editing multimedia resources, and creating interactive activities, we include in this category the peripheral devices such as cameras, scanners, and audio devices, which connect to a PC and so allow teachers to import images, photos, video clips, and scanned documents into the materials they create.

File editing tools Perhaps one of the best-known file editing tools is a word-processor. Word-processors come complete with tools that assist learners in the writing process, such as spell checkers and grammar checkers, and functions that make it easy to manipulate text (see Pennington, 2004). While there are potential limitations in the application of grammar checkers (Burston, 2001), they still have practical application in language learning contexts. There is also a multitude of tools that run on a single PC and allow teachers and students to produce files that can be printed or distributed via the web. While many word-processors have built-in functions to produce HTML versions of content, there are also specialist HTML editor programs, which allow web pages to be created in a "what you see is what you get" (WYSIWYG) editor. Many of these programs also include file transfer functionality, making it possible to move the HTML files from a PC to a website if desired. Teachers may also wish to create their own images, audio files, and video files and, of course, there are many tools for these tasks too. Examples of free and open source software are Gimp (images), Audacity (audio), and MovieMaker (video), while commercial applications include Fireworks (images), SoundForge (audio), and Vegas (video), although there are hundreds of other products that are constantly evolving.

Quiz authoring software Most of the LMSs mentioned earlier have their own tools for creating and editing quizzes online, but it is also possible to create quizzes that can function completely offline on a single computer. Two well-known and free tools are Hot Potatoes and Qedoc. The former has been freeware since September 2009 and allows teachers to create five kinds of interactive quizzes, namely cloze exercises, crosswords, jumbled sentences exercises, matching exercises, and more conventional quizzes, which contain a series of questions, to which students are expected to type or select a response. Having set up the quiz content and settings, the teacher generates HTML files that can be used on any PC that has a browser. The exercises can be done individually or chained together. If the exercises are put online, they become available anywhere on the Internet. They can also be administered through Moodle, which has the advantage that results can be collected to reveal interesting trends, such as common errors and average scores. Qedoc is a similar system, but it is more elaborate. It has more question types and greater control of the ordering and formatting of content. It can also function as a stand-alone set of exercises, or it can report results to an LMS that has suitable plug-in, such as the QuizPort module for Moodle.

Screen capture tools Screen capture tools are a useful way to provide support to students on how to use the technology they need to take part in a course. These digital recordings of events on a computer screen, or "screen-casts" as they are commonly known, are an opportunity for language teachers to give this support in the target language. Also, this software allows you to add text comments, background music, and voice-overs, as well as to insert video clips, and can be used to model activities, or even create presentations. Some screen capture tools, such as Captivate, will even allow insertion of interactive question-and-answer pages, which the students must complete in order to continue. The screencast is rendered as a Flash file that can be inserted into a web page and made available to the students. Screen capture tools also have practical applications for student tracking (see Chapter 2).

Self-study CD or DVD Despite losing popularity to the growing number of interactive sites and activities available online, there is still a lot of highly interactive and visually stimulating software distributed on compact disk (CD) or digital versatile disk (DVD). This type of software is installed on a single PC, and run from the PC's hard disk drive, which makes it possible to include large high-quality video or sophisticated functionality, such as voice recognition software. Not dependent on bandwidth, they may include game-like activities which elicit verbal responses from the user. For example, the user may be required to give directions verbally in order to navigate a maze, or may be required to say what things they want to buy in a shop. As with the online virtual worlds mentioned earlier, the multimedia and interactivity increases the user's engagement with the materials, and encourages users to practice speaking the target language. This technology is rarely free but it is generally very professionally developed. The software review section of the *CALICO Journal* is a good source of information regarding available software in a range of languages.

Mobile technologies

While mobile learning development is still in its infancy, assembling learning content which is accessible via mobile devices provides learners with "on the go" study material and can help improve time management and learner motivation (Vogel *et al.*, 2009). Up until now, research on mobile learning and language acquisition has focused on the use of mobile phones rather than on smart phones or media players with robust video, audio, and web browsing capabilities. Traditional mobile phones are not always suited for language study, due to undersized displays, data packet fees (Stockwell, 2008), and difficulties with mobile text input (Thornton and Houser, 2002). Newer mobile devices are becoming more ubiquitous in educational environments due to their larger screens with higher resolution, powerful multimedia capabilities, and web browsers, and the ability to connect to campus networks without data charges. While mobile devices offer new and exciting opportunities for language learning, there are some hurdles to overcome. Access to mobile devices may be limited and institutions may need to provide devices to students. Manipulating content on a mobile device, for example, can take longer than a computer with a traditional keyboard (Stockwell, 2010), but they allow better use of "dead time" (e.g. time spent commuting). In addition, while learners' preparedness to use mobile technology may vary (Stockwell, 2008), teachers can deliver the same material through different technologies allowing the learner to choose what device is best suited for accessing the content.

Mobile content delivery Mobile devices can be used to receive web-delivered media. Audio or video content, for example, can be distributed via podcasts. Educational podcasting includes both authentic broadcasts found throughout the web and local broadcasts produced by teachers and students. Podcasts can provide authentic language input, and can be used to engage learners through language production tasks (McCarty, 2005). Podcast recording applications ("apps") are available for popular mobile platforms such as iOS and Android. It is also possible to deliver a podcast from a mobile device by placing a voice call to a podcasting service. Podcasts are typically uploaded to social networking sites, blogging sites, or iTunes. Content such as information about vocabulary items can be sent to learners using email (Li *et al.*, 2010) or short message service (SMS) (Kennedy and Levy, 2008). Email can also be used to upload content from a mobile device to a web server (see the mobile examples below). Finally, advances in mobile processing speeds give mobile users a more genuine web browsing experience, making it possible to provide quite sophisticated software for learners (e.g. Stockwell, 2007b). News, social networking, and blogging sites often have mobile-optimized websites so learners have greater mobile options for participating in interactive online activities.

Mobile apps Software development kits (SDKs) are typically used to create apps. Often these apps are limited for educational use in that the content is not easily customized. To allow for greater flexibility, a template approach can be used to allow for embedding and editing of instructional content. Web apps are a simpler solution used to deploy cross-platform applications. Recent mobile web browsers can typically render most websites for viewing on small screens. Using a web-based application forgoes the need to enroll or distribute applications via online app stores, since applications can be deployed via the web. Coding web applications is also simpler and less expensive than coding native apps. The disadvantage of using web apps over native mobile apps is that you lose some flexibility with the ability to interact with the content. In addition, web apps that rely on Java or Flash are not compatible with every mobile browser; therefore, HTML5, CSS, and JavaScript are better suited for mobile app development.

Examples

Examples of multi-server and single-server technology

The objective of this project was to replicate a successful blended-learning English course and use it as a template to create new courses. After several years of teaching a general English course to students within the same university department, the teachers concerned felt confident they had developed an understanding of the students and a repertoire of learning activities that could be used to create similar courses for students.

Rationale for using technology The teachers set out to develop the documentation and materials collaboratively, and to this end, they used two file versioning systems: GoogleDocs and Subversion. The core documentation, comprising the syllabus, the technical specifications, and brainstormed ideas for activities and audio scripts, were stored in GoogleDocs, as this allowed either teacher to edit the documentation from any computer, at any time, using a standard browser, thereby giving both teachers immediate access to the latest documentation. The content files were maintained in a Subversion file repository. This enabled us to make duplicates of the content files in the LMSs where they were to be used. Also, we could create all the content files independently, using our preferred quiz, image, and audio editors on our own PCs, and then share those files, via the repository, with each other and with the various LMSs. Where possible, we used editors that allowed for tasks to be automated. For example, having recorded the audio tracks of the dialogs and vocabulary items and inserted markers to show the beginning and end of words and phrases, the audio editing software split up the audio track and saved each segment into a separate, sequentially numbered file automatically. The numbering of the audio files corresponded with the page and row in a central spreadsheet in which all the dialogs and vocabulary were stored.

In order to separate the content creation process from the delivery platform, the LMS materials were created using a "setup script," that is, a computer program which extracts the details stored in the main content spreadsheet, and creates courses, activities, and files suitable for the target LMS. There are several advantages of using a setup script, as opposed to creating activities directly in the LMS. Firstly, it becomes possible to use different setup scripts to convert the same content to different delivery platforms. In particular, the teachers hope to make the course available on mobile devices at some point. Also, a setup script allows for greater cohesion between the materials. For example, from a central vocabulary list, the program can ensure that exactly the same spellings and definitions are used in a glossary as in the vocabulary quizzes. Furthermore, the setup script can do tasks that would be very laborious and error-prone for a human to do, such as ensuring that items are selected evenly in random selections, converting the encoding of text, and formatting the text appropriately for the delivery platform.

We developed a setup script to assist in the creation of a Moodle course and activities. The script extracted the dialogs and vocabulary items from the content spreadsheet and created Hot Potatoes quiz files, which were added to the Moodle course in QuizPort activities. QuizPort is a third-party module for Moodle, which allows Hot Potatoes quizzes to be combined into chains of quizzes, in which post-conditions on each quiz control what a student is shown next after any given quiz is finished. The Hot Potatoes files could also be imported into the categories in the question bank for the Moodle course. We could then make Moodle Quiz activities in which each question was selected randomly from one of the question categories. Thus, each student was shown a different set of questions in the test, but every student knew that whatever questions they were given would also have been included in one of the QuizPort activities they were expected to have done earlier in the course. Finally, the setup script also created an import file for the Moodle glossary. For each word, phrase, or dialog line there was an English headword, a Japanese translation, and a link to the audio file for that item. Within the Moodle course, we enabled the media plug-ins filter so that the audio links would be converted to embedded media players. We also enabled glossary auto-linking, so that phrases appearing within the various activities would be linked to the glossary. Because the auto-linking of glossary entries is also done to text within Moodle Quiz questions, we had the setup script disable auto-linking in each phrase of open text in Hot Potatoes quizzes that were to be imported in the Moodle question bank. This is something that would be humanly impossible, given that there were hundreds of quiz files containing thousands of text phrases.

The teachers hoped to maintain and motivate the students by incorporating game-like features into the learning activities. These features included adding "levels" with achievable goals and clearly marked progress. Many of the students were familiar with these ideas from using video games on handheld game devices, and the intention was to apply these ideas to a web-based LMS, using score-boards and colors to give visual cues to students regarding their progress through the materials. Several features of the QuizPort module were useful in this regard. Firstly, we added timers to increase the urgency. Secondly, we required performance to a certain level on one task before proceeding to the next task. Finally, we displayed color-coded activity grades on the course page. By looking at the course page, students could quickly see what they had done, how well they had done it, and what they had to do next.

Overview of environment This project was conducted at a medium-size university in Japan. The two teachers involved in the project were each in charge of a compulsory course of basic English. They taught different cohorts of first-year students from the same university department. The classes took place in one of several large, computer-equipped classrooms, containing about fifty up-to-date PCs. Headphones were supplied by the university, but the majority of students preferred to use their own headphones. The course materials were distributed via a Moodle LMS. The teachers had access to several computers, such as desktop PCs at work, laptops at home, and smart phones while they were not at home or work. Hitherto, the students' motivation and expectations for these compulsory English classes had been low. The students are IT majors, so they have some familiarity with, and proclivity for, using computers to browse the web and edit documents.

Learner requirements The students were informed that in order to pass the course, they had to do all the activities listed on the course page of their online course. Some of the activities were self-study activities, which could be done at home or in class. However, in every class students were expected to show coursework to the teacher. This meant, in effect, that students had to attend every class. Students were also told to maintain a handwritten notebook, which would contain vocabulary lists, as well as rough drafts of the English dialogs and paragraphs that they produced.

Observations At the end of the course we used Moodle's feedback module to gather feedback from the students. Although the number of students was reasonably small, approximately eighty in all, the feedback suggests that the vast majority of the students, almost 90 percent, found the course effective and enjoyable. Some of the Japanese comments explain why; here are some of the comments translated into English: "It was fun," "I could study at home," "The words appeared several times, and I started to remember them," "I could go at my own pace," "I could listen many times," "Aiming for 100 percent felt like I was doing a game," "It was easier than a lesson with writing only." Some students also voiced concerns about the course, such as, "There were too many activities," "The buttons were difficult to push," "For someone who is not good at using computers, this course is really tough." Overall, though, the teachers feel that they have succeeded in their goal of using a variety of technologies to generate content efficiently and accurately, and then deploying that content to a large number of students in a blended-learning situation, in such a way that students are able to usefully engage with the materials to improve their motivation to study English and their ability to use it.

Example of mobile technology 1: in the classroom

Rationale for using technology The improved media handling capabilities of the operating systems on the latest mobile devices have expanded the potential for developing interactive language learning applications for mobile platforms. Given the physical limitations on the size of the screen and keyboard, applications that do not require extensive viewing of text or extensive text input are particularly suitable for mobile devices. A current project at Kochi Institute of Technology, Japan, set out to investigate the use of iPod Touch devices within a language class. The project was designed to determine if mobile devices could replace notebook or desktop computers for CALL instruction, as well as to ascertain whether self-paced learning using a handheld computer device could aid language acquisition.

Initially, it was envisaged that the content would be delivered to the students using a native iPhone application: that is, an application designed specifically for the iPhone and iPad family of devices. Such applications are generally quicker than web applications, and do not need a network connection, which is important if the devices are to be used outside of a wireless network. However, because of the high learning curve involved in development, the difficulty in adapting the application to other platforms, and concerns with application distribution, we decided to make the materials available via the web browser in the device.

Overview of the environment Four classes of 120 first-year engineering and science majors participated in the iPod Touch project. Language classes met twice a week and utilized a four skills English for specific purposes (ESP) textbook integrated with mobile media activities. Half of the students were assigned to an experimental group and performed the learning activities using the iPod Touch every other class. The control group completed language activities in a traditional teacher-led setting, in which students completed listening activities, worked through textbook activities, and listened to lectures at the same pace while being guided by the instructor.

Learner requirements We designed the web content to be easy to use for the students in the experimental group. Generally, the applications were a straightforward implementation of the activities in the students' language textbook. As the students worked through their paper textbooks, they used the iPods to complete the reading and listening activities, to study vocabulary using multimedia-enhanced flash cards, and to complete multiple choice, true/false, and cloze activities with supplementary audio, images, and feedback. Students were allowed to work through the activities at their own pace, and use the iPod devices as much or as little as they wanted to.

Observations While some students showed anxiety about using a new platform, most were able to navigate through the menus and activities with ease after one class. We noted that not all learners were initially captivated with the idea of self-study. Possibly, this was because they were looking forward to the increased social interaction that is possible in the smaller language classroom compared to larger lecture courses. However, we felt strongly that the self-paced study was a useful way to practice listening and vocabulary. In addition, the self-paced mobile learning materials were used only every other lesson, so students had opportunities to engage in interactive language activities with classmates in alternating classes. Finally, while not all students were initially open to the idea of self-study, they were all engaged in the language activities for the complete class. Although the self-study materials were basically done individually, the students were encouraged to interact with other classmates, or the instructor, if questions were raised.

Example of mobile technology 2: outside of the classroom

Rationale for using technology While many learners now possess a smart phone capable of running the multimedia web-based applications discussed in the previous section, the majority of mobile users in Japan use proprietary mobile handsets with rudimentary web browsers. Therefore, in order to leverage the potential of the availability of mobile devices among students, we developed a system to augment our CMS using mobile email functions. Email messages can be used to send and receive text, images, audio, and even video. The transmission can be initiated by the student sending in data, or by the server sending out prompts and reminders. This "prodding" of students is perhaps a unique feature of email, which is not possible using web pages alone.

Overview of the environment This project made use of a gateway between the school's CMS and a single email account. The gateway was set up to send data to, and receive data from, students' mobile devices. Using this system, students were able to upload content to the CMS, for example to their user profiles or blogs. The gateway took the form of a small script running on the server that automatically checks the course email account every five minutes, parses any messages it finds, and either posts the data to the CMS and/or sends data back to the student.

Learner requirements Students were required to use their mobile phones to take pictures of items of interest and send the images, along with some descriptive text, to the email server. When the gateway script detected new email messages, the images and text were added to the CMS. Where the device had included positional coordinates, these were referenced to a Google map embedded into the CMS. The gateway script was also used to send prompts in the target language to the students' mobile devices. One such task was for a test of English for international communication (TOEIC) vocabulary study. Students optionally signed up to receive TOEIC vocabulary items to their mobile device on a scheduled basis. The items involved both non-interactive content, such as vocabulary items with translations, and interactive content in the form of multiple choice questions, in which the student had to select the most appropriate reply to an email message.

Observations This system was very successful with projects done out of class, such as one in which students posted text, images, audio, or video to a gallery entitled "A day in the life of a Japanese university student." Students were very adept at capturing images on their mobile phones, and created some fascinating mobile blogs. Students would snap a photo and jot down some comments in an email during the course of their day and post to the gallery. The collection of lifestyle images with descriptions grew immensely over the years and became a valuable source of authentic learner content, which could be incorporated into other language activities. The email gateway was successful as a means of simplifying the practice of incorporating authentic student-generated material in classroom lessons.

Summary of mobile examples

These two examples of using mobile devices to support language instruction show just a couple of the many and diverse ways that mobile devices can be employed in CALL environments. With more traditional mobile devices, standard email offers interesting opportunities for sharing data between the learner and an online web environment, such as a CMS. With the advent of smart phones and mobile multimedia devices, so comes the potential for new and richer forms of language learning.

Implications

Teaching with technology requires a significant shift in the way of thinking by both practitioners and administrators. Today's learning agenda is experiencing a transformation. Traditional teacher-centered learning is changing to include informal learning spaces that promote learner autonomy and individualized learning, and competitive knowledge-based testing is being replaced by practical assessment of collaborative projects. Using tools, such as blogs and wikis, learners can construct digital portfolios, where the knowledge and content is emerging from the learner and knowledge and understanding of the process of completing a task takes precedence over the memorization of learning material. Progressive educational technologists even suggest that traditional educational institutions may change more radically, with traditional classrooms vanishing altogether, as information, content, conversations, and learners become distributed via global virtual classrooms (Siemens, 2008).

Designing CALL activities could include a multitude of technologies. When determining what technologies, if any, will better support a given language task, one must take into account a sizeable number of variables, such as learner and instructor accessibility, ease of use of application, platform dependencies, and financial constraints, not to mention the expertise and support that is available for any given technology.

While it may be fairly straightforward to exploit a new technology in a controlled environment (i.e. one's own computer or a classroom lab environment), it is most likely a much more daunting task to design technology-supported language learning tasks across an entire curriculum that includes several departments with possibly diverse educational goals, instructors with varying aptitude and inclination towards adopting technology, and users with different computing devices and technology skills. The implementation process may start with an assessment of the various tools that could assist with the particular language task at hand. A listening task, for example, could be made more learner-accessible via a podcast uploaded to a web service; a writing activity may be reinforced via practice exercises using Hot Potatoes, or submitted and graded online using an LMS; and a speaking activity could be made more authentic by setting up an online conference with a class from another country, or by having learners participate in a discussion using voice postings.

Another important criterion is hardware access. Will learners be completing the task or assignment during class time, in a lab, at home, or perhaps in a self-study area on campus? To make language material more accessible to learners, more institutions are starting to deploy mobile content, but because this medium is still in its infancy, hardware, as well as software, has compatibility issues. A consideration to add to this is the "IT gulf" that can exist between teachers who are technically inclined and those who are less so (Ruthven-Stuart, 2003), resulting in technology being adopted by only a small minority of teachers. One way to combat these issues is to control the hardware environment. More institutions or departments are participating in hardware loan arrangements where all students are given a laptop, a media player, or tablet device, or, as a less expensive option, purchasing classroom sets of mobile devices, such as the iPod Touch or iPad.

Finally, there is the problem of how to distribute the learning content. As most academic environments typically have some type of network access, web-based distribution is the norm. While this is generally not problematic when using traditional Windows or Macintosh devices, compatibility challenges often surface when developing or distributing web-based content for the new wave of operating systems such as Apple's iOS, Google's Android, or Microsoft's Windows Mobile. Successful CALL usage depends on viewing the variables in the technology and the environment, and providing access to hardware and content in a way that caters to this diversity.

Conclusions

Within the framework of four general categories, this chapter has given examples of computer-based technologies that have the potential to enhance and assist language learning. Given such a vast array of websites, software, and hardware, it becomes a major challenge for educators and institutions to get familiar enough with all the varieties of any given technology, such that an informed decision can be made about which technology, if any, should be used. These decisions need to be taken with great care, because they impact a great many people. Business administrators may be swayed by the glossy presentations of slick sales personnel, whereas teachers and students will want to have actual experience of using a technology before they commit to it. If an institution has made significant financial investment in a technology, the business managers will expect it to be used, and used to demonstrable effect, which applies further pressure on the teaching staff. This could be one reason why "free" websites and open source software have become so popular. They provide a way for teachers to try out technology with less financial commitment.

Once a successful methodology for a technology has been established, it encourages others to experiment and get involved. In this way, the grass-roots introduction of technology may well prove more effective in the long term than technology introduced top-down by management decree. Once a technology is introduced it may require extra staff, or new responsibilities for current staff, in order to maintain the technology, and support teachers who wish to use it. Successful incorporation of technology by the majority of teachers requires active support from the administration, technical support from computer staff, and ongoing training for the teachers (Ruthven-Stuart, 2006). To this end, it looks likely that the role of the educational technologist who has a wide knowledge not only of the technologies, but also of the issues involved in integrating these technologies into different educational contexts, will be more and more in demand.

9   Diversity in research and practice

Glenn Stockwell

Introduction

It is well established that research regarding the practical usage of technology in the language classroom is a central element of the field of computer-assisted language learning (CALL), with the primary aim of such research being to build upon our knowledge of how these technologies may best be used to enhance the language learning process. Those who are involved in using CALL, however, are often faced with a dilemma; on the one hand, there is a need to maintain practical solutions to problems they face in their daily teaching and learning environments, and on the other hand, there is pressure to publish research to satisfy institutional requirements. These two – often conflicting – perspectives mean that it is natural that there will be a great deal of variation in the way that both research and practice are undertaken, depending on the motivation behind undertaking them individually or in combination.

There has been a good deal of discussion about both research and practice in CALL, some focusing more on research (e.g. Egbert and Petrie, 2005; Felix, 2008), and others including a focus on practice (e.g. Egbert and Hanson-Smith, 1999; Beatty, 2003). While it might be said that research and practice are paramount in any discussion of second language acquisition, when it comes to CALL, there is a third major factor that needs to be taken into consideration – the technology. As Levy (2000) points out, in CALL research "technology always makes a difference; the technology is never transparent or inconsequential" (p. 190). The impact of its presence, however, may be brought to the forefront or placed in the background, depending on how research and practice are planned, designed, executed, evaluated, and disseminated.

This chapter looks at research and practice in CALL, and examines the role of technology in each. It does this by exploring the interdependent nature of the relationship between research, practice, and technology, followed by an examination of research collected from 2001 through to 2010 in order to identify how practice is framed, analyzed, and presented in CALL research over this ten-year period. Three examples demonstrating very different approaches to research, practice, and technology are presented, followed by a discussion of the starting points and outcomes of research in CALL, and how these both affect the research undertaken and classroom practice.

Overview and general issues

Interdependence of research, practice, and technology

How research and practice relate to one another has long been an issue of discussion in CALL. As early as 1997, the European Association for Computer Assisted Language Learning (EUROCALL) adopted the theme of "Where research and practice meet" for their annual conference held in Dublin, and it was at this conference where Garrett (1998) pointedly argued that research in CALL must maintain a close interrelationship with and play a key role in the development of practice in order to ensure the survival of CALL as a discipline.

As was discussed in Chapter 1, research in CALL is diverse in nature, as reflected in Egbert's (2005) description as "studies that take an analytic approach by looking at one or more ... variables [of context, task, tool, language, and people] in any number of ways or studies that look at the system of which these variables are part, at their interactions and complexities and their effects on each other" (p. 5). Practice in CALL is equally diverse, referring to how technology is actually implemented in achieving language learning goals, and includes the tasks and activities that are used, often related to an underlying pedagogical view. Given that practice is "dependent on the individual language-learning environment, the tools that are available ... and the expertise of teachers and learners" (Levy and Stockwell, 2006, p. 178), the complexities are clearly obvious.

The goals of research in CALL are highly varied and, depending on how the research is carried out, we might see situations where practice feeds into research or, alternatively, cases where research feeds back into practice. For instance, where the goal is primarily to investigate a technology or a technique or pedagogy that uses technology, the starting point would generally be some element of the learning environment. In this case, it is the practice in the environment which forms the foundation of the research. In contrast, when the goal is to replicate or refine previous work described in the literature, the starting point may be questions or hypotheses that have been formulated from previous research, and the learning environment acts as a platform through which this research may be conducted. Thus, in the first instance, research is shaped around the learning environment, whereas in the second instance, the research design takes precedence, meaning that the learning environment may be shaped in order to achieve the goals of the research. It is of course possible for a single study to exhibit qualities of both, and a study that examines a new technology in a learning environment may well start with questions that have been based on previous research, just as a replication study may be conducted within an intact learning environment with a view to better understand practice. It should be kept in mind that the role of technology in any kind of research will depend very much on what was being examined and for what reason. Technology is obviously present in all CALL research but whether it is the focus of the research or rather a means of facilitating the research is highly dependent upon the objectives of the research. When considering these factors, it is possible to see the complexity of the interplay that exists between research, practice, and technology. Exactly what effect each of these factors has on the others, however, requires a deeper investigation of the CALL research, as has been done in the following section.

Research and practice in CALL

Investigations into the nature of research in CALL are not new, and periodically researchers have stopped to take stock of where the field is, where it has been, and where it is heading. These have considered aspects such as research paradigms (Chapelle, 1997), the scope, goals, and methods of research (Levy, 2000), criteria for effective research (Huh and Hu, 2005), the technologies used for teaching language skills and areas (Stockwell, 2007a), and so forth. A few investigations have been rather critical of some of the research conducted in CALL, such as Hubbard (2005) who, among other things, argues that it is not uncommon for insufficient information to be collected about subjects, and Felix (2008), who points out that there is an element of CALL research which is poorly conceived and conducted. In saying, this, however, the majority of research in CALL is approached in a systematic manner, and has contributed to our understanding of both the processes and the outcomes of learning a language through technology. CALL research is dependent upon the technology that is selected for investigation, the way in which the technology is used, and the research design which is implemented. The affordances of technology can give us insights into learning processes in ways not possible pre-CALL (e.g. see Blake, 2000) and, as Garrett (1998, p. 8) suggests, CALL technology can not only "inform language learning and teaching but [also] actively shape it." For this to happen, however, we must be keenly aware of how CALL research is conducted in order to validate the findings.

In order to get a clearer idea of the way in which research is framed and carried out in CALL, a sample of articles in the CALL literature were examined and categorized. The sample included all articles (excepting software reviews, editorials, and commentaries) from 2001 through 2010 in four major English language CALL journals, *CALICO Journal, Computer Assisted Language Learning, Language Learning and Technology*, and *ReCALL*, coming to a total of 808 articles. These journals were selected as they focus specifically on computer-assisted language learning and because they have all been published for over ten years, hence were thought to provide the most consistent representation of CALL over this period. The aim was not to make definitive conclusions about research and practice in CALL, but rather to get a broad perspective of the nature of CALL research as seen through trends in the literature.

Table 9.1 provides an overview of the most commonly encountered types of research in the CALL literature according to this investigation. The descriptions of the research approaches were developed formatively during examination of the literature, and as such concrete counts were not recorded, but approximate figures were maintained. It should be pointed out that the research approaches in Table 9.1 do not cover all possibilities, and one notable omission from this table is that of technologies that were specifically designed for language learning purposes, such as research into commercial courseware. The reason for this omission is that, from the corpus of research that was investigated, this type of research has appeared with lower frequency in recent years, which is likely to be a reflection of a recent trend to use technologies that learners either already have access to and/or experience with outside the language learning environment rather than introducing new commercially available software. There are obviously cost reasons for using something that is already established elsewhere in the institution, that learners have already purchased themselves, or that can be used without cost, and while there are still examples of institutions purchasing commercial software for specific learning purposes, these are becoming less common, at least as far as the CALL literature is concerned. There is also a small amount of software designed for language learning which is made freely available to language teachers such as BETSY (e.g. Coniam, 2009) and FlashMeeting (Hopkins, 2010), but again, these do not appear frequently in the literature.

It should also be noted that the research approaches are not necessarily discrete or mutually exclusive, and in some cases studies contained elements that were representative of two or more approaches. In saying this, however, Table 9.1 gives a general overview of the kind of research that is being undertaken in CALL, which may be useful to get a broad picture of what the field is about. The first four approaches focus quite specifically on the interrelationship between technologies and practice, while the final three approaches are more concerned with the interplay between research and practice in CALL. Research, practice, and technology are of course present in each of the approaches, but they take on a more or less central role depending on the research approach being adopted.

In the first approach – research that investigates the use of a new or existing generic technology for its applicability to language learning – the technology serves as the starting point for the research. The technology used is described

Table 9.1 *Approaches to research in CALL*

Research approach	Examples
Investigate the use of a generic technology for its applicability to language learning	Brett, 2004; Rosell-Aguilar, 2007b; Sha, 2009; Peterson, 2010a
Describe the characteristics of a generic technology in a given language learning environment	Stockwell and Harrington, 2003; Wang, 2004; Li and Erben, 2007; Smith and Sauro, 2009
Describe the development and/or use of a technology created by the researcher or their institution individually or collaboratively	Corda and Jager, 2004; Hampel and Hauck, 2004; Lee *et al.*, 2009; Baturay *et al.*, 2010
Identify a problem in practice and find a solution using technology	Torlavić and Deugo, 2004
Identify a gap in research and build upon previous research	Yoshii and Flaitz, 2002; Lai and Zhao, 2006; Yoshii, 2006; Stockwell, 2010
Provide a meta-analysis of previous research	Levy, 2000; Felix, 2005a; Hubbard, 2005; Stockwell, 2007a
Discuss a concept, theory, or pedagogy related to CALL	Felix, 2002; Doughty and Long, 2003; Chapelle, 2005; Warschauer, 2005; Levy, 2007

as being "generic" as its original purpose was not for language learning purposes, but rather for use by either the larger community in general or other more specific non-language learning purposes. It is a technology which is new in its use within CALL, however, and in this sense is close to what Levy and Stockwell (2006) term as "emergent CALL," in that it is still not considered as being in the mainstream. As technologies are rarely classified as being "new" for any significant period of time, research of this nature is generally very time-sensitive, and what was considered as a new technology at one point will either move into the mainstream or essentially disappear from significant use in CALL contexts. Due to the fact that there is generally very little previous research into the use of the technology for language learning purposes, descriptions will generally consist of a detailed overview of what the technology is and how it may be used, and in some cases may also include a description of its actual usage. Examples of this include Peterson's (2010a) overview of Second Life, Rosell-Aguilar's (2007b) description of podcasting, and Brett's (2004) account of the speech synthesis and analysis software, PRAAT. In Peterson's study, there is a description of the actual use of the technology in order to investigate how learners interacted using this new medium, while Rosell-Aguilar and Brett provide a detailed overview of the technologies without including examples of actual usage. The focus of this kind of research remains very heavily on the actual technology itself, and discussion of its potential for future use in language learning often remains at a rather hypothetical level.

The next research approach looks at the characteristics of new or existing technologies in a given language learning environment. It differs from the first approach in that while the focus still remains on the technology to an extent, it moves beyond the hypothetical level that makes up much of the research in the previous category to focus rather on actual usage in language learning environments. The technology may still be emergent, but is more likely to be what Levy and Stockwell (2006) describe as "established" in that it is already in use in CALL, although how widely it is accepted or used will depend very much on the technology. The research is "more concerned with *what is* rather than *what might be* technologically" (Levy and Stockwell, 2006, p. 246), and the types of technologies that appear here include a variety of generic technologies that were already well established and used both in CALL and in the wider community at the time of publication. Examples might range from commonly used technologies such as email (e.g. Stockwell and Harrington, 2003) and word-processors (Rimrott and Heift, 2005), through to generic technologies that were gaining in popularity at the time of writing, such as instant messenger (Li and Erben, 2007) or NetMeeting (Wang, 2004). Rather than considering the technology from a general language learning perspective, studies of this nature generally embed the technology within a given language learning context and examine the learning process and/or outcomes.

The third approach investigates the development of what Levy (2000) refers to as new CALL artifacts, which are, as the name suggests, the software or hardware that are developed for language learning purposes. These artifacts may be developed primarily by the researcher(s) individually (e.g. Lee *et al.*, 2009), at an institutional level (e.g. Hampel and Hauck, 2004), or even at a cross-institutional level (e.g. Corda and Jager, 2004). Such artifacts vary greatly in their functionality and complexity, and in the majority of cases are designed for specific learning environments. Some artifacts can be very sophisticated – such as the ICALL system developed by Tokuda and Chen (2004), which automatically diagnoses learner translations and provides feedback based on their errors – or, in contrast, we may see artifacts that are created through existing authoring software, such as Hot Potatoes (e.g. Allum, 2004), where the basic template is already in place, but the content is completely created by the teacher. Research of this type may remain at a relatively hypothetical level (i.e. describe what is possible) or it may also provide examples of the artifact in actual practice with learners. In the majority of cases, however, the focus tends to remain on the technology itself in terms of its effectiveness.

The following research approach is concerned with identifying a problem in practice and finding a solution using technology. It is different from the earlier approaches in that this type of research does not start with a particular technology, but rather the choice of technology is made after identifying a specific learning goal or lack within a given learning environment, and matching this with the affordances that a technology provides. This approach is in line with what Colpaert (2006) refers to as a *pedagogy-based approach*, where design of a CALL environment begins from a "detailed specification of what is needed for language-teaching and learning purposes in a specific context" (p. 479). As Colpaert alludes to, this type of approach appears in the literature with surprisingly little frequency in favor of studies that focus on a pre-determined technology accompanied by a rationale to justify the usage and/or development of this technology. The problem with this research approach is the difficulty in viewing a learning context without some idea in advance of the technologies that are available at the institutional or the learner level. If, for instance, an institution has already incorporated an LMS such as WebCT, adopting or creating new technologies can be very risky, both in terms of institutional support and the potential load that learning a new system may place on learners (see Levy and Stockwell, 2006, for a discussion of integration of CALL). Similarly, deciding to use technologies already owned by learners such as mobile phones, for example, without being aware of the percentage of learners who possess them, has the potential to isolate those who do not, unless it is possible to provide phones for all learners as necessary. It is not surprising, then, that the example study given in Table 9.1 by Torlavić and Deugo (2004) does indicate that it was the intention of the authors in advance to create the Adverbial Analyzer artifact that is described in the study. What makes this different from the studies included in the third approach above is that rather than using the technology as the point of departure, they instead indicate the difficulties in teaching adverbs in their context, and describe the development of the system from a second language acquisition (SLA) perspective. Thus, the primary difference between this approach and the one that precedes it is the way in which the study is framed, although the line that defines them is not a clear-cut one.

In the fifth research approach, while of course the technology still plays a largely central role, the main goal is to build upon previous research. Stockwell (2010), for example, describes earlier studies carried out using mobile phones for language learning, but data were insufficient to identify the reasons why learners chose to use desktop computers in preference to mobile phones for completing vocabulary activities. As a result, the research was undertaken to identify possible reasons, specifically the effect of the platform used by learners to carry out the activities on scores and time taken to see if any causative relationship could be found. The study in this case built upon research that was specific to the technology being used, but there are also cases where the background research includes little or minimal reference to research incorporating technology. Also looking at vocabulary acquisition through technology, Yoshii and Flaitz (2002) investigated the effect of annotations on incidental vocabulary retention. Their description of the previous research focuses largely on the learning process itself, and the technology takes a more backseat position in both the previous research and the research design of their study. Despite the different angles of attack that were adopted, the intention of both studies is to achieve wider-reaching goals, which go beyond the specific environment being examined, in order to make a contribution to knowledge of affordances of a technology or language learning processes.

Meta-analyses, the sixth approach, are seen periodically in the research and are conducted by making a survey of certain literature, generally defined by the sources and the dates of the articles being investigated. Researchers will sometimes have concrete criteria in mind in advance of undertaking the meta-analysis, but it is also possible for criteria to be formed continually throughout the analysis (as has been done in the meta-analysis undertaken in this section). The topics and scope of meta-analyses are very broad. Hubbard (2008), for instance, looked at the range of theories used in CALL in a single journal, the *CALICO Journal*, over a twenty-five-year period, to investigate which theories were used in CALL research (see Chapter 1 for more details of this study). Levy (2000) examined research within a single year, 1999, looking at five journals and four books that dealt specifically with CALL, to determine the range and objectives of the research that took place in that year. The scope does generally tend to be somewhat wider than these two studies, as in Felix's (2005a) examination of twenty-two different journals from 2000 through 2004 to investigate how the effectiveness of CALL is portrayed in research, Hubbard's (2005) investigation of four major CALL journals from 2000 to 2003 for characteristics of subjects described in the CALL literature, and Stockwell's (2007a) study of four major CALL journals from 2001 to 2005 to determine the choice of technology for teaching specific language skills and areas. Meta-analyses can serve to either identify streams of research that can be followed by others (e.g. Levy, 2000), or to point out areas that provoke researchers to think about how their research is conducted (e.g. Felix, 2005b). In this sense, they have a more obvious relationship with research, but there are analyses that can also relate to improving practice in terms of being a benchmark of our current understanding of work done in the field.

The final approach includes discussions that are not about nor specific to a particular technology, but rather about concepts such as culture (Levy, 2007); research paradigms (Chapelle, 1997); theories such as constructivism (Felix, 2002); interactionism (Harrington and Levy, 2001; Chapelle, 2005), or socioculturalism (Warschauer, 2005); or even pedagogical approaches, such as Doughty and Long's (2003) overview of methodological principles and pedagogical procedures for optimizing a distance learning environment. Discussions in this approach will generally not include empirical data, but there are some exceptions where the discussion is accompanied by first-hand examples of actual usage (e.g. Levy and Kennedy, 2004). The general purpose of this approach to research is to make readers aware of the concept being discussed in order to improve research or practice in the field.

Looking at these research approaches, it is evident that the term "diversity" is directly relevant to research and practice in CALL in many regards. There was a good deal of variation in the frequencies of each of the approaches in the literature, however, with technology-centered approaches outweighing more research-centered ones. A large proportion of research described the characteristics of generic technologies, and while these technologies varied considerably, synchronous computer-mediated communication (CMC) technologies including chat, audio-, and video-conferencing were very common. Other approaches that featured heavily in the literature were the development and/ or use of a technology and the investigation of the use of a generic technology for its applicability to language learning. As pointed out above, research that identified problems in practice was very rare and, in many cases, descriptions appeared to justify use of a technology that had already been selected. Research that discussed concepts, theories, or pedagogies related to CALL appeared periodically in the literature, as did studies that identified gaps in research. Meta-analyses were generally reserved for more "experienced" researchers, and those who conducted one meta-analysis sometimes followed this up with other meta-analyses on a similar or different theme at a later date.

One trend that was evident in research over the ten-year period is a slow decline in studies about technologies that have been developed by the researcher or institution in favor of generic technologies. It is not clear whether this is a reflection of the lack of time and/or expertise to develop materials that would meet learner expectations, or of a greater interest in emerging generic technologies, but it is a trend that needs following more closely over the next few years. Another tendency that could be seen in the literature is a marked increase in the number of studies that investigate CMC technologies. This is probably not surprising given the increased accessibility to faster Internet services and improved functionality, making it possible to carry out interactions not only through text but also through audio and video, but it is perhaps also related to the fact that these technologies are readily available and studies can be carried out with little extra cost or time. There has also been an increase in the number of studies that include empirical data, where studies that included data collection and analysis comprised less than half the total articles in the early 2000s, these increased to around three-quarters of the total articles published in the journals over the past three years. This might be considered an indication of the increased expectations on researchers in CALL to examine their individual learning contexts rather than simply describing the possibilities of the technology. Care should be taken, however, not to fall into the trap of undertaking only outcomes-based CALL research (see Burston, 2003; Chapelle, 2010), which attempts to justify the existence of using technology for language teaching.

Rather, there is a need to explore the complexities involved in the interplay between research, practice, and technology, and to link this to further research and development in the future.

Examples

Three examples of studies from the CALL literature are described here in order to get an idea of the different ways in which research and practice can be approached. In the first example, Rosell-Aguilar (2007b) starts with a technology as the point of departure, and then describes how practice can be undertaken based on research of the technology. In the second example, Baturay *et al.* (2010) describe an online system they developed for learning grammar and its use in classroom practice, while in the final example, Yoshii (2006) examines existing research into vocabulary acquisition and then carries out his own study built on an area that he identified through this background research. Although each of these three examples involves research, practice, and technology, it is very clear that the centrality of each varies quite considerably, and this is relevant to both the execution of the study and to the outcomes. Each example is broken down into four sections; the purpose of the study, a brief overview of the study, a discussion of the interplay between research, practice, and the technology, and finally the conclusions.

Example 1: investigating applicability of a new technology

Purpose of the study This is a study of the use of podcasting for second language learning by Rosell-Aguilar (2007b). At the time of writing, podcasting was not a new technology, and had reached the mainstream for non-learning purposes from late 2004, initially for downloading radio programs (Hammersley, 2004). There had been a small number of instances of research into podcasting in the CALL literature, but as these remained rather limited in scope, this study aimed to "provide a taxonomy of podcast resources, review materials in the light of second language acquisition theories, argue for better design, and outline directions for future research" (Rosell-Aguilar, 2007b, p. 471).

Overview of the study The study begins with an overview of what podcasting is and a description of the origins of the term and how podcasts can be accessed. While there had already been a few studies incorporating podcasting, Rosell-Aguilar goes into quite a lot of detail into the possible applications of podcasting for second language learning, and describes a taxonomy of how podcasting may be used in language learning, divided up into the development of podcasting materials at an individual level or the use of existing resources.

This is followed by a lengthy discussion of podcasting and theories of learning, along with an overview of the potential advantages, challenges, and uses of podcasting in language learning. The study continues with a review of the currently available resources, and points out key issues such as design and pedagogy, as well as two examples of best practice. The study concludes with a discussion of the importance of establishing design principles and further research on podcasting in the future.

Research, practice, and technology The point of departure for the study is the investigation of the applicability of podcasting for language learning, so it is not surprising that the technology remains central throughout the paper. There are no empirical data collected in the study, and research revolves around work that has previously been carried out into podcasting and theories of language learning that may be applicable to learning through podcasting. While the study does not include first-hand examples of practice, Rosell-Aguilar still maintains a strong emphasis on practice through giving examples of resources that are available and specific advice regarding how podcasting may be used to facilitate second language acquisition.

Conclusions The conclusion is geared towards both practice and research. From a practice perspective, Rosell-Aguilar points out the importance of designing tasks and materials that follow second language acquisition theories, and gives concrete suggestions for both of these. From a research perspective, several specific questions are asked with a view to improving pedagogical design.

Example 2: describing the development and use of a technology

Purpose of the study This example outlines a web-based, multimedia-annotated grammar learning system called WEBGRAM, developed by the researchers as a supplement to in-class activities. Baturay *et al.* (2010) provide a detailed description of the functionality of the system and then describe how it was used with learners, focusing on learner participation and on how learners felt about using the system in terms of satisfaction, content, usability, practicality, and effectiveness.

Overview of the study The study is introduced with a general overview of the functions of technology in the language learning classroom followed by a review of recent research into computer-based grammar teaching. A short description is given of the WEBGRAM system, followed by the research questions, which seek to identify learner perceptions of the system. Details are then given of the participants in the study and the methods of data collection, which in this case are a checklist and an attention and satisfaction survey. Baturay *et al*. describe how the system was used with regard to other teaching materials, and give a brief outline of the activities that the system provided, including a number of screenshots. This is followed by the results of the checklist and survey, a discussion of the results in terms of the research questions and other related research, and lastly, the conclusion.

Research, practice, and technology The primary focus of the paper is the WEBGRAM system, which was developed by the authors, and the study revolves around evaluating this technology. Practice is defined as how the learners viewed the system as a learning tool rather than how they used it or any specific benefits that were achieved by learners beyond their own perceptions. To this end, the research is in essence an evaluation of the technology with regard to learner satisfaction.

Conclusions Given that the purpose of the study is to evaluate the WEBGRAM system, the conclusions are very much limited to what could be inferred from the checklist and survey data. Some general comments are given regarding the importance of design in integrating technology into the curriculum, but there are no specific suggestions for practice or research based on the outcomes of the study.

Example 3: identifying a gap in research

Purpose of the study This study examines the effectiveness of first language (L1) and second language (L2) glosses on incidental vocabulary learning. It builds upon previous CALL and non-CALL research into the use of glosses from which Yoshii (2006) formulates research questions regarding whether the choice of language of the glosses or the modes used in the glosses will have an impact on the learning process. The study incorporates a pre-test, a post-test, and a delayed post-test, which are carried out on 195 learners at two universities, and statistical measures are applied to investigate the effect of the variables described.

Overview of the study The study begins with a review of literature into L1 and L2 glosses. While Yoshii does not indicate whether this research comes from CALL or non-CALL contexts, an examination of the references shows that sources from both contexts are included in this discussion. This is followed by an overview of the effects of multimedia glosses in order to identify specifically the characteristics of these glosses and their effects on retention. The discussion is also not limited only to CALL contexts, and again non-CALL examples are cited by Yoshii, but here they are related to similar studies conducted using technology. Yoshii then goes on to describe a model of how words are represented in L2 learners' knowledge, and this model forms the foundation for the research questions. The study includes a detailed overview of the procedure, instruments, and data analysis methods used in the study, as well as basic information regarding the participants. The results are broken down according to the pre-test and the two post-tests, which are further divided into the tests that were administered to the learners. The discussion largely follows the research questions, outlining how the results relate to the questions, and possible reasons for phenomena that were revealed in the results. The study then concludes with a brief summary and a number of implications for teaching and research.

Research, practice, and technology While technology most certainly maintains an important presence in the study, it could be argued that this presence is largely an unseen one. Almost no information is given about the technology that was used beyond being a "reading program on the Internet" (Yoshii, 2006, p. 89), which is indicative of Yoshii's intention to focus on the research into glosses. Practice is also given a relatively minor role in the study, with little being mentioned of the language learning environment apart from the fact that the subjects were studying English at university level. Thus, while the purpose of the research is to further our knowledge of glosses in order to improve practice, this is for the most part implicit and up to readers to infer for themselves.

Conclusions The conclusion continues the focus on research that has been maintained throughout the paper. Implications for both research and practice are included, however, and Yoshii provides a list of suggestions for further research as well as some tentative suggestions for practice based on the results of the study.

Implications

Selecting a starting point for research

Each of the three studies listed above has a very different point of departure. In the first study, the starting point is clearly the technology with a view to showing how it can be used in language teaching and learning. Rosell-Aguilar (2007b) argues that the technology is applicable to language learning with regard to its affordances, available resources that may be used in language teaching, and theories of language learning. The starting point of the second study by Baturay *et al.* (2010) is also a technology, but in this case it is a technology that has been developed by the authors themselves, and as a result the authors' aim appears to be to show that the technology is appropriate for language learning and that it was viewed positively by the learners. The final study has research questions as its starting point, where Yoshii (2006) identifies an area of inquiry from the literature and seeks to investigate this in a thorough and methodical manner. These three very different starting points – a generic technology, a self-developed technology, and research questions – have very much dictated the way in which the study was framed and presented. The reasons behind these different starting points are, however, considerably more difficult to determine.

Without being familiar with each of the researchers who carried out these studies it is impossible to tell what their individual motivations might have been. It may be possible, however, to consider some of the possible reasons for carrying out research in CALL and the factors that may contribute to the types of research that appear in the CALL literature. Just as learners who use CALL are varied in their backgrounds, training, and experience with technology, motivation, goals, and their individual personalities, we could say that the same applies to those who carry out research into CALL. Teachers who have previously learned through CALL as a student will have the benefit of seeing it through the learners' eyes (Kolaitis *et al.*, 2006), just as formal training in CALL can give teachers a wider perspective and grounding that will likely have a large effect on how CALL materials are designed and/or implemented (see Hubbard and Levy, 2006, for details on teaching education in CALL). Similarly, attempting to learn how to implement CALL without sufficient support can result in teachers using very simple materials or even opting to not use it at all (Stockwell, 2009). Of course, experience as a researcher is another essential factor, and this will have an effect on how research is approached. A background in research into SLA, for example, might lead to a stronger focus on the learning process rather than the technology, which again will affect both what is researched and how the research is conducted.

The motivation for using CALL in the first place will also greatly affect the research approach. There will likely be a difference between a teacher who wants to try technology out of interest, a teacher who identifies a learning need in their given learning context and decides to adopt technology to fill this need, and a teacher who is forced to use technology because of institutional pressures. Goals with technology may be very small, such as using authoring software like Hot Potatoes to create quizzes in a single class, or they may be somewhat grander, such as creating a system that will be used by several institutions by learners of different languages. As with any endeavor, the individual personality of the teacher will also impact what is researched and how it is undertaken, even if all other factors are more or less equal. Someone with a desire to try new things may be more adventurous in the technologies they select, whereas someone who is more conservative may choose to stick with something more mainstream. Similarly, the ability to view an environment holistically or discretely will likely affect not only how technologies are implemented, but also how the research methodology is designed.

An important underlying factor behind CALL research is the environment in which the learning takes place. There will be differences in the technologies that are appropriate for use in, for instance, a face-to-face and a distance environment (see Chapter 5). Even within the same face-to-face environment, other differences will emerge dependent upon the technologies that are available, both at an institutional and individual level. Approaches to undertaking research may also vary depending on whether there are pressures to research, either self-imposed or external, and the expected outlets for publication if research is to be published. More "prestigious" journals will generally require a more rigid research framework to be put in place, which in turn can directly affect what happens in the language learning environment. It becomes evident, then, that it is all of these factors – personal, environmental, and institutional – which come together to guide the way in which CALL practitioners make decisions about how to undertake research.

Diverse outcomes of research

If the starting points of the research are different, then it follows naturally that the outcomes of the research will also be very different. If the goal of research is to describe a new technology for use in language learning, then the outcomes of such research might be, as was the case with Rosell-Aguilar (2007b), a list of suggestions of how this technology might be used in teaching, and perhaps also thoughts for research for others who are considering using the technology in the future. Where the starting point is to see how a self-designed artifact such as the WEBGRAM system created by Baturay *et al.* (2010) is viewed by learners, the outcomes may be more localized. While Baturay and her colleagues provide design principles for those who may plan to develop similar systems, a secondary outcome of this type of research might be to show that a project was successful, which would be of particular importance if there are financial stakeholders associated with it. Finally, when the point of departure is to investigate a particular aspect based on research, the outcomes will, as Yoshii (2006) proposes, suggest how the results fit in with previous research and what further research is still required. Research of this kind has the potential to inform further research, not only in CALL but potentially in other aspects as well. Thus, the outcomes of the research will be determined by the starting point of the research in terms of the applicability to practice and further research, and how much these results can be of use to a wider audience.

This brings us to a rather pointed comment by Pica, which is of some relevance to the CALL community as well, when she suggests that "many teachers believe that research on L2 learning has little to say to their everyday class-room needs and decisions" (1994, p. 49). It is not difficult to see how CALL practitioners may also feel that research on CALL has little to say to their everyday classroom needs and decisions, in particular when it describes a par-ticular technology that cannot readily be obtained or a teaching approach that does not suit the goals or the environment they are teaching in. Without being critical of the study by Baturay *et al.* (2010), it is all too easy for outcomes from research to have a very limited audience to whom it can be useful, and this is a trend that is often seen in research surrounding self-developed arti-facts. This problem can be alleviated somewhat by taking the time to include details of how the implications can be of relevance to others outside the scope of the specific environment being described when disseminating the research. As the conductor of the research, the researcher is in the best position to exam-ine all aspects of the environment along with any limitations and shortcomings that may have arisen. Armed with this knowledge, the researcher has the ability to frame the outcomes of the study such that it can be of relevance for others undertaking similar work, even in the case of self-developed artifacts. Bearing in mind the difference between research for evaluative purposes (i.e. for in-house justification or improvement) compared with research for dissemination purposes (i.e. for the wider CALL community), can make it easier to frame the results in a way that can be of benefit for both research and practice at a local and wider level.

Considering research outcomes is of course not only limited to self-devel-oped artifacts, but is also relevant to other approaches to research as well. When examining a generic technology for its applicability for language learning, moving beyond the hypothetical to the actual can provide a valuable founda-tion for others who are also investigating the possibilities of using this technol-ogy. While of course the suggestions provided by Rosell-Aguilar (2007b) on podcasting are very useful and have the potential to shape practice and further research, conclusions based on empirical research can give deeper insights into the applicability of a technology and its pedagogical applications. Moreover, well-thought-out suggestions for teaching based on personal experiences can make a difference, not only to future research that is undertaken, but also as a guide to teachers who may decide to use the technology without undertaking formal research on it, thus directly impacting actual practice as well.

Conclusion

Research and practice are two essential and central aspects of the field of CALL, and they interact with one another in ways that can have a great effect on how each is undertaken. They are also constantly shaped by the technology, the environment, and the characteristics of the teachers and the learners, which results in a dynamic and sometimes unpredictable combination. Given these variables, even if a decision is made to research the same technology, there will likely be differences in both the starting points and the outcomes of research as a result of the specific context. Carrying out research and/or practice in the midst of this diversity in a meaningful way requires CALL practitioners to take stock of the implications and effects of each of these factors, and lay out clear goals, while being mindful of the motivations behind these goals.

Whether it starts from a technology, a problem in practice, a research question, or a concept or theory, continued research is necessary in CALL. In undertaking such research, however, it is important to look past the complexities of the immediate context to see what aspects can be of use to other contexts, and to make this clear to consumers of the research. Well-conceived research can bring forth important developments in practice, and being aware of the interplay between research and practice in CALL can lay the foundations for the continued development and refinement of both.

10   Conclusion

Glenn Stockwell

Introduction

The diversity that exists in the field of computer-assisted language learning (CALL) will undoubtedly go beyond what has been described in this book. Indeed, the diversity in the way that each of the chapters has been written, and the varying views of the theme of diversity itself, is a testimony of the dynamic and, in some ways, unpredictable nature of research and practice in CALL. Researchers and practitioners will naturally have different priorities in their perspectives of CALL, and this will have an impact on the outcomes which we see in the literature and on what happens in the classroom. The chapters in this book shed some light on these complexities and, at the same time, demonstrate that careful consideration and examination of the learning context in terms of the objectives, the learners, the content, and the technologies can enrich learning, not only in terms of what knowledge learners can acquire, but also how it is acquired and how learners perceive this process. The immediate relevance of this fact is evident for practice but also serves to act as a guide for areas where further research is needed in CALL. Although technology is often the point of departure for both research and practice, the contextual factors must be kept clearly in mind, and while knowledge of the technologies and their affordances is essential, actual practice within diverse contexts also forms an essential agenda for CALL research.

Levels of diversity

When examining any context in which CALL might be used, it becomes immediately obvious that there is diversity at a range of different levels that go beyond simply what happens within a single class or course. This diversity may be seen at the individual level, the institutional level, or the societal level, each of which come together in a way that impacts how CALL can be implemented and used. Table 10.1 outlines some of the diverse aspects that may fit into each of these different levels.

Table 10.1 *Levels of diversity in CALL*

Level	Aspects of diversity
Individual	Learner background, skills, and goals
	Teacher experience, skills, and teaching styles
	Attitudes towards technology for language learning
	Technological affordances
	Classroom dynamics
Institutional	Educational policy and curriculum
	Institution-wide technology use
	View of teacher training
	Technological and financial support
	Attitudes towards specific needs for language learning
Societal	Availability and costs of technologies
	Technology standards
	Access to relevant information and organizations

The various aspects of diversity that fit into each level are described below. It should be pointed out, however, that the levels do not exist independently of one another, but rather each one both shapes and is shaped by the others to form the complex matrix that is the language learning context. Individuals will necessarily be influenced by the institution where they are studying and the society in which they live. The institution will also be heavily affected by the society within which it is located, but it can also receive quite significant influence from individuals. Society undergoes change as a result of both individuals and indeed even institutions, sometimes at a slow and almost imperceptible pace, and at other times in a relatively short period of time.

Diversity at an individual level

The first level, the individual level, includes the different features of the individual aspects in the immediate teaching and learning environment. As has been pointed out at various points throughout this book (see Chapters 1, 2, and 3), learners engage with technology differently depending on their experiences, skills, preferences, and individual learning and even personal goals (see Colpaert, 2010). Those learners who have used CALL before may hold views – either positive or negative – based on their previous experiences, and this is likely to affect how they view and undertake CALL activities. Learners who are more motivated may well take the initiative and engage in study of their own volition, and may seek extra learning resources using the Internet or even more opportunities for communication using computer-mediated communication (CMC) or social networking sites. In addition to factors inherent to individual learners, differences can also be related to external factors in the classroom, including the interactional dynamics with other learners. This may be seen, for example, in email exchanges (e.g. Stockwell and Levy, 2001) or during collaborative learning around a computer in a face-to-face environment (e.g. Jeon-Ellis *et al.*, 2005), where the other participants in the learning activity may affect not only what is learned, but how it is learned and how the learning process itself is viewed by the learners.

The characteristics of teachers will also have an impact on the context, such as their familiarity with and attitudes towards technology for language learning. There has been evidence to suggest the positive effect of teacher training on CALL use, such as empowering teachers to "take control of their own professional development" (Rickard *et al.*, 2008, p. 215). Teachers can undergo training in a variety of different ways, starting at a department or faculty-wide level (Iskold, 2003), an institution-wide level (Leahy, 2006), or a cross-institutional level (Murray, 1998). Alternatively, teachers may choose to enroll in other formal courses for pre-service and in-service teachers (e.g. Son, 2002; Rilling *et al.*, 2005; Hanson-Smith, 2008), or if access to courses is limited, they may also choose to study about CALL alone (e.g. Kolaitis *et al.*, 2006), although self-study without some kind of support is extremely difficult (Stockwell, 2009). The diversities of the individual technologies is also one aspect that cannot be ignored and, as was explained in Chapter 1, technologies bring with them affordances that affect both the processes and the products of language learning (see Levy, 2002). Consideration of the affordances of individual technologies is essential to order to make the correct choices about which technologies to use to meet not only learners' needs, but also to match teachers' skills and experience.

Diversity at an institutional level

The second level is the institutional level, and it refers to the differences in the context that arise as a result of the institution within which CALL is implemented. It is natural that institutions will have varying opinions regarding how much importance is to be placed on technology based on their educational policies and provision of technical support (see Levy and Stockwell, 2006). Some institutions are very enthusiastic about using technology with a strong view that it enhances the learning environment, and as such may choose to use a standardized learning management system (LMS) such as Blackboard or Moodle at an institution-wide level, or alternatively, they may choose to distribute a certain technology to all staff and students like portable MP3 players (e.g. McCarty, 2005). Aggressive implementation of technology of this kind will generally be accompanied by support at various levels, such as in-house training programs or technical support to deal with problems as they arise. In contrast to these institutions that hold a more proactive view regarding technology, there are others that take a more conservative stance, choosing to introduce only the bare minimum in technical requirements for both staff and students. This may include setting up some kind of computer laboratory or establishing a framework for basic support for staff and students in case of technical difficulties. While the institution may not oppose technology use, it does not actively encourage it either. Institutions may have varied reasons for taking this position, not least of which is the potential for ongoing high costs and insufficient usage to warrant any further outlays (see Cuban, 2001). The two examples here certainly do not represent a dichotomy, and there are likely countless other combinations which would fit somewhere between them, such as where technology is widely used but not standardized or supported with teacher training. The position taken regarding technology use at an institution-wide level will naturally have far-reaching implications for how technology is used for language learning purposes. If a certain technology has been implemented at an institutional level, it can be difficult to go against the policies regarding use of this technology to introduce something different and, in many cases, language teachers find themselves having to make do with what is already in place (e.g. see Möllering, 2000). If no such infrastructure is in place, there may be some advantages in not needing to use pre-determined resources that might not necessarily suit the learning goals, but there can be greater pressure on teachers who are implementing technology in the first place to find sufficient technical and financial support.

The attitudes that the institution have regarding the specific needs for language teaching and learning can also have a significant impact on the technologies that can be used in the language classroom. Administrators may be more willing to purchase a technology if it can be used across the entire curriculum than if it is aimed towards a relatively small proportion of the student population, as is sometimes the case with language programs within a larger curriculum. This will affect not only the amount of financial and technical support that is made available to language teachers, but also the training that may be available to them. While there may be some overlaps, training in technology for generic purposes is not the same as training in CALL technologies, and language learning has particular requirements that many generic technologies – even those for general education – are simply not designed to handle. Thus, it is clear that the institutional level is indeed a complex one, and while administrators most likely attempt to keep an eye on both the individual and societal factors in their views of technology usage, they are often limited by the available financial and human resources.

Diversity at a societal level

The third level, the societal level, considers the context in its widest capacity, the society in which it is situated. There are obvious differences in the availability of technologies, both geographically and socioeconomically. Regional or national differences are often the result of relatively unforeseen factors. For instance, in days gone by – although there still is some relevance today – we could see the National Television System Committee (NTSC) video format used in the US, Korea, and Japan; phase alternating line (PAL) in the UK and Australia; and séquentiel couleur à mémoire (SECAM, known as sequential color memory) in Spain and Russia, to name a few. While there were no doubt very good reasons for each of these video formats being devised and implemented, the final outcome was a range of systems that, in the absence of suitable decoders, made videos region-specific. This meant that if a video was bought in the US, for example, it could not be played in Australia, or the other way around. Another case is the use of short message service (SMS) for texting on mobile phones. In Europe, this has been considered as the standard way of sending messages. However, in Japan, where mobile phones have their own individual email addresses, the concept of SMS itself is not widely known, and many phones do not have the capacity to send or receive SMS messages from people overseas. As a more recent example, social networking sites have been gaining in popularity in many parts of the world, with the major sites in many English-speaking countries including Facebook and MySpace (see Chapter 5). Although these social networks do have a presence in other language areas, there are several sites specific to other regions and language groups, including, for instance, 51.com and RenRen for Chinese speakers, V Kontakte for Russian speakers, Skyrock for French speakers (also popular with English speakers), Mixi for Japanese speakers, and Cyworld for Korean speakers. Other crucial factors that have an impact on technology use at a societal level include accessibility and cost of Internet access, Internet connection speed, and the penetration rate of technologies such as mobile phones, MP3 players, and other portable devices such as laptop or tablet computers.

This regional (or in some cases linguistic) diversity in technologies will have implications for language teaching as well. For instance, research into text-only SMS is of limited relevance to regions where mobile email is used, which often has more advanced functionality than SMS such as emoticons and picture and video attachments. Similarly, introducing Facebook as a social networking site where an alternative is more commonly used could have negative ramifications, such as a lower acceptance rate by learners. In addition, if costs of using the Internet at home are high or if there are download limits, then this will also affect decisions pertaining to use it. Video-conferencing, for example, is very heavy on bandwidth, and excessive usage could result in losing Internet access for the rest of the month or having to pay extra costs. Thus, expectations about what technologies can be used for language learning will depend very much on the societal context within which they are to be used. Seeing how technology is used within an individual society is important to determine how it will ultimately be used for language learning (see Levy, 1997), and familiarity with technologies has the potential to positively impact their use in language learning situations as well.

Another issue is that of socioeconomic diversity. The digital divide has been described as "the troubling gap between those who use computers and the internet and those who do not" (Mehra *et al.*, 2004, p. 782), and while it may of course occur at an individual level (where some learners may find costs of certain technologies too prohibitive), it is also evident at regional and national levels. There are differences in the costs of technologies in different countries and as a result it is feasible to imagine schools in less developed countries that are starved of access to technology compared to schools in more developed countries that have sophisticated equipment that is not used to its maximum potential. In saying this, and as has been raised earlier in the book, having the latest technologies is no guarantee that they will be more effective; innovative and well-thought-out design and use of CALL materials can make up for the advantages of having more sophisticated technologies. In situations where the cost of technology is prohibitive, there is a need to consider ways of removing the financial burden from the learners to avoid an even greater gap appearing between individuals based on their financial situations. A number of other issues relevant to this discussion are also raised in Chapter 6, such as the priorities regarding implementation of open educational resources in developed and developing countries.

The majority of the discussion above regarding diversity at a societal level has revolved around the learners' standpoint, but of course the teacher is also affected by societal aspects as well. Though the issue of the use of technologies within a given society remains equally relevant for teachers, another important factor to bear in mind is how teachers can have access to information regarding CALL implementation and usage. Academic publications can be quite costly, and although there are some journals that are freely available online, the publishers of the majority of the respected journals need to charge subscription costs to survive. Similarly, organizations such as the Computer Assisted Language Instruction Consortium (CALICO) in the US, the European Association for Computer Assisted Language Learning (EUROCALL) in Europe, and the Japan Association for Language Teaching Computer Assisted Language Learning Special Interest Group (JALT CALL SIG) in Japan will generally hold annual conferences that can be attended by both local and international researchers. While they provide an excellent source of information regarding trends in the field and a forum for discussion, they are also limited to those who can attend. There are many regions where a dedicated organization of this type does not exist, and although organizers of conferences such as Globalization and Localization in Computer Assisted Language Learning (GloCALL) and WorldCALL do attempt to hold their conferences in varied locations to access those in lesser developed areas, it is physically not possible to reach all the locations where teachers wishing to use CALL may be. This can lead to paucity in information in regions where this access is too expensive, meaning that even if they have adequate technologies, teachers who wish to use CALL may inadvertently retrace the steps of work that has been previously done. Given, then, that the degree of access to information about CALL has the potential to greatly affect both research and practice, efforts should be made to disseminate information in such a way that it can be made available to as wide an audience as possible. Finding a viable means of achieving this without impacting too heavily upon the financial interests of publishers and other organizations that provide this information, however, will likely prove to be a very difficult task indeed.

Embracing or dealing with diversity?

One of the primary objectives of this book has been to illustrate the diversity that exists in the research and practice in CALL to encourage a better understanding of the issues that impact the implementation of technologies in language learning. As was pointed out in Chapter 1, the view of diversity can be either a positive or a negative one, depending on whether it is seen as a way of providing more options or as a hindrance due to the sheer mass of information that needs to be sifted through to make sense of the field. In a positive sense, we may argue that we should embrace this diversity as a welcome aspect of the field, whereas in the negative sense, this diversity may be seen as something to deal with, a problem that somehow needs to be solved. It is unlikely that many people will hold a completely positive or a completely negative view, and the majority will likely welcome some aspects of diversity but find others difficult to contend with.

When we look at the field of CALL over the past several decades, it becomes immediately obvious that it is far more diverse now than it was in the early years. This would be expected to be quite natural given the huge developments that have happened over this time, and the changes that have appeared in the context in terms of the individual, institutional, and societal levels that are explained above. Early CALL was based on similar types of systems with comparable capabilities, general computers that were used on a stand-alone basis or linked to one another in a closed network. At that time, nearly everything was a new experience to the teachers, the learners, and the institution. Many of the teachers were people who were enthusiastic about technology, and for the most part had more knowledge of the system they were using than the learners did. The institution perhaps had a tempered view of the potential, and usually little pressure was placed on teachers to use the technology, who were basically left to their own devices. The use of technology in society was limited at best, and for the most part non-existent except for an elite few, meaning that students were unlikely to have had very much experience with computers outside of the educational environment. When we look at the current environment, the differences in all of these areas can be quite mind-boggling, where the relatively level playing field of previous times has been replaced by learners who own sophisticated mobile devices, engage in social networking in their spare time, and, in some cases, have a better knowledge of the technologies used around them than their teachers. Institutions apply pressure for results to justify the high costs involved in purchasing and maintaining technology, and technologies of various shapes and forms are an integral part of our everyday lives. The fact that the field of CALL has witnessed these changes in one sense is a testimony to its coming of age, where it does not simply sit on the coattails of other disciplines, but rather has been shaped by changes in our lives that are quite independent of development of theories of second language acquisition or cognitive psychology. This does not mean that CALL will not continue to benefit greatly from research in these fields, but that such research will be applied in different ways depending upon the reality of CALL contexts in this changing world.

Continued diversity in CALL is inevitable. Many of the technologies that are available to us now were not even thought of some twenty years ago, and it is conceivable that technologies that will appear in twenty years from now will be completely different from what we might imagine now. If we have diversity, where we are surrounded by new and different options at one end of the spectrum, then arguably at the other end we might expect to find the concept of normalization. According to Bax (2003), normalization is "the stage when a technology is invisible, hardly even recognised as a technology, taken for granted in everyday life" (p. 23). In an environment where new technologies continue to be developed and diversified, is it feasible that they could become invisible? If normalization were viewed as a static or unchanging state, then the answer to this would be no. However, normalization must be viewed as an ongoing process, which can only be made possible by constant changes in the environment such as making the technology more accessible, providing training, adapting the pedagogy, and strengthening links between CALL and non-CALL aspects of the curriculum (Levy and Stockwell, 2006). It is also important to realize that not all technologies will become normalized, and some technologies that were normalized will cease to be so, depending on further developments in technology. Specialized software for a certain learning purpose such as pronunciation training (e.g. Brett, 2004) is very unlikely to reach a stage where it is normalized in the sense of being invisible or taken for granted, whereas other technologies that are used in our everyday lives, such as email, may be considered as much closer to reaching this state. Other technologies such as videodisks and Hypercard were at one point commonly used in the language classroom, but have all but disappeared now, replaced with more functional and robust ones. This ongoing process of change is one that will likely continue to be representative of CALL, and while there will be technologies that may evolve with the times, we will likely see shifts in research and practice in CALL towards newer technologies and away from many older ones.

Conclusion

Although this chapter forms the conclusion of this book, it should be pointed out first of all that it would be unrealistic to attempt to summarize the potential conclusions and implications that can be made from the explanations and examples that arise throughout this book. There were, however, a number of points raised that are pivotal in enhancing both research and practice in CALL.

- Implementation of CALL is highly dependent upon the intersection of the varied factors that make up the context in which it is used (Chapter 1).
- Being aware of what learners actually do with CALL materials and why, can help to provide training that is relevant to learner needs (Chapter 2; Chapter 4).
- Learner training depends not only on the individual but also on the group (Chapter 3).
- Different technologies bring with them varying affordances that affect what can be learned and how this occurs (Chapter 5, 6, and 7).
- Teachers must continually keep up with developments in technology and how they can facilitate language learning (Chapter 8).
- Research, practice, and technology in CALL are inextricably entwined with one another, and it is difficult to view one without some consideration of the others (Chapter 9).

CALL is a dynamic field that is dependent upon diverse factors both inside and outside of the classroom. Successful research and practice in CALL relies on keeping a willingness to accept diversity in various aspects of the teaching environment, but at the same time remaining wary about the potential dangers that too much diversity can bring, both to teachers and to learners. What must always be kept in mind is that CALL is about providing the optimum environment to maximize language learning opportunities for our learners. CALL is not a result of endeavoring to use the latest technologies, but rather exploring the technological options that are available and choosing what is the most appropriate following a sound pedagogy. In the midst of this diversity, rather than forcing conformation or singularism, adoption of a pluralist standpoint allows us to view contexts from different perspectives and get different insights into the complexities of language learning. The range of technological options will continue to grow, and the decisions regarding which options are the best will depend on an understanding of the context in all of its complexity.

Appendix   List of websites

51.com: www.51.com
Active Worlds: www.activeworlds.com
Adobe Connect Pro: www.adobe.com/products/adobeconnect.html
Adobe Dreamweaver: www.adobe.com/products/dreamweaver
Android: www.android.com
Apple: www.apple.com
aTutor: http://atutor.ca
Audacity: http://audacity.sourceforge.net
Big Blue Button: http://bigbluebutton.org
Blackboard: www.blackboard.com
Captivate: www.adobe.com/products/captivate
Commonwealth of Learning: www.col.org/Pages/default.aspx
Creative Commons: www.creativecommons.org
CVS: www.nongnu.org/cvs
Cyworld: www.cyworld.co.kr
Diigo: www.diigo.com
DimDim: www.dimdim.com
DynEd: www.dyned.com
EdModo: www.edmodo.com
EduBlogs: www.edublogs.org
Eluminate: www.elluminate.com
Ever Quest II: www.everquest2.com
Facebook: www.facebook.com
Fireworks: www.adobe.com/products/fireworks
FLAX: http://flax.nzdl.org/greenstone3/flax
Gimp: www.gimp.org
GIT: http://git-scm.com
Glogster: www.glogster.com
GNU General Public License: www.gnu.org/gnu/gnu.html
Google: www.google.com
Greenstone: www.greenstone.org
Hot Potatoes: http://hotpot.uvic.ca
HyperCam: www.hyperionics.com
iOS: www.apple.com/iphone/ios4
iPad: www.apple.com/ipad
iPaper: www.scribd.com/ipaper

iPhone: www.apple.com/iphone
iPod: www.apple.com/ipod
iPod Touch: www.apple.com/ipodtouch
iTunes: www.apple.com/itunes
Live Meeting: http://office.microsoft.com/en-us/live-meeting
Mahara: http://mahara.org
Microsoft: www.microsoft.com
Mixi: http://mixi.jp
Moodle: http://moodle.org
MovieMaker: www.microsoft.com/windowsxp/using/moviemaker
MySpace: www.myspace.com
Open University Virtual MPhil: http://virtualmphil.open.ac.uk
PRAAT: www.fon.hum.uva.nl/praat
Prezi: http://prezi.com
Qedoc: www.qedoc.org
QuizPort: http://docs.moodle.org/en/QuizPort_module
ReallyEnglish: www.reallyenglish.com
RenRen: www.renren.com
Sakai: http://sakaiproject.org
ScreenCam: www.smartguyz.com
Scribd: www.scribd.com
Second Life: www.secondlife.com
Skyrock: www.skyrock.com
SlideShare: www.slideshare.net
Smart.fm: http://smart.fm/home
SnapzProX: www.ambrosia.com
SoundForge: www.sonycreativesoftware.com/soundforgesoftware
Stanford University Entrepreneurship Corner: http://ecorner.standford.edu
Subversion: http://subversion.tigris.org
The Sims: http://thesims.ea.com
Traveler: www.digitalspace.com/avatars/traveler.html
Twitter: www.twitter.com
Udutu: www.udutu.com
Vegas: www.sonycreativesoftware.com/vegassoftware
V Kontakte: http://vkontakte.ru
VoiceThread: http://voicethread.com
WebCT: www.webct.com
Webex: www.webex.com
Wii: www.nintendo.com/wii
Wikipedia: www.wikipedia.org
Windows Media Player: http://windows.microsoft.com/en-US/windows/products/
windows-media
Windows Mobile: www.microsoft.com/windowsphone/en-us/default.aspx
WiZiQ: www.wiziq.com
Wordle: www.wordle.net
WordPress: http://wordpress.org
Yahoo: www.yahoo.com
YouTube: www.youtube.com
Yugma: www.yugma.com

Glossary

Affordance. When something is made possible. Generally used in CALL to show the facilitating or restrictive effects of a technology for language learning.

App. A self-contained piece of software that does a useful task on a mobile computing device ("app" is an abbreviation of "application").

Asynchronous. Something that happens out of sequence or with a delay. Asynchronous communication refers to communication that does not occur in real time, as in email.

Avatar. A digital representation of a computer user, chosen by a user from a menu of possible representations, often three-dimensional and resembling a human being, but sometimes resembling an animal or an object, that can appear to move about the screen, for example, by walking or flying.

Blog. An online journal or personal website that is updated often, and to which readers can add comments to the articles and posts. "Blog" is a contraction of "web log."

Bottom-up. An approach to listening that focuses on individual sounds and words as a way to build up overall meaning.

Chat. A kind of synchronous communication whereby two or more computer users exchange text messages over a computer network.

Cloud. A collection of sophisticated computing services and massive data storage that is ubiquitously available via the Internet.

Collaboration. The act of working together to achieve a particular goal, as in collaborative learning.

Computer-assisted language learning (CALL). The use of computer-based resources and materials in the learning of additional languages, either through stand-alone computers or via the Internet. CALL also explicitly recognizes that computing resources and pedagogical approaches for their use are closely interwoven.

Computer literacy. Learners' general familiarity with computers and ability to do a wide range of activities on computers, not necessarily related to language learning.

Computer log. A list of students' interactions with a program, typically in the form of a text file.

Courseware. Dedicated CALL software, as opposed to web-based resources.

Creative Commons. A non-profit organization, based in the US, which has developed a set of free public licenses to enable authors to define the basis on which they will share their intellectual property or creative works with others. Creative Commons licenses contrast with copyright.

Digital natives.   Individuals who have grown up using digital technology.

Distance learning.   A way of learning where the students are situated geographically far from the institution where they are studying, so are not able to physically attend classes.

Distributed spaces.   Spaces for communication or collaboration which can be shared by non-co-located partners to progress a project, task, or conversation online.

Flash.   A multimedia platform that is commonly used to add animation and interactivity to web pages.

FLAX.   An open source software tool used to extract and store linguistic and multimedia materials within the Greenstone Digital Library environment.

General technology competence.   *See* computer literacy.

GNU.   A computer operating system similar to Unix that is made up entirely of free software. The name is a recursive acronym for "GNU's Not Unix."

GNU general public license (GPL).   A widely used free software license agreement. Under the agreement any derived products from freely obtained software code can be used or altered, but then must be made publicly available. The term "free" thus relates to open access to, and distribution of, programming code, as opposed to its financial cost.

HTML5.   The next major revision of HTML, the standard for structuring and presenting web content. It allows for easier embedding of video and audio.

Iconic.   Something which takes the form of an icon (e.g. an iconic sign), or which relies on an icon in order to generate meaning (an example of an iconic sign is an image of a waste paper bin, signifying that items dragged across the screen to that image are to be deleted).

Java.   A versatile programming language that is widely used to add interactivity to web pages, and build web applications to run on a server.

JavaScript.   A programming language that is used to add interactivity to web pages. It is a very different language from Java.

Language support.   Resources and systems for facilitating language learning outside the classroom.

Learner autonomy.   The ability to take responsibility for one's own learning.

Learner training.   Specific instruction to facilitate the growth of autonomous learner skills in using technology for language learning.

Learning management system (LMS).   Software platform that supports teaching and learning processes through a variety of communication, file storage, and file management tools.

Media.   The images, audio, video, and other non-text items that are embedded into a web page.

Modality.   The conditions through which the material for the creation of meaning are made available to users. For example, the relationship between any technological feature (e.g. a hyperlink) and a semiotic resource (e.g. the meanings in the pop-up that appears when the hyperlink is clicked) is a relationship of modality.

Moodle.   An open source LMS software platform originally developed in Australia by programmer Martin Dougiamas, but now in use throughout the world.

MP3 player.   A portable device for playing MP3 audio files.

Multimodality.   The co-availability of several modalities. For example, a semiotic resource (e.g. spoken language) may be associated with a single modality (e.g. speech from an audio channel). Equally, a semiotic resource (e.g. written language) may be associated with two different modalities (e.g. user-generated meanings such as chat messages and system-generated ones such as icons or pop-ups).

Negotiation of meaning.   A process where speakers ask questions or give confirmation to reach a clear mutual understanding of one another.

Open educational resources (OER).   The open provision of educational resources and expertise, through information and communication technologies, for consultation, use, and adaptation by a community of users for non-commercial purposes.

Open source software (OSS).   Software that is free to use, download, and modify, as long as changes are made available to the community that uses and develops the software.

Pedagogical training.   Specific instruction for learners that focuses on pedagogical techniques, including those that language instructors normally use.

Podcast.   A series of digital audio or video files that are released periodically and distributed via the Internet to be played back on a computer or media player. "Podcast" is a contraction of "iPod broadcast."

Podcasting.   The recording of online broadcasts that can be saved for playback later, generally using a portable player such as an MP3 player.

Portable document format (PDF).   A file format that allows documents to be laid out, displayed, and printed identically on different operating systems.

Processing.   The mechanism by which sounds or visual representations of language are converted to information.

Recast.   The paraphrasing of an utterance changing certain elements of the original utterance but maintaining the same central meaning.

Role-playing game.   A game where learners assume certain roles to interact with one another and the environment they are in. They often refer to fantasy and other non-realistic-type games.

SCORM.   A collection of standards for defining web-based eLearning activities. SCORM stands for "sharable content object reference model."

Server.   A computer connected to a computer network for the purposes of distributing data to other computers on the network.

Shadowing.   A technique used in language learning where learners simply listen to a speaker or recorded text and simply follow along, trying to say exactly the same thing as the speaker continues.

Simulation game.   A game where learners assume certain roles to interact with one another, imitating a situation that may be found in real life.

Smart phone.   A mobile phone that has many features of a PC, such as the ability to display web pages, play videos, and play interactive games.

Social networking.   The act of interacting with others to exchange information. In recent years, this is often conducted online through social networking sites.

Socio-affective.   Relates to social interaction and is designed to appeal to affect, rather than to cognition. For example, socio-affective discourse includes greetings, apologies, compliments, offers of support, expressions of empathy, etc.

Socio-constructivist.   Reflects a view of learning as a social process, in which the main ways of building up knowledge and meaning is through learners collaborating and negotiating with each other as they carry out a task.

Strategy training.   Specific instruction for learners that focuses on how to approach resources in order to get the most benefit from them.

Synchronous.   Something that happens at the same time with no delay. Synchronous communication refers to communication that occurs at the same time, like chat.

Tandem learning.   Learning that occurs when the participants mutually benefit from language exchange with one another.

Tandem partner.   A participant in a tandem learning project. Tandem learning involves two learners with different native languages. The learning is a formal or an informal arrangement, in which partner A teaches their native language to partner B, who in return teaches their native language to partner A.

Teacher education.   The provision of training for teachers to give them instruction that is of assistance to their professional development.

Technical training.   Specific instruction for learners that focuses on technical skills useful for language learning with computers.

Telepresence.   Ways in which users of computer-assisted communication may signal to non-co-located partners that they are present online, and whether they are fully attending to the task or are in a lesser attentional state (for example, temporarily away from the computer).

Top-down.   An approach to listening that focuses on overall meaning first, then breaks the content down into smaller and smaller sections, eventually leading to individual words and sounds.

Tracker.   A device used to capture students' actions while using software.

User-extendable.   That which may be added to by the user, through coding (as in user-extendable databases) or through selecting and combining items (for example, in virtual environments) in order to create new limits to these environments or new objects within them.

Video clip.   A short video, especially one that is an excerpt from a longer video.

Virtual environment.   An environment that is computer simulated to feel like a real environment.

Washback effect.   The influence that a test or other factor has on instruction and learning.

Web 2.0.   Technologies that focus on Internet-based activities such as media sharing, media manipulation, online gaming and virtual worlds, blogging, social bookmarking, and syndication for the purposes of social networking, collaboration, and production of user-generated content.

Wiki.   Software that allows people to collaborate on the creation of the pages of a website using only their browser.

References

Abelson, H. (2008). The creation of OpenCourseWare at MIT. *Journal of Science Education and Technology*, **17**(2), 164–174.

Abrams, Z. I. (2003a). Flaming in CMC: Prometheus' fire or Inferno's? *CALICO Journal*, **20**(2), 245–260.

(2003b). The effect of synchronous and asynchronous CMC on oral performance in German. *Modern Language Journal*, **87**(2), 157–167.

(2008). Sociopragmatic features of learner-to-learner computer-mediated communication. *CALICO Journal*, **26**(1), 1–27.

Alford, D. and Pachler, N. (2007). *Language, Autonomy and the New Learning Environments*. Frankfurt am Main, Germany: Peter Lang.

Allen, I. E., Seaman, J., and Garrett, R. (2007). *Blending In: the Extent and Promise of Blended Learning in the United States*. Needham, MA: Sloan Consortium.

Allum, P. (2004). Evaluation of CALL: initial vocabulary learning. *ReCALL*, **16**(2), 488–501.

Alm, A. (2006). CALL for autonomy, competence and relatedness: motivating language learning environments in Web 2.0. *The JALT CALL Journal*, **3**(2), 29–38.

Appel, C. and Gilabert, R (2002). Motivation and task performance in a task-based web-based tandem project. *ReCALL*, **14**(1), 16–31.

Atkins, D. E., Brown, J. S., and Hammond, A.L. (2007). *A Review of the Open Educational Resources (OER) Movement: Achievements, Challenges, and New Opportunities*. Report to the William and Flora Hewlett Foundation. Retrieved June 15, 2010, from: www.hewlett.org/library.

Baraniuk, R. G. and Burrus, C.S. (2008). Viewpoint: global warming toward open educational resources. *Communications of the ACM*, **51**(9), 30–32.

Barrette, C. (2001). Students preparedness and training for CALL. *CALICO Journal*, **19**(1), 5–36.

Baturay, M. H., Dalaglu, A., and Yildirim, S. (2010). Language practice with multimedia supported web-based grammar revision material. *ReCALL*, **22**(3), 313–331.

Bax, S. (2003). CALL – past, present and future. *System*, **31**, 13–28.

Beatty, K. (2003). *Teaching and Researching Computer-assisted Language Learning*. Harlow, UK: Longman.

Beller-Kenner, S. (1999). CALL issues: introducing students to computers. In J. Egbert and E. Hanson-Smith (eds.), *CALL Environments: Research, Practice, and Critical Issues* (pp. 362–385). Alexandria, VA: TESOL.

Belz, J. (2001). Institutional and individual dimensions of transatlantic group work in network-based language teaching. *ReCALL*, **13**(2), 213–231.

(2007). The role of computer mediation in the instruction and development of L2 pragmatic competence. *Annual Review of Applied Linguistics*, **27**, 45–75.

Belz, J. and Kinginger, C. (2002). Cross-linguistic development of address from using in telecollaborative language learning: two case studies. *The Canadian Modern Language Review/La Revue Canadienne des Langues Vivantes*, **59**(2), 189–214.

Belz, J. and Thorne, S. (eds.) (2006). *Internet-mediated Intercultural Foreign Language Education*. Boston, MA: Thomson-Heinle.

Benson, P. (2001). *Teaching and Researching Autonomy in Language Learning*. London: Longman.

Berk, R. A. (2009). Multimedia teaching with video clips: TV, movies, YouTube, and mtvU in the college classroom. *International Journal of Technology in Teaching and Learning*, **5**(1), 1–21.

Blake, R. (2000). Computer-mediated communication: a window on L2 Spanish interlanguage. *Language Learning and Technology*, **4**(1), 120–136.

(2005). Bimodal CMC: the glue of language learning at a distance. *CALICO Journal*, **22**(3), 497–511.

(2007). New trends in using technology in the language curriculum. *Annual Review of Applied Linguistics*, **27**, 76–97.

(2009). The use of technology for second language distance learning. *Modern Language Journal*, **93**, 822–835.

Bland, S., Noblitt, J., Gay, G., and Armington, S. (1990). The naïve lexical hypothesis: evidence from CALL. *Modern Language Journal*, **74**(4), 440–450.

Blin F. (2004). CALL and the development of learner autonomy: towards an activity-theoretical perspective. *ReCALL*, **16**(2), 377–395.

Bloch, J. (2007). Abdullah's blogging: a generation 1.5 student enters the blogosphere. *Language Learning and Technology*, **11**(2), 128–141.

Boling, E. and Soo, K. (1999). CALL issues: designing CALL software. In J. Egbert and E. Hanson-Smith (eds.), *CALL Environments: Research, Practice, and Critical Issues* (pp. 442–456). Alexandria, VA: TESOL.

Borras, I. and Lafayette, R. C. (1994). Effects of multimedia subtitling on the speaking performance of college students of French. *Modern Language Journal*, **78**(1), 61–75.

Brammerts, H. (1996). Language learning in tandem using the Internet. In M. Warschauer (ed.), *Telecollaboration in Foreign Language Learning*. Hawaii: University of Hawaii.

Brandl, K. (1995). Strong and weak students' preferences for error feedback options and responses. *Modern Language Journal*, **79**(2), 194–211.

Breen, M. and Mann, S. (1997). Shooting arrows at the sun: perspectives on pedagogy for autonomy. In P. Benson and P. Voller (eds.), *Autonomy and Independence in Language Learning* (pp.132–149). London: Longman.

Brett, D. (2004). Computer generated feedback on vowel production by learners of English as a second language. *ReCALL*, **16**(1), 102–113.

Brine, J. and Franken, M. (2006). Student perceptions of a selected aspect of a computer-mediated academic writing program: an activity theory analysis. *Australian Journal of Educational Technology*, **22**(1), 21–38.

Brine, J. and Johnson, E. M. (2008). Collaborative development of EFL in Vietnam through open source software. *Proceedings of WorldCALL 2008: Bridging the World Through Technology Enhanced Language Learning*. Fukuoka, Japan.

Brown, I., Campbell, A. P., and Weatherford, Y. (2008). Using DynEd and ALC with low-level university freshmen. *The JALT CALL Journal*, **4**(3), 37–53.

Burston, J. (1996). CALL at the crossroads: myths, realities, promises, and challenges. *Australian Review of Applied Linguistics*, **19**(2), 27–36.

(2001). Exploiting the potential of a computer-based grammar checker in conjunction with self-monitoring strategies with advanced level students of French. *CALICO Journal*, **18**(3), 499–515.

(2003). Proving it works. *CALICO Journal*, **20**(2), 219–226.

Bush, L. (2009). Viva VoiceThread: integrating a Web 2.0 tool in the additional language classroom. In I. Gibson, R. Weber, K. McFerrin, R. Carlsen, and D. A. Willis (eds.), *Proceedings of Society for Information Technology and Teacher Education International Conference 2009* (pp. 3,247–3,250). Chesapeake, VA: Association for the Advancement of Computing in Education (AACE).

Butler, P. (2006). *Managing Organizational Change*. Presented at the Virtual Learning Environment (VLE): pedagogy and implementation online conference. Retrieved November 20, 2006, from www.online-conference.net/vle2006/introduction.htm.

Calvert, M. (1992). Working in tandem: peddling an old idea. *Language Learning Journal*, **6**, 17–19.

Campbell, C. and Fulford, D. (2009). *From Knowledge Generation to Knowledge Integration: Analysis of How a Government Uses Research*. Paper presented to the annual conference of the American Educational Research Association (AERA), San Diego, CA.

Campbell, D. F. (2004). Delivering an online translation course. *ReCALL*, **16**(1), 114–123.

Cárdenas-Claros, M. and Gruba, P. (2009). Help options in CALL: a systematic review. *CALICO Journal*, **27**(1), 69–90.

Chanier, T. and Vetter, A. (2006). Multimodalité et expression en langue étrangère dans une plate-forme audio-synchrone. *Apprentissage des Langues et Systèmes d'Information et de Communication*, **9**, 61–101.

Chapelle, C. (1997). CALL in the year 2000: still in search of research paradigms. *Language Learning and Technology*, **1**(1), 19–43.

(2001). *Computer Applications in Second Language Acquisition: Foundations for Teaching, Testing and Research*. Cambridge, UK: Cambridge University Press.

(2003). *English Language Learning and Technology: Lectures on Applied Linguistics in the Age of Information and Communication Technology*. Amsterdam: John Benjamin Publishing.

(2005). Interactionist SLA theory in CALL research. In J. Egbert and G. M. Petrie (eds.), *CALL Research Perspectives* (pp. 53–64). Mahwah, NJ: Lawrence Erlbaum Associates.

(2007). Technology and second language acquisition. *Annual Review of Applied Linguistics*, **27**, 98–114.

(2009). The relationship between second language acquisition theory and computer-assisted language learning. *Modern Language Journal*, **93**, 741–753.

(2010). The spread of computer-assisted language learning. *Language Teaching*, **43**(1), 66–74.

Chapelle, C. and Mizuno, S. (1989). Students' strategies with learner-controlled CALL. *CALICO Journal*, **7**(1), 25–47.

Chun, D. (2001). L2 reading on the web: strategies for accessing information in hyper-media. *Computer Assisted Language Learning*, **14**(4), 367–403.

(2007). Come ride the wave: but where is it taking us? *CALICO Journal*, **24**(2), 239–252.

Chun, D. and Payne, J. S. (2004). What makes students click: working memory and look-up behavior. *System*, **32**(4), 481–503.

Chun, D. and Plass, J. (1996). Effects of multimedia annotations on vocabulary acqui-sition. *Modern Language Journal*, **80**(2), 183–198.

Chun, L. and Zhao, Y. (2006). Noticing and text-based chat. *Language Learning and Technology*, **10**(3), 102–120.

Clarebout, G. and Elen, J. (2008). Advice on tool use in open learning environments. *Journal of Educational Multimedia and Hypermedia*, **17**(1), 81–97.

Clark, R. (1983). Reconsidering research on learning from media. *Review of Educational Research*, **53**(4), 445–459.

Cobb, T. and Stevens, V. (1996). A principled consideration of computers and reading in a second language. In M. Pennington (ed.), *The Power of CALL* (pp. 115–136). Houston, TX: Athelstan.

Coffin, J. (2006). Analysis of open source principles in diverse collaborative communi-ties. *First Monday*, **11**(6). Retrieved April 20, 2009, from http://firstmonday.org/issues/issue11_6/coffin/index.html.

Coleman, J.A. (2005). Call from the margins: effective dissemination of CALL research and good practices. *ReCALL*, **17**(1), 18–31.

Collentine, J. (2000). Insights into the construction of grammatical knowledge provided by user-behavior tracking technologies. *Language Learning and Technology*, **3**(2), 44–57.

Colpaert, J. (2006). Pedagogy-driven design for online language teaching and learning. *CALICO Journal*, **23**(3), 477–497.

(2010). Elicitation of language learners' personal goals as design concepts. *Innovation in Language Learning and Teaching*, **4**(3), 259–274.

Conacher, J. E. and Kelly-Holmes, H. (2007). Thinking beyond the technology: towards a broader understanding of new language-learning environments. In J. E. Conacher and H. Kelly-Holmes (eds.), *New Learning Environments for Language Learning. Moving Beyond the Classroom?* (pp. 931). Frankfurt am Main, Germany: Peter Lang.

Coniam, D. (2009). Experimenting with a computer essay-scoring program based on ESL student writing scripts. *ReCALL*, **21**(2), 259–279.

Convery, A. (2009). The pedagogy of the impressed: how teachers become victims of technological vision. *Teachers and Teaching: Theory and Practice*, **15**(1), 25–41.

Corda, A. and Jager, S. (2004). ELLIPS: providing web-based language learning for higher education in the Netherlands. *ReCALL*, **16**(1), 225–236.

Crabbe, D. (1999). Fostering autonomy from within the classroom: the teacher's respon-sibility. *System*, **21**(4), 443–452.

Crook, C. (2008). *Web 2.0 Technologies for Learning: the Current Landscape – Opportunities, Challenges and Tensions*. Retrieved December 13, 2010, from the BECTA website: www.becta.org.uk.

Cuban, L. (2001). *Oversold and Underused: Computers in the Classroom*. Cambridge, MA: Harvard University Press.

Cunningham, S. J., Knowles, C., and Reeves, N. (2001). An ethnographic study of technical support workers: why we didn't build a tech support digital library. In E. A. Fox and C. L. Borgman (eds.), *Proceedings of the 1st ACM/IEEE-CS Joint Conference on Digital Libraries* (pp. 189–198). Roanoke, VA: Association for Computing Machinery (ACM).

Cushion, S. (2004). Increasing accessibility by pooling digital resources. *ReCALL*, **16**(1), 41–50.

Dall, S. (2001). Technology in the classroom: teaching the process of editing. *CALICO Journal*, **18**(2), 401–403.

Dam, L. (1995). *From Theories to Classroom Practice*. Dublin: Authentik.

Danan, M. (2004). Captioning and subtitling: undervalued language learning strategies. *Meta: Translators Journal*, **49**(1), 67–77.

Daniels, P. (2008). Designing CMS modules to support language learning. *The JALT CALL Journal*, **4**(1), 93–104.

D'Antoni, S. (2008). *Open Educational Resources: the Way Forward. Deliberations of an International Community of Interest*. Paris, France: UNESCO.

   (2009). Open educational resources: reviewing initiatives and issues. *Open Learning: The Journal of Open and Distance Learning*, **24**(1), 3–10.

Darhower, M. (2002). Interactional features of synchronous computer-mediated communication in the intermediate L2 class: a sociocultural case study. *CALICO Journal*, **19**(2), 249–277.

   (2007). A tale of two communities: group dynamics and community building in a Spanish-English telecollaboration. *CALICO Journal*, **24**(3), 561–589.

   (2008). The role of linguistic affordances in telecollaborative chat. *CALICO Journal*, **26**(1), 48–69.

Davis, J. and Lyman-Hager, M. (1997). Computers and L2 reading: student performance, student attitudes. *Foreign Language Annals*, **30**(1), 58–72.

Dazakiria, H. (2008). Students' accounts of the need for continuous support in a distance learning programme. *Open Learning: The Journal of Open and Distance Learning*, **23**(2), 103–111.

De Ridder, E. (2000). Are we conditioned to follow links? Highlights in CALL materials and their impact on the reading process. *Computer Assisted Language Learning*, **13**(2), 183–195.

   (2002). Visible or invisible links: does the highlighting of hyperlinks affect incidental vocabulary learning, text comprehension, and the reading process? *Language Learning and Technology*, **6**(1), 123–146.

   (2003). *Reading from the Screen in a Second Language: Empirical Studies on the Effect of Marked Hyperlinks on Incidental Vocabulary Learning, Text Comprehension and the Reading Process*. Antwerp, Belgium: Garant.

DeLano, L., Riley, L., and Crookes, G. (1994). The meaning of innovation for ESL teachers. *System*, **22**(4), 487–496.

Desmarais, L., Duquette, L., Renié, D., and Laurier, M. (1998). Evaluating learning and interactions in a multimedia environment. *Computers and the Humanities*, **31**(3), 327–349.

Deutschmann, M., Panichi, L., and Molka-Danielsen, J. (2009). Designing oral participation in Second Life – a comparative study of two language proficiency courses. *ReCALL*, **21**(2), 206–226.

Dippold, D. (2009). Peer feedback through blogs: student and teacher perceptions in an advanced German class. *ReCALL*, **21**(1), 18–36.

Dörnyei, Z. (2001). *Teaching and Researching Motivation*. Harlow, UK: Longman.

Dörnyei, Z. and Ushioda, E. (2011). *Teaching and Researching Motivation* (2nd edn.). London: Longman.

Doughty, C. and Long, M. (2003). Optimal psycholinguistic environments for distance foreign language learning. *Language Learning and Technology*, **7**(3), 50–80.

Dougiamas M. (1998). *A Journey into Constructivism*. Retrieved December 31, 2010, from http://dougiamas.com/writing/constructivism.html.

Downes, S. (2007). Models for sustainable open educational resources. *Interdisciplinary Journal of Knowledge and Learning Objects*, **3**, 29–44.

Egbert, J. (2005). Conducting research on CALL. In J. Egbert and G. M. Petrie (eds.), *CALL Research Perspectives* (pp. 3–8). Mahwah, NJ: Lawrence Erlbaum Associates.

Egbert, J., Chao, C.-C., and Hanson-Smith, E. (1999). Computer-enhanced language learning environments: an overview. In J. Egbert and E. Hanson-Smith (eds.), *CALL Environments: Research, Practice, and Critical Issues* (pp. 1–13). Alexandria, VA: TESOL.

Egbert, J. and Hanson-Smith, E. (eds.) (1999). *CALL Environments: Research, Practice, and Critical Issues*. Alexandria, VA: TESOL.

Egbert, J. and Petrie, G. M. (eds.) (2005). *CALL Research Perspectives*. Mahwah, NJ: Lawrence Erlbaum Associates.

Ellis, N. (1996). Sequencing in SLA. Phonological memory, chunking, and points of order. *Studies in Second Language Acquisition*, **18**, 91–126.

Erben, T. (1999). Constructing learning in a virtual immersion bath: LOTE teacher education through audiographics. In R. Debski and M. Levy (eds.), *WORLDCALL: Global Perspectives on Computer-assisted Language Learning* (pp. 229–248). Lisse, The Netherlands: Swets and Zeitlinger.

Ercetin, G. (2003). Exploring ESL learners' use of hypermedia reading glosses. *CALICO Journal*, **20**(2), 261–283.

Felix, U. (2001). The web's potential for language learning: the student's perspective. *ReCALL*, **13**(1), 47–58.

(2002). The web as a vehicle for constructivist approaches in language teaching. *ReCALL*, **14**(1), 2–15.

(2003). Pedagogy on the line: identifying and closing the missing links. In U. Felix (ed.), *Language Learning Online: Towards Best Practice* (pp. 147–170). Lisse, The Netherlands: Swets and Zeitlinger.

(2005a). Analysing recent CALL effectiveness research: towards a research agenda. *Computer Assisted Language Learning*, **18**(1–2), 1–32.

(2005b). What do meta-analyses tell us about CALL effectiveness? *ReCALL*, **17**(2), 269–288.

(2008). The unreasonable effectiveness of CALL: what have we learned in two decades of research? *ReCALL Journal*, **20**(2), 141–161.

Figura, K. and Jarvis, H. (2007). Computer-based materials: a study of learner autonomy and strategies. *System*, **35**, 448–468.

Fischer, R. (1999). *Student Control and Student Learning*. Paper presented at EUROCALL 1999, University of Franche Comté, Besançon, France.

(2000). *Locus of Control and Achievement in Multimedia CALL.* Paper presented at EUROCALL 2000, University of Abertay, Dundee, Scotland.

(2004a). *How Do Students Use CALL Reading Materials, and How Do We Know that They Do?* Paper presented at CALL 2004, University of Antwerp, Belgium.

(2004b). *How Interactive Is Interactive CALL?* Paper presented at CALICO 2004, Carnegie Mellon University, Pittsburgh, PA.

(2004c). *The Relationship Between Student Usage and Student Learning in Multimedia CALL.* Paper presented at EUROCALL 2004, University of Vienna, Austria.

(2007). How do we know what students are actually doing? Monitoring students' behavior in CALL. *Computer Assisted Language Learning*, **20**(4), 409–442.

Fotos, S. and Browne, C. (eds.) (2004). *New Perspectives on CALL for Second Language Classrooms.* Mahwah, NJ: Lawrence Erlbaum Associates.

Fullan, M. (2001). *The New Meaning of Educational Change.* New York: Teachers' College Press.

Ganderton, R. (1999). Interactivity in L2-web-based reading. In R. Debski and M. Levy (eds.), *WORLDCALL: Global Perspectives on Computer-assisted Language Learning* (pp. 49–66). Lisse, The Netherlands: Swets and Zeitlinger.

Garrett, N. (1991). Technology in the service of language learning: trends and issues. *Modern Language Journal*, **75**(1), 74–101.

(1998). Where do research and practice meet? Developing a discipline. *ReCALL*, **10**(1), 7–12.

(2008). The reinvention of different kinds of wheels. *CALICO Journal*, **25**(3), 385–386.

(2009). Computer-assisted language learning trends and issues revisited: integrating innovation. *Modern Language Journal*, **93**, 719–740.

Garrison, D. R. and Vaughan, N. D. (2008). *Blended Learning in Higher Education: Framework, Principles, and Guidelines.* San Franciso, CA: John Wiley and Sons.

Geser, G. (ed.) (2008). Open educational practices and resources. *OLCOS Roadmap 2012.* Salzburg, Austria: EduMedia Group.

Gibson, J. J. (1977). The theory of affordances. In R. Shaw and J. Bransford (eds.), *Perceiving, Acting, and Knowing: Toward an Ecological Psychology* (pp. 67–82). Hillsdale, NJ: Lawrence Erlbaum Associates.

Glendenning, E. and Howard, R. (2003). Lotus ScreenCam as an aid to investigating student writing. *Computer Assisted Language Learning*, **16**(1), 31–46.

GNU/GPL (2009). GNU General Public License. Retrieved December 15, 2010, from www.gnu.org/gnu/gnu.html 15 April 2009.

Goldberg, A. K. and Riemer, F. J. (2006). All aboard – destination unknown: a sociological discussion of online learning. *Educational Technology and Society*, **9**(4), 166–172.

Goodfellow, R. (2008). New directions in research into learning cultures in online education. *Sixth International Conference on Networked Learning.* Halkidiki, Greece.

Goodfellow, R. and Lamy, M.-N. (2009). Conclusion: directions for research in online learning cultures. In R. Goodfellow and M.-N. Lamy (eds.), *Learning Cultures in Online Education* (pp. 170–183). London: Continuum Books.

Gourley, B. and Lane, A. (2009). Re-invigorating openness at the Open University: the role of open educational resources. *Open Learning: The Journal of Open and Distance Learning*, **24**(1), 57–65.

Grgurovic, M. and Hegelheimer, V. (2007). Help options and multimedia listening: students' use of subtitles and the transcript. *Language Learning and Technology*, **11**(1), 45–66.

Griffiths, C. (ed.) (2008). *Lessons from Good Language Learners*. Cambridge, UK: Cambridge University Press.

Gromik, N. (2005). EFL learner use of podcasting resources: a pilot study. *The JALT CALL Journal*, **4**(2), 47–60.

Hammersley, B. (2004). Audible revolution. *The Guardian*, p. 27 (December 13).

Hampel, R. (2006). Rethinking task design for the digital age: a framework for language teaching and learning in a synchronous online environment. *ReCALL*, **18**(1),105–121.

Hampel, R. and Hauck, M. (2004). Towards an effective use of audio conferencing in distance learning courses. *Language Learning and Technology*, **8**(1), 66–82.

Hampel, R. and Stickler, R. (2005). New skills for new classrooms: training tutors to teach languages online. *Computer Assisted Language Learning*, **18**(4), 311–326.

Hanson-Smith, E. (2008). Communities of practice for pre- and in-service teacher education. In P. Hubbard and M. Levy (eds.), *Teacher Education in CALL* (pp. 301–315). Philadelphia, PA: John Benjamins.

Hara, N. and King, R. (1999). Students' frustrations with a web-based distance education course. *First Monday*, **4**(12). Retrieved December 31, 2010, from http://firstmonday.org/htbin/cgiwrap/bin/ojs/index.php/fm/article/viewArticle/710/620.

Harrington, M. and Levy, M. (2001). CALL begins with a "C": interaction in computer-mediated language learning. *System*, **29**, 15–26.

Healey, D. (1999). Theory and research: autonomy and language learning. In J. Egbert and E. Hanson-Smith (eds.), *CALL Environments: Research, Practice, and Critical Issues* (pp. 391–402). Alexandria, VA: TESOL.

Healey, D., Hegelheimer, V., Hubbard, P., Ioannou-Georgiou, S., Kessler, G., and Ware, P. (2009). *TESOL Technology Standards Framework*. Alexandria, VA: TESOL.

Heift, T. (2001). Error-specific and individualised feedback in a web-based language tutoring system: do they read it? *ReCALL*, **13**(1), 99–109.

(2002). Learner control and error correction in ICALL: browsers, peekers, and adamants. *CALICO Journal*, **19**(2), 295–313.

(2004). Corrective feedback and learner uptake in CALL. *ReCALL*, **16**(4), 416–431.

(2007). Learner personas in CALL. *CALICO Journal*, **25**(1), 1–10.

(2008). *Errors and Intelligence in CALL: Bridging a World of Diverse Learners*. Keynote address presented at WorldCALL, Fukuoka, Japan.

(2010). Prompting in CALL: a longitudinal study of learner uptake. *Modern Language Journal*, **94**(2), 198–216.

Heift, T. and Schulze, M. (2007). *Errors and Intelligence in Computer-assisted Language Learning: Parsers and Pedagogues*. New York: Routledge.

Hernández-Ramos, P. (2006). How does educational technology benefit humanity? Five years of evidence. *Educational Technology and Society*, **9**(4), 205–214.

Ho, C. M. L., Rappa, N. A., and Chee, Y. S. (2009). Designing and implementing virtual role-play and structured argumentation: promises and pitfalls. *Computer Assisted Language Learning* **22**(5), 381–408.

Holec, H. (1981). *Autonomy and Foreign Language Learning*. Oxford, UK: Pergamon Press.

Hong, K. H. (2010). CALL teacher education as an impetus for L2 teachers in integrating technology. *ReCALL*, **22**(1), 53–69.

Hopkins, J. E. (2010). Distance learners' perceptions of assessed, student-led speaking tasks via a synchronous audiographic conferencing tool. *Innovation in Language Learning and Teaching*, **4**(3), 235–258.

Hron, A. and Friedrich, H. (2003). A review of web-based collaborative learning: factors beyond technology. *Journal of Computer Assisted Learning*, **19**(1), 70–79.

Hubbard, P. (2004). Learner training for effective use of CALL. In S. Fotos and C. Browne (eds.), *New Perspectives on CALL for Second Language Classrooms* (pp. 45–68). Mahwah, NJ: Lawrence Erlbaum Associates.

(2005). A review of subject characteristics in CALL research. *Computer Assisted Language Learning*, **18**(5), 351–368.

(2008). Twenty-five years of theory in the *CALICO Journal*. *CALICO Journal*, **25**(3), 387–399.

Hubbard, P. and Bradin-Siskin, C. (2004). Another look at tutorial CALL. *ReCALL*, **16**(2), 448–461.

Hubbard, P. and Levy, M. (2006). The scope of CALL education. In P. Hubbard and M. Levy (eds.), *Teacher Education in CALL* (pp. 2–20). Philadelphia, PA: John Benjamins.

Huh, K. and Hu, W.-C. (2005). Criteria for effective CALL research. In J. Egbert and G. M. Petrie (eds.), *CALL Research Perspectives* (pp. 9–21). Mahwah, NJ: Lawrence Erlbaum Associates.

Hulstijn, J. (1993). When do foreign-language readers look up the meaning of unfamiliar words? The influence of task and learner variables. *Modern Language Journal*, **77**(2), 139–147.

Hunter, L. (2008). Moodle in the writing lab: foregrounding task design as topic in instructor-learner exchange. *The JALT CALL Journal*, **4**(1), 85–92.

Hurd, S. (2005). Autonomy and the distance language learner. In B. Holmberg, M. Shelley, and C. White (eds.), *Distance Education and Languages: Evolution and Change* (pp. 1–19). Clevedon, UK: Multilingual Matters.

Hutchby, I. (2001). *Conversation and Technology: From the Telephone to the Internet*. Cambridge, UK: Polity Press.

Hylén, J. (2006). *Open Educational Resources: Opportunities and Challenges*. Retrieved December 15, 2010, from the Organisation for Economic Co-operation and Development (OECD) website www.oecd.org/home/0,2987,en_2649_201185_1_1_1_1_1,00.html.

Iiyoshi, T., Kumar, M. S. V., and Brown, J. S. (2008). *Opening Up Education: the Collective Advancement of Education Through Open Technology, Open Content, and Open Knowledge*. Cambridge, MA: The MIT Press.

Internet World Stats (2009). *Vietnam Internet Usage Stats and Marketing Report*. Retrieved April 20, 2009, from www.internetworldstats.com/asia/vn.htm.

Iskold, L. V. (2003). Building on success, learning from mistakes: implications for the future. *Computer Assisted Language Learning*, **16**(4), 295–328.

Jeon-Ellis, G., Debski, R., and Wigglesworth, G. (2005). Oral interaction around computers in the project-oriented CALL classroom. *Language Learning and Technology*, **9**(3), 121–145.

Johnson, E. M. (2008). An investigation into pedagogical challenges facing international tertiary-level students in New Zealand. *Higher Education Research and Development*, **27**(3), 231–243.

Johnson, E. M., Barnard, R., Witten, I., and Finch, L. (2006). *E-Learning Initiatives to Support Postgraduate Teaching in Vietnam* (pp. 1–23). Final (public) report for Export Education Innovation Programme: EEIP 08, Innovative Projects Development Fund. Ministry of Education, Wellington (October 31).

Johnson, E. M. and Walker, R. M. (2007). The promise and practice of e-learning within complex tertiary environments. In J. M. Spector, D. G. Sampson, T. Okamoto, Kinshuk, S. A. Cerri, M. Ueno, and A. Kashihara (eds.), *Proceedings of the International Conference on Advanced Learning Technologies (ICALT 2007)* (pp. 753–757). Los Alamitos, CA: IEEE Computer Society.

Jones, J. (2001). CALL and the responsibilities of teachers and administrators. *ELT Journal*, **55**, 360–367.

Jones, L. (2009). Supporting student differences in listening comprehension and vocabulary learning with multimedia annotations. *CALICO Journal*, **26**(2), 267–289.

Jones, L. and Plass, J. (2002). Supporting listening comprehension and vocabulary acquisition in French with multimedia annotations. *Modern Language Journal*, **86**(4), 546–561.

Kassen, M. and Lavine, R. (2007). Developing advanced level foreign language learners with technology. In M. Kassen, R. Lavine, K. Murphy-Judy, and M. Peters (eds.), *Preparing and Developing Technology-Proficiency L2 Teachers* (pp. 233–262). San Marcos, TX: CALICO.

Kelly, G. A. (1955). *The Psychology of Personal Constructs*. New York: Norton.

Kelly, J. A. (2010). Social network sites and the ideal L2 self: using MySpace in a Chinese EFL class. *The JALT CALL Journal*, **6**(1), 17–33.

Kennedy, C. and Levy, M. (2008). L'italiano al telefonino: using SMS to support beginners' language learning. *ReCALL*, **20**(3), 315–350.

Kern, R. (1995). Restructuring classroom interaction with networked computers: effects on quantity and characteristics of language production. *Modern Language Journal*, **79**(4), 457–476.

Kessler, G. (2009). Student-initiated attention to form in wiki-based collaborative writing. *Language Learning and Technology*, **13**(1), 79–95.

Kessler, G. and Bikowski, D. (2010). Developing collaborative autonomous learning abilities in computer mediated language learning: attention to meaning among students in wiki space. *Computer Assisted Language Learning*, **23**(1), 41–58.

Kessler, G. and Plakans, L. (2008). Does teachers' confidence with CALL equal innovative and integrated use? *Computer Assisted Language Learning*, **21**(3), 269–282.

Kiernan, P. and Aizawa, K. (2004). Cell phones in task based learning: are cell phones useful language learning tools? *ReCALL*, **16**(1), 71–84.

Knight, S. (1994). Dictionary use while reading: the effects on comprehension and vocabulary acquisition for students of different verbal abilities. *Modern Language Journal*, **78**(2), 285–299.

Knowles, M. S. (1975). *Self-directed Learning: a Guide for Learners and Teachers*. Englewood Cliffs, NJ: Cambridge Adult Education.

Kolaitis, M., Mahoney, M. A., Pomann, H., and Hubbard, P. (2006). Training ourselves to train our students for CALL. In P. Hubbard and M. Levy (eds.), *Teacher Education in CALL* (pp. 317–332). Amsterdam: John Benjamins.

Kopyc, S. (2006). Enhancing teaching with technology: are we there yet? *Innovate: Journal of Online Education*. Retrieved December 5, 2006, from www.innovate online.info/index.php?view=article&id=74.

Kötter, M. (2003). Negotiation of meaning and codeswitching in online tandems. *Language Learning and Technology*, **7**(2), 145–172.

Krashen, S. (1981). *Second Language Acquisition and Second Language Learning*. Toronto, Canada: Pergamon Press.

Kress, G. and van Leeuwen, T. (2001). *Multimodal Discourse. The Modes and Media of Contemporary Communication*. London: Arnold.

Lafford, B. (2009). Toward an ecological CALL: update to Garrett (1991). *Modern Language Journal*, **9**(3), 673–696.

Lai, C., Fei. F., and Roots, R. (2008). The contingency of recasts and noticing. *CALICO Journal*, **26**(1), 70–90.

Lai, C. and Zhao, Y. (2006). Noticing and text-based chat. *Language Learning and Technology*, **10**(3), 102–120.

Lamy, M.-N. (2006). Usages, contre-usages: nouvelles cultures des formations virtuelles. In M.-J. Barbot, C. Debon, and V. Glikman (eds.), *Pédagogie et Numérique. Contradictions? Convergences?* Special issue of *Education Permanente*, **169**(4), 79–88.

Lamy, M.-N. and Goodfellow, R. (1999). Reflective conversation in the virtual language classroom. *Language Learning and Technology*, **2**(2), 43–61.

Lamy, M.-N. and Hampel, R. (2007). *Online Communication for Language Teaching and Learning*. London: Palgrave Macmillan.

Lane, A. (2008). Who puts the education into open educational content? In R. N. Katz (ed.), *The Tower and the Cloud: Higher Education in the Age of Cloud Computing* (pp. 158–168). Educause. Retrieved April 11, 2009, from www.educause.edu/ books.

Lantolf, J. (2000). Introducing sociocultural theory. In J. Lantolf (ed.), *Sociocultural Theory and Second Language Learning* (pp.1–26). Oxford, UK: Oxford University Press.

    (2005). Sociocultural and second language learning research: an exegesis. In E. Hinkel (ed.), *Handbook of Research in Second Language Teaching and Learning* (pp. 335–353). Mahwah, NJ: Lawrence Erlbaum Associates.

Laufer, B. and Hill, M. (2000). What lexical information do L2 learners select in a CALL dictionary and how does it affect word retention? *Language Learning and Technology*, **3**(2), 58–76.

Lázaro, N. and Reinders, H. (2007). Innovation in self-access: three case studies. *CALL-EJ*, **8**(2). Retrieved January 6, 2011, from http://call-ej.org.

    (2004). Researching language learning processes in open CALL settings for advanced learners. *Computer Assisted Language Learning*, **17**(3–4), 289–313.

Leahy, C.(2006). Introducing ICT to teachers of an institution-side language programme: principal considerations. *The JALT CALL Journal*, **2**(3), 3–14.

Leakey, J. and Ranchoux, A. (2006). BILINGUA: a blended language learning approach for CALL. *Computer Assisted Language Learning*, **19**(4), 357–372.

Lee, C., Wong, K. C. K., Cheung, W. K., and Lee, F. S. L. (2009). Web-based essay critiquing system and EFL students' writing: a quantitative and qualitative investigation. *Computer Assisted Language Learning*, **22**(1), 57–72.

Lee, L. (2001). Online strategies: negotiation of meaning and strategies used among learners of Spanish. *ReCALL*, **13**(3), 232–244.

(2009). Promoting intercultural exchanges with blogs and podcasting: a study of Spanish–American telecollaboration. *Computer Assisted Language Learning*, **22**(5), 425–443.

(2010). Exploring wiki-mediated collaborative writing: a case study in an elementary Spanish course. *CALICO Journal*, **27**(2), 260–276.

Lehrer, J. (2009). *How We Decide*. New York: Houghton Mifflin Harcourt.

Lemke, J. (2006). Towards critical multimedia literacy: technology, research, and politics. In M. McKenna, L. Labbo, D. Reinking, and R. Kieffer (eds.), *International Handbook of Literacy and Technology Volume III* (pp. 3–14). Mahwah, NJ: Laurence Erlbaum Associates.

Leow, R. P. (1995). Modality and intake in second language acquisition. *Studies in Second Language Acquisition*, **17**, 79–89.

Levin, B. (2004). Making research matter more. *Education Policy Analysis Archives*, **12**(56), October 17. Retrieved July 30, 2009, from http://epaa.asu.edu/epaa/v12n56.

Levy, M. (1997). *Computer Assisted Language Learning: Context and Conceptualization*. Oxford, UK: Clarendon Press.

(2000). Scope, goals and methods in CALL research: questions of coherence and autonomy. *ReCALL*, **12**(2), 170–195.

(2002). CALL by design: discourse, products and processes. *ReCALL*, **14**(1), 58–84.

(2007). Culture, culture learning and new technologies: towards a pedagogical framework. *Language Learning and Technology*, **11**(2), 104–127.

Levy, M. and Hubbard, P. (2005). Why call CALL "CALL"? *Computer Assisted Language Learning*, **18**(3), 143–149.

Levy, M. and Kennedy, C. (2004). A task-cycling pedagogy using stimulated reflection and audio-conferencing in foreign language learning. *Language Learning and Technology*, **8**(2), 50–69.

Levy, M. and Stockwell, G. (2006). *CALL Dimensions: Options and Issues in Computer-assisted Language Learning*. Mahwah, NJ: Lawrence Erlbaum Associates.

Li, J. and Erben, T. (2007). Intercultural learning via instant messenger interaction. *CALICO Journal*, **24**(2), 291–311.

Li, M., Ogata, H., Hou, B., Hashimoto, S., Uosaki, N., Liu, Y., and Yano, Y. (2010). Development of adaptive vocabulary learning using mobile phone email. *Proceedings of the 2010 International Conference on Wireless, Mobile and Ubiquitous Technologies in Education (WMUTE)* (pp. 34–41). Kao-hsiung, April 12–16.

Liddell, P. and Garrett, N. (2004). The new language centers and the role of technology: new mandates, new horizons. In S. Fotos and C. Browne (eds.), *New Perspectives on CALL for Second Language Classrooms* (pp. 27–40). Mahwah, NJ: Lawrence Erlbaum Associates.

Lightbown, P. and Spada, N. (2006). *How Languages Are Learned* (3rd edn.). Oxford, UK: Oxford University Press.

Lin, M.-C. and Chiu, T.-L. (2009). The impact of an online explicit lexical program on EFL vocabulary gains and listening comprehension. *The JALT CALL Journal*, **5**(2), 3–14.

Little, D. and Dam, L. (1998). Learner autonomy: what and why? *The Language Teacher Online*, **22**(10). Retrieved January 5, 2011, from http://jalt-publications .org/tlt/files/98/oct/littledam.html.

Littlejohn, A. and Pegler, C. (2007). *Preparing for Blended E-Learning*. New York: Routledge.

Littlewood, W. (1996). "Autonomy": an autonomy and a framework. *System*, **24**(4), 427–435.

Lund, A. (2008). Wikis: a collective approach to language production. *ReCALL*, **20**(1), 35–54.

Mateas, M. and Lewis, S. (1996). A MOO-based virtual training environment. *Journal of Computer-mediated Communication*, **2**(3) December. Retrieved December 15, 2010, from http://jcmc.indiana.edu/vol2/issue3/mateas.html#RTFToC9.

McAndrew, P. and Wilson, T. (2008). *Pocketing the Difference: Joint Development of Open Educational Resources*. Eighth IEEE International Conference on Advanced Learning Technologies, July 1–5. Santander, Cantabria, Spain.

McCarty, S. (2005). Spoken Internet to go: popularization through podcasting. *The JALT CALL Journal*, **1**(2), 67–74.

Mehra, B., Merkel, C., and Bishop, A. P. (2004). The Internet for empowerment of minority and marginalized users. *New Media and Society*, **6**(6), 781–802.

Meskill, C. (2005). Triadic scaffolds: tools for teaching English language learners with computers. *Language Learning and Technology*, **9**(1), 46–59.

Meskill, C. and Anthony, N. (2007). Form-focused communicative practice via CMC: what language learners say. *CALICO Journal*, **25**(1), 69–90.

Mitchell, R. and Myles, F. (2004). *Second Language Learning Theories* (2nd edn.). London: Hodder Arnold.

Möllering, M. (2000). Computer mediated communication: learning German in Australia. *ReCALL*, **12**(1), 27–34.

Morgan, M., Butler, M., and Power, M. (2007). Evaluating ICT in education: a comparison of the affordances of the iPod, DS and Wii. *ICT: Providing Choices for Learners and Learning. Proceedings ascilite Singapore 2007* (pp. 717–726).

Mork, C. (2009). Using Twitter in EFL education. *The JALT CALL Journal*, **5**(3), 41–56.

Morris, F. (2005). Child-to-child interaction and corrective feedback in a computer mediated L2 class. *Language Learning and Technology*, **9**(1), 29–45.

Murray, L. (1998). CALL and web training with teacher self-empowerment: a departmental and long-term approach. *Computers and Education*, **31**, 17–23.

Murray, L. and Hourigan, T. (2008). Blogs for specific purposes: expressivist or socio-cognitivist approach? *ReCALL*, **20**(1), 82–97.

Nagata, N. (1993). Intelligent computer feedback for second language instruction. *Modern Language Journal*, **77**(3), 330–338.

    1995). An effective application of natural language processing in second language instruction. *CALICO Journal*, **13**(1), 47–67.

    (1996). Computer versus workbook instruction in second language acquisition. *CALICO Journal*, **14**(1), 53–75.

Naiman, N., Frohlich, M., Stern, H. H., and Todesco, A. (1978). *The Good Language Learner*. Toronto: Ontario Institute for Studies in Education.

Neergaard, H. and Ulhøi, J. P. (2007). *Handbook of Qualitative Research Methods in Entrepreneurship*. Cheltenham, UK: Edward Elgar Publishing.

Nelson, W., Bueno, K., and Huffstutler, S. (1999). If you build it, they will come. But how will they use it? *Journal of Research on Computing in Education*, **32**(2), 270–286.

Neumann, W. L. (2003). *Social Research Methods: Qualitative and Quantitative Approaches* (5th edn.). Boston, MA: Allyn and Bacon.

Noblitt, J. and Bland, S. (1991). Tracking the learner in computer-aided language learning. In B. Freed (ed.), *Foreign Language Acquisition Research and the Classroom* (pp. 120–131). Lexington, MA: D. C. Heath.

Nozawa, K. (2008). Muudoru-ni yoru kyozai kanri [Managing teaching materials in Moodle]. In H. Yoshida, K. Matsuda, R. Uemura, and K. Nozawa (eds.), *Gaikokugo kyoiku to ICT* [Foreign language education and ICT] (pp. 100–118). Tokyo: Council for Improvement of Education through Computers.

Oakley, B., Felder, R. M., Brent, R., and Elhajj, I. (2004). Turning student groups into effective teams. *Journal of Student Centered Learning*, **2**(1), 9–34.

O'Bryan, A. (2008). Providing pedagogical learner training in CALL: impact on student use of language-learning strategies and glosses. *CALICO Journal*, **26**(1), 142–159.

O'Bryan, A. and Hegelheimer, V. (2007). Integrating CALL into the classroom: the role of podcasting in an ESL listening strategies course. *ReCALL*, **19**(2), 162–180.

Okada, A. (2008). OpenLearn and knowledge maps for language learning. In R. D. C. V. Marriott and P. L. Torres (eds.), *Handbook of Research on E-Learning Methodologies for Language Acquisition* (pp. 84–103). Hershey, PA: Information Science Reference.

Organisation for Economic Co-operation and Development (OECD) (2007). *Giving Knowledge for Free: the Emergence of Open Educational Resources*. Paris, France: OECD Education and Skills.

Orsini-Jones, M. (2004). Supporting a course in new literacies and skills for linguists with a virtual learning environment. *ReCALL*, **16**(1), 189–209.

Otto, S. and Pusack, J. (2009). Computer-assisted language learning authoring issues. *Modern Language Journal*, **93**, 784–801.

Oxford, R. (1990). *Language Learning Strategies: what Every Teacher Should Know*. New York: Newbury House/Harper and Row.

Oxford, R. and Nyikos, M. (1989). Variables affecting choice of language learning strategies by university students. *Modern Language Journal*, **73**(3), 291–300.

Pasfield-Neofitou, S. (2010). An analysis of L2 Japanese learners' social CMC with native speakers: interaction, language use, and language learning. Unpublished doctoral dissertation, Monash University, Melbourne.

Pellettieri, J. (2000). Negotiation in cyberspace: the role of chatting in the development of grammatical competence. In M. Warschauer and R. Kern (eds.), *Network-based Language Teaching: Concepts and Practice* (pp. 59–86). Cambridge, UK: Cambridge University Press.

Pennington, M. (2004). Electronic media in second language writing: an overview of tools and research findings. In S. Fotos and C. Browne (eds.), *New Perspectives on CALL for Second Language Classrooms* (pp. 69–92). Mahwah, NJ: Lawrence Erlbaum Associates.

Peterson, M. (2004). MOO virtual worlds in CMC-based CALL: defining an agenda for future research. In J.-B. Son (ed.), *Computer-assisted Language Learning: Concepts, Contexts and Practices* (pp. 39–58). New York: iUniverse Inc.

(2008). Virtual worlds in language education. *The JALT CALL Journal*, **4**(3), 29–37.

(2010a). Learner participation patterns and strategy use in Second Life: an exploratory case study. *ReCALL*, **22**(3), 273–292.

(2010b). Massively multiplayer online role-playing games as arenas for second language learning. *Computer Assisted Language Learning*, **23**(5), 429–440.

Peterson, P. (2001). Skills and strategies for proficient listening. In M. Celce-Murcia (ed.), *Teaching English as a Second or Foreign Language* (3rd edn.) (pp. 87–100). Boston, MA: Heinle.

Pica, T. (1994). Questions from the language classroom: research perspectives. *TESOL Quarterly*, **28**(1), 49–79.

Pinkman, K. (2005). Using blogs in the foreign language classroom: encouraging learner independence. *The JALT CALL Journal*, **1**(1), 12–24.

Plass, J., Chun, D., Mayer, R., and Leutner, D. (1998). Supporting visual and verbal learning preferences in a second-language multimedia learning environment. *Journal of Educational Psychology*, **90**(1), 25–36.

Prensky, M. (2001). Digital natives, digital immigrants. *On the Horizon*, **9**(5), 1–6.

Prichard, C. (2010). Using social bookmark sites for independent reading projects. *The JALT CALL Journal*, **6**(2), 115–128.

Pujolà, J.-T. (2001). Did CALL feedback feed back? Researching learners' use of feedback. *ReCALL*, **13**(1), 79–98.

(2002). CALLing for help: researching language learning strategies using help facilities in a web-based multimedia program. *ReCALL*, **14**(2), 235–262.

Purushotma, R. (2005). Commentary: you're not studying, you're just... *Language Learning and Technology*, **9**(1), 80–96.

Raby, F. (2005). A user-centered ergonomic approach to CALL research. In J. Egbert and G. M. Petrie (eds.), *CALL Research Perspectives* (pp. 179–190). Mahwah, NJ: Lawrence Erlbaum Associates.

Ranalli, J. (2008). Learning English with The Sims: exploiting authentic computer simulation games for L2 learning. *Computer Assisted Language Learning*, **21**(5), 441–455.

Rankin, Y., Gold, R., and Gooch, B. (2006a). Evaluating interactive gaming as a language learning tool. *Conference Proceedings of SIGGRAPH 2006*. Boston, MA, July 30–August 3.

(2006b). 3D role-playing games as language learning tools. *Conference Proceedings of EuroGraphics 2006, Vol. 25*. Vienna, Austria, September 4–8.

Reinders, H. (2005). Non-participation in a university language programme. *JALT Journal*, **27**(2), 209–226.

(2006). Supporting self-directed learning through an electronic learning environment. In T. Lamb and H. Reinders (eds.), *Supporting Independent Learning: Issues and Interventions* (pp. 219–238). Frankfurt am Main, Germany: Peter Lang.

(2007). Big brother is helping you. Supporting self-access language learning with a student monitoring system. *System*, **35**(1), 93–111.

Reinders, H. and White, C. (2010). The theory and practice of technology in materials development and task design. In N. Harwood (ed.), *Materials in ELT: Theory and Practice*. Cambridge, UK: Cambridge University Press.

Rich, J. (1981). *Innovation in Education: Reformers and Their Critics*. Boston, MA: Allyn and Bacon.

Rickard, A., Blin, F., and Appel, C. (2008). Training for trainers: challenges, outcomes, and principles of in-service training across the Irish education system. In P. Hubbard and M. Levy (eds.), *Teacher Education in CALL* (pp. 203–218). Philadelphia, PA: John Benjamins.

Rilling, S., Dahlman, A., Dodson, S., Boyles, C., and Pazvant, O. (2005). Connecting CALL theory and practice in preservice teacher education and beyond: processes and products. *CALICO Journal*, **22**(2), 213–235.

Rimrott, A. and Heift, T. (2005). Language learners and generic spell checkers in CALL. *CALICO Journal*, **23**(1), 17–48.

Robb, T. (2006). Helping teachers to help themselves. In P. Hubbard and M. Levy (eds.), *Teacher Education in CALL* (pp. 335–347). Amsterdam: John Benjamins

Roby, W. (1999). What's in a gloss? *Language Learning and Technology*, **2**(2), 94–101.

Romeo, K. and Hubbard, P. (2010). Pervasive CALL learner training for improving listening proficiency. In M. Levy, F. Blin, C. Siskin, and O. Takeuchi (eds.), *WorldCALL: International Perspectives on Computer Assisted Language Learning* (pp. 215–229). New York: Routledge.

Rosell-Aguilar, F. (2007a). Changing tutor roles in online tutorial support for open distance learning through audio-graphic SCMC. *The JALT CALL Journal*, **3**(1–2), 81–94.

  (2007b). Top of the pods: in search of a podcasting "podagogy" for language learning. *Computer Assisted Language Learning*, **20**(5), 471–492.

Ruthven-Stuart, P. (2003). A website: a first step to bridging the IT gulf. Retrieved December 28, 2010, from www.cis.doshisha.ac.jp/kkitao/organi/kyoto/book/peter .pdf.

  (2006). Integrating ICTs into a university language curriculum. Retrieved December 28, 2010, from www.hokuriku-u.ac.jp/library/pdf/kiyo27/gai12.pdf.

Sampson, N. (2003). Meeting the needs of distance learners. *Language Learning and Technology*, **7**(3), 103–118.

Savignon, S. J. and Roithmeier, W. (2004). Computer-mediated communication: texts and strategies. *CALICO Journal*, **21**(2), 265–290.

Schacter, D. L. (2001). *The Seven Sins of Memory: How the Mind Forgets and Remembers*. Boston, MA: Houghton Mifflin.

Schneider, J. and von der Emde, S. (2006). Conflicts in cyberspace: from communication breakdown to intercultural dialogue in online collaborations. In J. A. Belz and S. L. Thorne (eds.), *AAUSC 2005 – Internet-mediated Intercultural Foreign Language Education* (pp. 178–206). Boston, MA: Thomson-Heinle.

Schwienhorst, K. (2003). Learner autonomy and tandem learning: putting principles into practice in synchronous and asynchronous telecommunication environments. *Computer Assisted Language Learning*, **16**(5), 427–443.

Scollon, R. and Scollon, S.W. (2003). *Discourses in Places. Language in the Material World*. London and New York: Routledge.

Sha, G. Q. (2009). AI-based chatterbots and spoken English teaching: a critical analysis. *Computer Assisted Language Learning*, **22**(3), 269–281.

Sharma, P. and Barrett, B. (2007). *Blended Learning: Using Technology In and Beyond the Language Classroom*. Oxford, UK: Macmillan.

Shetzer, H. and Warschauer, M. (2000). An electronic literacy approach to network-based language teaching. In M. Warschauer and R. Kern (eds.), *Network-based Language Teaching: Concepts and Practice* (pp. 171–185). Cambridge, UK: Cambridge University Press.

Shield, L. (2003). MOO as a language learning tool. In U. Felix (ed.), *Language Learning Online: Towards Best Practice* (pp. 97–122). Lisse, The Netherlands: Swets and Zeitlinger.

Shield, L., Weininger, M. J., and Davies, L. B. (1999). MOOing in L2: constructivism and developing learner autonomy for technology-enhanced language learning. *C@lling Japan* **8**(3). Retrieved October 27, 2009, from http://jaltcall.org/cjo/10_99/mooin.htm.

Siemens, G. (2008). A world without courses. Retrieved June 22, 2008, from www.elearnspace.org/media/worldwithoutcourses/player.html.

Sinclair, B. (2006). Learner training: part I. *Independence*, **38**, 21–22. Retrieved January 6, 2011, from www.learnerautonomy.org/issue38learnertrainingarticle1.html.

Skehan, P. (1989). *Individual Differences in Second Language Learning*. London: Edward Arnold.

Skourtou, E. (2002). Connecting Greek and Canadian schools through an Internet-based sister-class network. *International Journal of Bilingual Education and Bilingualism*, **5**(2), 85–95.

Smith, B. (2003). Computer-mediated negotiated interaction: an expanded model. *Modern Language Journal*, **8**(1)7, 38–57.

Smith, B. and Sauro, S. (2009). Interruptions in chat. *Computer Assisted Language Learning*, **22**(3), 229–247.

Smith, M. S. (2009). Opening education. *Science*, **323**, 89–93.

Somekh, B. (2001). The role of evaluation in ensuring excellence in communication technology initiatives. *Education, Communication and Information*, **1**(1), 75–101.

Son, J.-B. (2002). Online discussion in a CALL course for distance language teachers. *CALICO Journal*, **20**(1), 127–144.

Sotillo, S. (2005). Corrective feedback via instant messenger learning activities in NS-NNS and NNS-NNS dyads. *CALICO Journal*, **22**(3), 467–496.

Stevens, V. (2006). Second Life in education and language learning. *TESL-EJ*, **10**(3). Retrieved December 15, 2010, from www.tesl-ej.org/pdf/ej39/int.pdf.

Stevick, E. (1980). *Teaching Languages: a Way and Ways*. Rowley, MA: Newbury House Publishers.

Stockwell, G. (2003). Effects of topic threads on sustainability of email interactions between native speakers and nonnative speakers. *ReCALL*, **15**(1), 37–50.

  (2007a). A review of technology choice for teaching language skills in the CALL literature. *ReCALL*, **19**(2), 105–120.

  (2007b). Vocabulary on the move: investigating an intelligent mobile phone-based vocabulary tutor. *Computer Assisted Language Learning*, **20**(4), 365–383.

  (2008). Investigating learner preparedness for and usage patterns of mobile learning. *ReCALL*, **20**(3), 253–270.

(2009). Teacher education in CALL: teaching teachers to educate themselves. *International Journal of Innovation in Language Learning and Teaching*, **3**(1), 99–112.

(2010). Using mobile phones for vocabulary activities: examining the effect of the platform. *Language Learning and Technology*, **14**(2), 95–110.

Stockwell, G. and Harrington, M. W. (2003). The incidental development of L2 proficiency in NS-NNS email interactions. *CALICO Journal*, **20**(2), 337–359.

Stockwell, G. and Levy, M. (2001). Sustainability of email interactions between native speakers and nonnative speakers. *Computer Assisted Language Learning*, **14**(5), 419–442.

Stracke, E. (2007). A road to understanding: a qualitative study into why learners drop out of a blended language learning (BLL) environment. *ReCALL*, **19**(1), 57–78.

Strambi, A. and Bouvet, E. (2003). Flexibility and interaction at a distance: a mixed-mode environment for language learning. *Language Learning and Technology*, **7**(3), 81–102.

Svensson, P. (2003). Virtual worlds as arenas for language learning. In U. Felix (ed.), *Language Learning Online: Towards Best Practice* (pp. 123–142). Lisse, The Netherlands: Swets and Zeitlinger.

Swain, M. (1995). Three functions of output in second language learning. In G. Cook and B. Seidlhofer (eds.), *Principle and Practice in Applied Linguistics: Studies in Honor of William E. Rutherford* (pp.125–144). Oxford, UK: Oxford University Press.

Tamai, K. (2002). On the effects of shadowing on listening comprehension – keynote lecture at the 3rd annual conference of JAIS. *Interpretation Studies*, **2**, 178–192.

Tanaka, N. (2005). Collaborative interaction as the process of task completion in task-based CALL classrooms. *The JALT CALL Journal*, **1** (2), 21–40.

Tanaka-Ellis, N. (2010). Factors limiting learners' success in achieving task outcomes in CALL. *Innovation in Language Learning and Teaching*, **4**(3), 213–233.

Thang, N. N. and Quang, T. (2007). International briefing 18: training and development in Vietnam. *International Journal of Training and Development*, **11**(2), 139–149.

Thomas, M. (ed.) (2009). *Handbook of Research on Web 2.0 and Second Language Learning*. Hershey, PA: Information Science Reference.

Thorne, S., Black, R., and Sykes, J. (2009). Second language use, socialization, and learning in Internet interest communities and online gaming. *Modern Language Journal*, **93**, 802–821.

Thorne, S. and Payne, S. (2005). Evolutionary trajectories, Internet-mediated expression, and language education. *CALICO Journal*, **22**(3), 371–397.

Thorne, S. L. (2003). Artifacts and cultures-of-use in intercultural communication. *Language Learning and Technology*, **7**(2), 38–67.

Thornton, P. and Houser, C. (2002). M-learning: learning in transit. In P. Lewis (ed.), *The Changing Face of CALL: a Japanese Perspective* (pp. 229–243). Lisse, The Netherlands: Swets and Zeitlinger.

Tokuda, N. and Chen, L. (2004). A new KE-free online ICALL system featuring error-contingent feedback. *Computer Assisted Language Learning*, **17**(2), 177–201.

Torlavić, E. and Deugo, D. (2004). Application of a CALL system in the acquisition of adverbs in English. *Computer Assisted Language Learning*, **17**(2), 203–235.

Toyoda, E. and Harrison, R. (2002). Categorization of text chat communication between learners and native speakers of Japanese. *Language Learning and Technology*, **6**(1), 82–99.

Trinder, K., Guiller, J., Margaryan, A., Littlejohn, A., and Nicol, D. (2008). *Learning from Digital Natives: Bridging Formal and Informal Learning*. Glasgow, UK: The Higher Education Academy. Retrieved January 6, 2011, from www.academy.gcal .ac.uk/ldn.

Tudini, V. (2003). Using native speakers in chat. *Language Learning and Technology*, **7**(3), 141–159.

Ulitsky, H. (2000). Language learner strategies with technology. *Educational Computing Research*, **22**(3), 285–322.

UNESCO (2002). *Forum on the Impact of Open Courseware for Higher Education in Developing Countries (Final Report)*. Paris, France. Retrieved January 6, 2011, from www.wcet.info/resources/publications/unescofinalreport.pdf.

(2009). *Access to Open Educational Resources*. Retrieved March 8, 2009, from http:// oerwiki.iiep-unesco.org/index.php?title=Access2OER/Access_Issues.

Ushioda, E. (1996). *Learner Autonomy 5: the Role of Motivation*. Dublin: Authentik.

Van der Linden, E. (1993). Does feedback enhance computer-assisted language learning? *Computers in Education*, **21**(1), 61–65.

van Lier, L. (1996). *Interaction in the Language Curriculum: Awareness, Autonomy and Authenticity*. London: Longman

(2000). From input to affordance: social-interactive learning from an ecological perspective. In J. Lantolf (ed.), *Sociocultural Theory and Second Language Learning* (pp. 245–261). New York: Oxford University Press.

Vandergrift, L. (2004). Listening to learn or learning to listen? *Annual Review of Applied Linguistics*, **24**, 3–25.

VietnamNetBridge (2007). *Vietnam OpenCourseWare's First Day of School*. Retrieved June 9, 2008 from http://english.vietnamnet.vn/education/2007/12/759480.

Vogel, D., Kennedy, D., and Kwok, R. C. (2009). Does using mobile device applications lead to learning? *Journal of Interactive Learning Research*, **20**(4), 469–485.

Volle, L. M. (2005). Analyzing oral skills in voice email and online interviews. *Language Learning and Technology*, **9**(3), 146–163.

Wang, Y. (2004). Supporting synchronous distance language learning with desktop videoconferencing. *Language Learning and Technology*, **8**(3), 90–121.

(2007). Task design in videoconferencing-supported distance language learning. *CALICO Journal*, **24**(3), 591–630.

Ward, M. (2002). Reusable XML technologies and the development of language learning materials. *ReCALL*, **14**(2), 285–294.

Ward, M. and Genabith, J. (2003). CALL for endangered languages: challenges and rewards. *Computer Assisted Language Learning*, **16**(2–3), 233–258.

Warschauer, M. (2005). Sociocultural perspectives on CALL. In J. Egbert and G. M. Petrie (eds.), *CALL Research Perspectives* (pp. 41–51). Mahwah, NJ: Lawrence Erlbaum Associates.

Warschauer, M. and Kern, R. (eds.) (2000), *Network-based Language Teaching: Concepts and Practice*. Cambridge, UK: Cambridge University Press.

Weasenforth, D., Biesenbach-Lucas, S., and Meloni, C. (2002). Realizing constructivist objectives through collaborative technologies: threaded discussions. *Language Learning and Technology*, **6**(3), 58–86.

Wesche, M. and Paribakht, T. (2000). Reading based exercises in second language vocabulary learning: an introspective study. *Modern Language Journal*, **84**(2), 196–214.

White, C. (2006). State of the art article: the distance learning of foreign languages. *Language Teaching*, **39**(4), 247–264.

Wiley, J. (2006). *A Brief History of OER*. OECD Centre for Educational Research and Innovation, Expert Meeting on Open Educational Resources. Retrieved April 13, 2009, from www.hewlett.org/library.

Winke, P. and Goertler, S. (2008a). An introduction to distance language learning. In S. Goertler and P. Winke (eds.), *Opening Doors Through Distance Language Education: Principles, Perspectives, and Practices* (pp. 1–10). San Marcos, TX: CALICO.

(2008b). Did we forget someone? Students' computer access and literacy for CALL. *CALICO Journal*, **25**(3), 483–509.

Witte, J. (2007). Why the tail wags the dog: the pernicious influence of product-oriented discourse on the provision of educational technology support. *Annual Review of Applied Linguistics*, **27**, 203–215.

Witten, I. H., Loots, M., Trujillo, M. F., and Bainbridge, D. (2001). The promise of digital libraries in developing countries. *Communications of the ACM*, **44**(5), 82–85.

Woolsey, K. (2008). Where is the new learning? In R. N. Katz (ed.), *The Tower and the Cloud: Higher Education in the Age of Cloud Computing* (pp. 212–218). Educause. Retrieved April 11, 2009, from www.educause.edu/books.

Wright, C., Dhanarajan, G., and Reju, S. A. (2009). Recurring issues encountered by distance educators in developing and emerging nations. *International Review of Research in Open and Distance Learning*, **10**(1), 1–25.

Wu, S., Franken, M., and Witten, I. (2009). Refining the use of the web (and web search) as a language teaching and learning resource. *International Journal of Computer Assisted Language Learning*, **22**(3), 247–265.

Wu, S. and Witten, I. (2007). Content-based learning in a digital library. Unpublished manuscript. Hamilton, New Zealand: The University of Waikato.

Xie, T. (2002). Using Internet relay chat in teaching Chinese. *CALICO Journal*, **19**(3), 513–524.

Yamada, M. and Akahori, K. (2007). Social presence in synchronous CMC-based language learning: how does it affect the productive performance and consciousness of learning objectives? *Computer Assisted Language Learning*, **20**(1), 37–65.

Yanguas, Í. (2010). Oral computer-mediate interaction between L2 learners: it's about time! *Language Learning and Technology*, **14**(3), 72–93.

Yates, N. (2008). Wikis and constructivism: exploring the links. *The JALT CALL Journal*, **4**(3), 15–28.

Yoshii, M. (2006). L1 and L2 glosses: their effects on incidental vocabulary learning. *Language Learning and Technology*, **10**(3), 85–101.

Yoshii, M. and Flaitz, J. (2002). Second language incidental vocabulary retention: the effect of text and picture annotation types. *CALICO Journal*, **20**(1), 33–58.

Zhao, Y. (2003). Recent developments in technology and language learning: a literature review and meta-analysis. *CALICO Journal*, **21**(1), 7–27.

Index